Collaborative Advantage

Collaborative Advantage

*Forging Green Industries
in the New Global Economy*

JONAS NAHM

OXFORD
UNIVERSITY PRESS

OXFORD
UNIVERSITY PRESS

Oxford University Press is a department of the University of Oxford. It furthers
the University's objective of excellence in research, scholarship, and education
by publishing worldwide. Oxford is a registered trade mark of Oxford University
Press in the UK and certain other countries.

Published in the United States of America by Oxford University Press
198 Madison Avenue, New York, NY 10016, United States of America.

© Oxford University Press 2021

Library of Congress Cataloging-in-Publication Data
Names: Nahm, Jonas, author.
Title: Collaborative advantage : forging green industries in the new global economy / Jonas Nahm.
Description: 1 Edition. | New York : Oxford University Press, 2021. |
Includes bibliographical references and index.
Identifiers: LCCN 2021014209 (print) | LCCN 2021014210 (ebook) |
ISBN 9780197555378 (paperback) | ISBN 9780197555361 (hardback) |
ISBN 9780197555392 (epub) | ISBN 9780197555408
Subjects: LCSH: Clean energy industries—Case studies. |
Strategic alliances (Business) | Partnership. | Cooperation. |
Organizational effectiveness. | International economic integration.
Classification: LCC HD9502.5.C542 N34 2021 (print) |
LCC HD9502.5.C542 (ebook) | DDC 333.79/4—dc23
LC record available at https://lccn.loc.gov/2021014209
LC ebook record available at https://lccn.loc.gov/2021014210

DOI: 10.1093/oso/9780197555361.001.0001

1 3 5 7 9 8 6 4 2

Paperback printed by LSC Communications, United States of America
Hardback printed by Bridgeport National Bindery, Inc., United States of America

Contents

Acknowledgments

Collaboration was central to the making of this book. The seeds for this project were planted at MIT more than a decade ago, when conversations about globalization, innovation, and the climate crisis loomed large at the institute. Edward Steinfeld, Suzanne Berger, and Richard Lester encouraged me to connect the dots between the three. They shared the vision that a PhD program should be an apprenticeship, so the first set of collaborations focused on learning the skills of the trade. Richard introduced me to conducting research as part of large, interdisciplinary research teams that included both social scientists and engineers. The ability to communicate across disciplinary lines has been central to much of this project. I learned to conduct interviews from Suzanne, who joined me in the field on several trips to visit renewable energy firms. While driving thousands of miles across Germany, most recently in the fall of 2019, long conversations helped distinguish the trunk from the branches of this study. I am especially indebted to Ed, who believed in this project from the very beginning and has supported me through the end. Understanding China's approach to manufacturing was a joint endeavor, carried out roughly equally through site visits to industrial parks in China and long conversations over coffee in Lexington.

At Brown, I met an interdisciplinary gang of postdocs who all worked on making their projects accessible to a broader audience. Julia Chuang, Janice Gallagher, Michelle Jurkovich, Deepak Lamba-Nieves, Atul Pokharel, and Elena Shih became collaborators in solving the challenges of academic life. Our friendships and two Providence winters was what it took to find my voice in this project. I am grateful to Rick Locke for bringing us together and to Ed for keeping us there.

In 2016, I found a new base from which to continue this research at the Johns Hopkins School of Advanced International Studies, an institution whose geographical reach mirrors the scope of this book. The small faculty apartments above the library in the Hopkins Nanjing Center became a home away from home over the years, as I continued to visit renewable energy firms in China. At SAIS, I gained a deep bench of collaborators who, like me, aspire to use social science research to tackle global problems and from whom I continue to learn. I am lucky to have such great colleagues and grateful to Johannes Urpelainen for championing the importance of firm-level work in solving the challenge of climate change.

This book, too, relied on global networks. Rick Doner, Peter Evans, Gary Herrigel, Margaret Pearson, Meg Rithmire, and Edward Steinfeld went out of their way to read the manuscript and spend a day with me at Brown to workshop the project. I am grateful for their advice and encouragement. Friends and colleagues around the world read chapter drafts and provided feedback at conferences that helped shape the manuscript into its final form: Bentley Allan, Ling Chen, Nathan Cisneros, Kristin Fabbe, Carla Freeman, John Helveston, David Hart, Jesse Jenkins, Joanna Lewis, Kathy Hochstetler, Llewleyn Hughes, Kyle Jaros, Valerie Karplus, Andrew Kennedy, Genia Kostka, Boy Lüthje, Jonas Meckling, Greg Nemet, Hiram Samel, Debbi Seligsohn, Kyoung Shin, Leah Stokes, and Eric Thun helped make sense of the story in China and connect it to the rest of the world. Yan Fan, Regina Rossman, and Sam Smith were the research assistants of my dreams and graduated way too quickly. Stephen Sears and Stacy VanDeveer told me to keep going when I needed to hear it.

My field research relied on the generosity of many who shared their networks, spare bedrooms, and insights on renewable energy industries. In China, Victor Bekink, Wang Lei, and Li Shuai opened doors I didn't know existed. Without Li Shuai's ability to charm executive assistants, many interviews would not have happened. I am especially grateful to all those who made time to be interviewed for this project and who allowed me to tell this story.

No collaboration was more joyful and enduring than the one with Meg Rithmire, who was there from the beginning and who showed me that it could be done. I relied on Meg for too many things to list here, including finding the title for this book. For a social creature, the process of writing the manuscript would have been impossible without this friendship that kept me company on every page.

Writing this book and doing the research leading up to it has impacted no one more than Jason, who truly lived with this project for the last ten years. His patience, love, and support through the ups and downs of the process, including many months of fieldwork, have meant the world to me.

1

Introduction

It was a humid summer afternoon when I arrived at an industrial park on the outskirts of Shanghai to tour a solar photovoltaic (PV) firm. In the lobby of the main office building, glass displays advertised the latest technology breakthroughs, touting the firm's efficiency records for converting sun to electricity with different solar technologies. Across town, in one of the firm's manufacturing plants, robotic arms whizzed past in rapid succession to assemble individual solar cells into modules that would be mounted on residential rooftops in Europe. The firm I was visiting constituted part of a group of Chinese companies that had, in just a few years, multiplied global production capacity for renewable energy technologies while rapidly reducing costs. Over the course of ten years, global production of solar PV modules had increased by a factor of 40, much of it driven by Chinese factories. By 2012, barely a decade after the first solar manufacturing plants opened in China, the nation accounted for more than 60 percent of the world's solar manufacturing capacity.

Touring the Shanghai plant, I recognized that the ability to deliver ever more efficient solar panels at lower prices was emblematic of a broader phenomenon. The steady presence of research and development (R&D) teams in China suggested that the rapid rise of this nation's renewable energy industries was not simply the result of greater investments in production capacity. Something else was at play, as well. Chinese firms were succeeding because they were *innovating*, and at a level not conventionally associated with low-cost manufacturing.

In China's leading wind and solar firms, R&D teams were preoccupied with technological improvements that would enable faster and cheaper manufacturing. Solar PV manufacturers all over China had installed "Golden Lines," separate production facilities set up solely for R&D efforts, allowing engineering teams to work without interfering with manufacturing operations. Bringing mass production to emerging renewable energy industries was a feat not just of supportive government policies but also of technological innovation.

At the same time, a steady flow of foreign engineers through China's economic development zones signaled that China's rise as a center for clean energy industries also relied on technological capabilities that had originated in other parts the world. JA Solar, the firm I visited in Shanghai, had worked with Innovalight, a start-up from Silicon Valley, to commercialize a new material for solar PV production—a silicon ink. Innovalight had originally sought to become a solar manufacturer in its own right. But the American firm lacked manufacturing skills and the type of financing and government support that would allow it to scale its technology easily. Innovalight ultimately signed a joint development agreement with JA Solar in Shanghai. After a year of collaborative research, the team successfully commercialized the technology, yielding a new generation of high-efficiency panels.[1]

The collaboration extended beyond just JA Solar and Innovalight. Like many of its peers, JA Solar sourced components and production equipment from European firms such as Schmid, a German supplier of production equipment for the solar industry. Founded in 1864, Schmid produced saws for lumber mills and manufacturing equipment for furniture before developing printers for electronic circuit boards in the 1960s. In the early 2000s, the company became one of the first producers of designated manufacturing equipment for the solar photovoltaic industry, much of it eventually destined for Chinese plants.[2]

The solar modules rolling off production lines in the industrial suburbs of Shanghai were not solely the result of Chinese innovation. Yet neither were they solely the result of innovation *outside* China, as observers in the West often made it seem.[3] The renewable energy firms dotting China's economic development zones offered a model of industrial innovation that was at once global and local. The technological capabilities and R&D efforts underpinning JA Solar's solar panels and other renewable energy firms in China relied on a global network of highly specialized firms that collaborated on technological innovation. At the same time, these firms' specialized skills remained deeply reliant on institutions, public resources, and government policies in their countries of origin. Their global partners made use of local, publicly funded institutions ranging from vocational training for small and medium-sized manufacturers in Germany's Black Forest to government research programs underpinning the tech firms of Silicon Valley. Renewable energy manufacturers in China also relied on public support, as provincial and municipal governments in China created a vast infrastructure for mass production in the nation's economic development zones. This infrastructure proved instrumental in allowing Chinese wind and solar manufacturers to focus on scale and cost in the commercialization of new technologies. The rise of this global division of labor in industrial innovation, and its links to changes in the organization of the global economy, national policies, and institutions form the subject of this book.

---

[1] Nahm and Steinfeld 2014, 297.
[2] Nahm 2017b, 83.
[3] Fialka 2016.

A Global Division of Labor

This is a book about the development and persistence of distinct national industrial profiles in a global division of labor. My aim is to demonstrate that new opportunities for collaboration in the global economy have reinforced national patterns of industrial specialization in technological innovation and the institutions that support them. As I show in the chapters that follow, this is the case particularly in emerging industries, such as wind and solar, where the absence of incumbent firms would lead us to expect nations to break more readily with industrial practices of the past.

In the decades before international economic integration made it easier for firms around the world to work together on tasks ranging from innovation to production, differences in national capitalisms—the institutions, actors, and relationships governing the domestic market economy—yielded equally distinct national industrial profiles for innovation, production, and competitiveness. National economies specialized in inventing and producing different types of products precisely because domestic arrangements did not lend themselves equally to all types of competitive strategies.[4] Entire industrial sectors were contained within national borders. Trade enabled the exchange of products and led to direct competition between economies that contained similar industries.

Economic globalization has changed this arrangement permanently. Many of the activities that make up the global economy now lie beyond the territorial reach of individual economies, challenging the primacy of states as organizing units for industrial sectors. These changes have been accompanied by concerns about the ability of states to preserve national differences in economic practices, industrial capabilities, and the institutions that support them.[5] A core contribution of this book is to show not only that the forces of international economic integration continue to be mediated by distinct domestic institutions but also that they actually strengthen divergent national capitalisms over time. My central argument is that globalization causes a persistent and consequential divergence of industrial specializations and national institutions.

Let's return to the example of the Shanghai solar manufacturer. JA Solar operated its manufacturing plants with a division of labor between firms from three different continents: from China, JA Solar contributed skills in manufacturing innovation; from Germany, Schmid delivered production equipment; and from the United States, Innovalight offered a novel material to increase the efficiency of solar panels. Although each firm maintained a set of skills in keeping with

---

[4] See, for instance, Hall and Soskice 2001.
[5] For a review of arguments about convergence as a result of competitive pressures in the international economy, see Berger 2000.

traditional industrial strengths within its country of origin, the collaboration among the three companies made each individual specialization functionally viable and economically successful in the emerging global solar industry.

The Chinese manufacturer did not replace the skills of its German and US partners with a set of capabilities established in-house, even if the Chinese government openly wished for more national autonomy in technological innovation.[6] The firm focused, instead, on a set of core skills in commercialization while relying on partnerships with others to access expertise in the development of new technologies and production equipment that were not well supported in China's domestic economy. These relationships between firms with complementary skills challenge prevailing expectations that the dynamics of our global economy undermine distinct national competitive strategies and the institutions that support them—particularly those in advanced industrialized economies. They also suggest the need for a new account of the linkages between changes in the global economy, national institutions, and firms' specialization in distinct sets of technological capabilities.

Changes in the international economy and their domestic effects have long been the subject of research in the social sciences. Throughout the 1980s and 1990s, new digital technologies, changes in global financial markets, and the evolution of international economic institutions spurred a reorganization of global production. This rise of cross-national supply chains changed industries that had previously existed within national borders. Where national industries once rivaled one another, competition now shifted to contending networks, each of which linked or connected firms from industrial backgrounds and geographical locations.[7] The present study contributes to these debates by offering a "shop floor" account of how the reorganization of the international economy made it easier for firms to enter new industries through ever-narrower specialization while relying on collaboration with others to access skills that they no longer possessed in-house or could source from their own domestic economy.

I employ the concept of *collaborative advantage* to capture the connection between these changes in the global economy, firms' competitive strategies, and their engagement in domestic political economies. Collaborative advantage describes the creative process through which firms insert themselves into globalized production systems. Two types of experimental action enable firms to reap benefits from participating in the global economy (Figure 1.1). First, thanks to new opportunities for collaboration, firms can participate in a global division of labor that allows them to specialize. This *economic* manifestation of collaborative advantage captures the creative process through which firms identify and act on

---

[6] Kennedy 2013.
[7] Camuffo 2004; Langlois 2002.

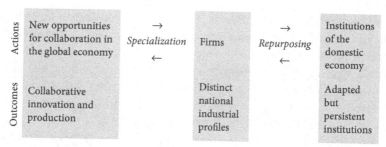

Figure 1.1 Collaborative Advantage

opportunities to compete in global industries. Second and in turn, these new possibilities for specialization allow firms to repurpose existing institutions for application in new industries. This *political* manifestation of collaborative advantage drives the persistence of legacy institutions within the domestic economy and causes their iterative reorientation toward new, global industrial sectors. As the two actions that constitute collaborative advantage, specialization and institutional repurposing together explain why distinct national industrial profiles persist in today's global economy.

Economically, collaborative advantage describes the importance of specialization in the global economy. As I show in the case of wind and solar industries in China, Germany, and the United States, globalization has created new possibilities for collaboration that relieve firms of the need to establish in-house the full range of production and innovation capabilities required to bring a new product to market. The existence of other specialized firms has made it possible for these firms to access necessary skills through collaboration in global supply chains. Globalization has made it easier to find such partners, even if they are dispersed geographically. When collaboration enables firms to specialize, the skills required for innovation—defined here as the process by which new and improved technologies are developed and brought to market—are rarely organized within a single enterprise or even a single economy. Firms and the economies in which they are located no longer have to be self-sufficient. They no longer need to be located near one another. What's more, local strengths in a particular type of industrial activity no longer necessarily lead to the attraction of related skills into the local economy. Simply put, these firms are able to compete in global industries through specialization while relying on collaboration with others.

Politically, collaborative advantage manifests in the ability of firms to repurpose existing institutions for application in new industries. Rather than establish in-house the full range of skills required to bring a new product to market, firms can pick among individual steps in the development, commercialization, and production process when strategizing how to enter new industrial sectors.

Firms use these new opportunities for specialization to make their way into new economic sectors that build on existing industrial capabilities within the firm and the domestic institutions that support them. Such institutions include the domestic financial sector, the labor market and vocational training institutions, and government programs to support R&D. Specialization allows firms to appropriate and repurpose these resources to compete in new industries sometimes far removed from their founding or original purpose.

Although industrial legacies and the presence of different types of institutions constrain what types of activities can be carried out in different economies, institutions are not incapable of change. Under the right circumstances, they can be reinvented and support firms as they respond to new opportunities in the global economy. Globalization allows firms to repurpose existing institutions for new industrial contexts, presenting a set of resources for experimentation and adaptation. These resources, in turn, ignite imagination. Globalization allows for creativity and experimentation precisely because it has opened up new possibilities for specialization. Domestic institutions no longer fully define how firms choose to enter new industries or which firms are able to do so.

The distinct national industrial profiles that I document in this book resulted from just such creativity and inventiveness. They built on domestic institutional resources while taking advantage of new opportunities for specialization. It is precisely because collaboration allowed for industrial specialization that firms in Germany were able to enter wind and solar industries that made use of traditional vocational training institutions and banking relationships. It was for the same reason that Chinese firms were able to break into global supply chains with R&D skills in commercialization: they experimented with the manufacturing infrastructure established since the beginning of economic reforms by China's subnational governments. Collaborative advantage reverses the logic that has portrayed distinct national political economies as fundamentally threatened by the competitive pressures resulting from three decades of globalization: specialization and repurposing explain why globalization leads to persistent and consequential divergence of institutions and national industrial specializations over time.

' In my opening vignette, we saw a set of firms with industrial specializations that depended on one another yet remained deeply grounded in domestic institutions in their home economies. By exploring this phenomenon through the lens of collaborative advantage, this book brings together two perspectives that have often been considered separately in research on globalization, technological innovation, and industrial specialization: a focus on the policies and institutions that influence firm behavior at the national and subnational level, and the analysis of changes in the global organization of production and innovation. Collaborative advantage contests depictions of globalization as being solely or even primarily about competition, and offers an interpretation of the nature, drivers, and consequences of international economic integration through the lens of collaboration. Using the empirical cases of global renewable energy industries, I aim to show not just that collaboration is central to shaping the international division of labor but also that it fundamentally changes how firms respond to the policies and institutions of the state.

While this book is not the first to link these debates, it offers a novel perspective on the mechanisms behind institutional endurance—and on the nature of globalization more broadly. Over the past three decades, explaining the consequences of globalization has become a central area of inquiry for scholars of political economy. One avenue of research has understood globalization primarily as a process of reaping gains from international trade based on comparative advantage. Grounded in the notion that factor endowments shape nations' relative opportunity costs for specializing in the production of some goods over others, this position has focused on the circumstances that allow and prevent nations from realizing the benefits of greater economic integration.[8] A second avenue of research, centered on increasing competition, has approached international economic integration from a domestic perspective. Without refuting potential gains from trade, such research has nonetheless focused on the constraints imposed on states by the international economy. Research in this tradition has examined what options remain for policymakers to respond to an ever more unpredictable global economic context—and how political choices shape the ability of domestic firms to engage the global economy.[9]

The analytical approach I have taken builds on these approaches and stresses both the interdependence of firms' choices about participation in the global economy and the embeddedness of these firms in domestic institutions. I unpack not only how firms in emerging industries collaborate to develop new technologies, but also how such relationships change the ways in which firms engage domestic political economies. In particular, I make the point that international economic integration and distinct domestic political economies are not locked into a zero-sum game in which states actively try to push back on global competitive pressures to maintain national differences. By showing how specialization allows firms to engage the global economy in new ways that build on and support existing domestic institutions, this book instead makes the case for a firm-based mechanism for institutional endurance.

The remainder of this chapter places governmental goals to create innovative domestic industries within the broader context of changes in the global economy. I argue that the reorganization of the international economy necessitates both a

[8] Samuelson 1938, 265.
[9] Baldwin 2016, chapters 7–8; Breznitz 2007, 4–6.

new understanding of technological innovation and a recasting of state-business relations. I then briefly introduce the core empirical outcome explained in this book—the development of distinct patterns of industrial specialization in wind and solar industries in China, Germany, and the United States—and I suggest that renewable energy sectors provide a particularly compelling analytical window into the drivers behind the global division of labor in technological innovation.

Innovation and the State in a Changing Global Context

The creation of innovative domestic industries has long captured the attention of policymakers. Government officials in China, Germany, and around the world continue to look to the United States—and Silicon Valley in particular—as a model of the powerful economic forces unleashed by technological innovation. The flow of political delegations through the district most known for its global technology giants demonstrates the importance governments worldwide have attached to technological innovation, and it reflects the status ascribed to the United States as a seedbed for innovative firms.[10] Hoping to replicate the region's success, governments have attempted to encourage similar clusters of high-technology enterprises at home.[11] Silicon Roundabout in Britain, Silicon Saxony in Germany, and Optics Valley in China all exemplify the belief that firms capable of high-technology innovation are critical to a modern economy and that governments play an important role in facilitating their creation.

In the postwar decades, governments in rapidly developing East Asian economies employed strategic intervention to encourage domestic enterprises to catch up with the innovative firms in the West. Underlying such government ambition was the notion that economic development entailed the progressive advancement from commodity production to the invention and commercialization of new technologies. To help domestic enterprises compete with incumbent firms in global industries, the state channeled support to select industrial groups. As Alice Amsden documented in the case of South Korea, a set of performance requirements made government support conditional on the continuous improvement of R&D capabilities to avoid the corruption and rent-seeking often associated with state subsidies.[12] Through a mix of public and private efforts, Korean and Japanese conglomerates rose through the ranks of global electronics

---

[10] Boudreau 2012; Kopytoff 2014; Traufetter 2013.
[11] Gunnar Trumbull has detailed state efforts to remake a domestic Silicon Valley in France. See Trumbull 2004.
[12] Amsden 2001, 8–12.

and auto industries, some eventually beating firms in advanced economies at their own innovative game.[13]

Governments in the West were also unwilling to leave innovation to market forces, a reluctance driven by reasons ranging from national competitiveness to national security. In the United States, the Cold War strengthened the impetus for public investments in R&D and helped lead to the eventual development of new civilian technologies—and the high-technology clusters such as Silicon Valley that sprang up around them.[14] Meanwhile, among European economies weakened by World War II, concerns about permanently falling behind the growing capabilities of the US economy drove state support for innovation. Public R&D funding for research institutes and enterprises aimed to encourage the competitiveness of domestic industries, particularly those of broader societal and economic importance. In addition to basic research and research with defense applications, governments funded innovation in sectors from automobiles and aerospace to health and energy.

In advanced and developing economies alike, public support for innovation rested on the assumption that the invention of new technologies would attract industrial activities beyond innovation itself. In the postwar decades, technological innovation often required the establishment of manufacturing facilities on site or nearby, as well as large numbers of suppliers who could successfully bring products from the laboratory to market. With their engineering teams focused on the various stages of product development and commercialization, large enterprises proved particularly capable of managing the linkages between these myriad R&D activities and local suppliers.[15] Public support for R&D was driven not by concerns about which elements of a broader division of labor to establish within national borders, but by the expectation that investments in R&D would lead entire industries to locate domestically. Public support for innovation was thus the lynchpin of broader governmental initiatives for industrial development and economic growth more generally.

Since 2000, government delegations touring Silicon Valley have retained the hope that public support for innovation will create thriving domestic industrial sectors.[16] High-technology industries, the conventional wisdom has held, create jobs not just in R&D but also in a broad range of connected activities along the trajectory from lab to market, including in manufacturing. Public investments

---

[13] Such accounts of the East Asian the role of industrial policy in the developmental states were not uncontested. See, for instance, Krugman 1994; Samuels, 1987; World Bank 1993.

[14] Lécuyer 2007.

[15] Chandler and Hikino 1997.

[16] There are, of course, economic benefits from high-tech sectors even without the simultaneous attraction of supplier industries and manufacturing. For a study of the benefits of attracting high-tech industries into US urban economies, see Moretti 2012.

in R&D in Germany have been expected to yield German industries that would compete, for instance, with French industries across the border.

Yet as my opening example of Shanghai's solar PV manufacturer illustrates, the organization of the international economy differed from the situation faced by firms in postwar East Asian developing economies and their European and American contemporaries. Rapid economic development had established China as the world's second-biggest economy in just a few decades. Starting in the early 1990s, a series of novel digital technologies had made it feasible to physically separate early R&D and commercialization, as blueprints and production specifications could be electronically transmitted around the world. Many firms subsequently focused on core skills in the development of new technologies while moving production activities to low-cost locations abroad.[17] In the United States in particular, financial markets began to reward such restructuring: these shifts relieved corporations of the financial burden associated with the capital-intensive construction of new manufacturing facilities.[18]

But these changes were not one-dimensional. Although the inventors of Silicon Valley were no longer geographically tethered to many commercialization and production activities that used to occur within their four walls, policymakers continued to presume tight managerial and geographical linkages between innovation and production. The emergence of truly global supply chains transformed the connections between the activities required to bring new technologies to market: economic globalization made it easier to access a broad range of technologies and skills through collaboration, while it also dispersed these same technologies and skills geographically. Rather than establish in one place the full range of R&D capabilities required to develop, commercialize, and produce new technologies, firms began to specialize and make use of new opportunities for collaboration in their global networks. The fragmentation of production and the rise of global supply chains further accelerated this process. Now capable of far narrower activities than the firms of the past, the players in this new global economy learned to access needed skills through collaboration. The United States continued to lead in the number of start-ups created domestically; in the context of economic globalization, however, these start-ups also proved far more likely to rely on technological capabilities located elsewhere to bring their products to market. Skills in commercialization and mass production, for instance, became increasingly rare domestically, as the center of global manufacturing shifted to China (Figure 1.2).

---

[17] Baldwin and Clark 2000; Berger 2005a, chapter 4; Sturgeon 2002.
[18] Gerald F. Davis documents how financial markets forged the restructuring of the US model of industrial organization beginning in the 1990s. See Davis 2009.

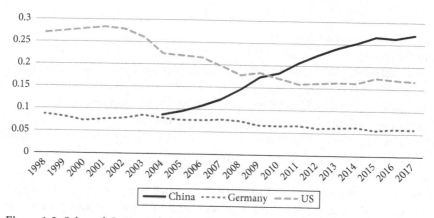

Figure 1.2 Selected Countries' Shares of Global Manufacturing Value Added.
Source: UN National Accounts Main Aggregates Database, value added by economic activity, at current prices—US dollars.

The image of Silicon Valley as the paragon of innovation-based economic success has remained prominent among policymakers around the world. Yet the global organization of production and innovation, the linkages between the activities required to bring new technologies to market, and the geography of actors involved in such activities had fundamentally changed since the postwar decades. If there was a lesson to be learned during my visit to Shanghai's solar manufacturer, it was that the payoffs from government investments in technological innovation were no longer guaranteed to manifest domestically. This book examines the division of labor in technological innovation in this new global context.

Renewable Energy Industries in the New Global Economy

What drives national patterns of industrial specialization in an era when many of the activities that make up the global economy have shifted beyond the territorial reach of individual states? What can states do to support the growth of innovative industries in their home economies within this new reality? How do firms engage their domestic economic institutions as they reach for new opportunities in global supply chains? I examine these questions through a comparative investigation of the development of wind and solar sectors in China, Germany, and the United States. Three factors make renewable energy industries a particularly compelling window onto these national patterns as they are unfolding.

First, wind and solar industries evolved *after* the reorganization of the global economy. Existing literatures have long examined the transformative effects of globalization on innovation and industrial organization in legacy industries. Such research has attributed changes in the location of major industrial activities to the competitive forces of globalization. Some scholars have traced the impact of digital production technologies on the global organization of the computer industry.[19] Others have examined the effect of globalization—including the establishment of NAFTA, China's WTO accession, and other changes in international economic institutions—on the structure of the global auto industry.[20]

In contrast to established industries, whose origins long predate the reorganization of the international economy, firms that produced wind turbines or manufactured solar panels did not reach scale-economies until the early 2000s.[21] By focusing on postglobalization industries, this book removes from the analysis the politically contentious process of restructuring legacy industries: put another way, wind and solar sectors allow us to separate the effects of globalization on preexisting industries from the development of new industrial sectors that sprang up under globalization. My argument is that collaborative advantage has the strongest effect in industries lacking powerful incumbent firms and legacy production structures. It is here we see significant impact on the division of labor and domestic institutions.

Second, I focus on wind and solar industries because they are based on two very different underlying technologies. These technologies result in divergent production requirements, supply chain structures, and engineering challenges. Wind turbines, with many moving parts, long lists of components, and sophisticated material needs, require complex production arrangements across a large number of firms. An average wind turbine contains components assembled from more than 8,000 individual parts, which are produced by more than 1,000 different suppliers.[22] The production of solar panels, by contrast, comprises far fewer actors and thus has a much shorter supply chain. Manufacturing of crystalline silicon solar PV modules, the dominant technology in the solar industry, occurs in five major steps, sequentially arranged from the production of silicon through the cutting of wafers to the production of cells and subsequent assembly of modules. The production of solar panels based on second-generation thin film technologies is concentrated even further in a single production line.[23]

Why do these differences matter? They help demonstrate that the argument presented here applies across technologies and supply chain structures. In the wind industry, international economic integration enabled the globalization of clusters of firms. Since many component parts of wind turbines are too heavy to

---

[19] Baldwin and Clark 2000.
[20] Doner, Noble, and Ravenhill 2006; Thun 2006.
[21] Berger 2013b, 40–41.
[22] American Wind Energy Association 2015.
[23] Shah and Greenblatt 2010, 77–98.

be shipped economically, assembly frequently occurs in close proximity to the final site of installations. Wind manufacturing firms and their suppliers therefore established clusters in close proximity to final markets around the world, not dissimilar to the car industry. The solar sector, by contrast, presents a case of transnational supply chains, in which different production steps occur in different parts of the world, and components are easily shipped from one location to another as they progress toward the final product. Comparing cross-national patterns of technological innovation across two such different technologies and supply chain structures allows my research to isolate the influence of technology: if collaborative advantage in the global economy enables firms in a particular economy to specialize in similar technological activities across two different industrial sectors, then specialization must be the result of factors other than the technology itself.

Third and most important, renewable energy industries offer a particularly lucid empirical context for investigating the changing impact of state-business relations on national patterns of industrial specialization. Arguably more than any other set of industries, renewable energy sectors have come to exemplify the aspiration of governments to cultivate domestic high-technology industries through targeted state intervention over the past two decades. In 2014, more than seventy countries used subsidies and energy market regulation to stimulate domestic demand for renewable energy technologies. Advanced and developing economies from Algeria to Yemen set targets for the share of domestic energy to be generated from renewable sources. Globally, governments spent more than USD 5 billion on renewable energy R&D in 2014 alone.[24]

Government support for renewable energy industries has, of course, been justified by the need to switch to cleaner sources of energy for environmental reasons. Concerns about climate change have motivated citizens and governments alike to encourage energy transitions away from fossil fuels.[25] Yet few governments have supported wind and solar sectors solely on environmental grounds, despite their significance for combating the effects of climate change. Political support for renewable energy transitions and the public funds required to initiate and sustain technological change have depended on the promise of tangible benefits for the broader economy, in particular through the creation of domestic industries. These promised benefits took on added importance as clean energy industries became sizable global sectors. In 2018, the world spent more than USD 300 billion on low-carbon energy technologies (Figure 1.3).

States that have successfully supported the establishment of renewable energy firms have been able to adopt more ambitious climate policies with the help of

---

[24] REN21 2015, reference tables.
[25] REN21 2020.

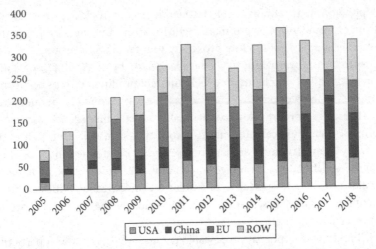

Figure 1.3 New Investment in Clean Energy Technologies (USD Billions)
Source: Bloomberg New Energy Finance

industrial coalitions and public support.[26] Other governments have seen wind and solar sectors as purely export-oriented industries, supporting them despite a lack of any ambition to use them for domestic green energy transitions in the short term.[27] As a consequence, these governments have justified the use of public funds for wind and solar industries by pointing to the potential for job creation, national competitiveness, and the need to target emerging high-technology firms in strategic industrial sectors.[28] For these states, environmental benefits alone are not enough.

Despite their differences, governments pursued remarkably similar industrial policy goals when they encouraged the development of renewable energy industries. In China, Germany, and the United States, the cases examined in this book, the state encouraged technological innovation through R&D policies, at least partly in the hope that the development of new wind and solar technologies would spur the growth of competitive domestic industries. But because electricity generated from renewable sources was not yet competitive with conventional sources of energy, governments in all three economies also employed subsidies and energy market regulation to create domestic demand for wind and solar technologies. Clearly, cross-national differences existed in the implementation of such policies, in the size and duration of subsidies, and in the conditions for

[26] Laird and Stefes 2009; Meckling et al. 2015.
[27] Zhang, Andrews-Speed, and Ji, 906–8.
[28] Zysman and Huberty 2013, xi–58.

government support. Yet by combining push-and-pull, technology-and-demand approaches to industrial policy and technological innovation, governments in China, Germany, and the United States came to share something in common: the aspiration to create firms capable of inventing, commercializing, and manufacturing renewable energy technologies domestically.[29]

The core empirical contribution of this book concerns the persistent and consequential divergence of national industrial specializations. Such divergence occurred despite similarities in state goals and industrial policies and, as mentioned previously, applied to both industries in spite of differences in underlying technologies and supply chain organization. Modern renewable energy industries emerged virtually simultaneously in China, Germany, and the United States, yet firms in each location established distinct industry profiles and distinct national patterns of technological specialization. A large literature in political economy has shown that sectoral dynamics and firms' positions in global supply chains shape firms' policy preferences, including on trade and domestic economic policy. This book, instead, explains why firms in different economies are more likely to choose different technological specializations within the same industrial sectors and, as such, achieve more prominence in some segments of the global supply chains than others.[30]

In the United States, wind and solar firms have typically taken the form of start-ups with skills in the *invention* of new technologies, but with far fewer capabilities in the commercialization and production of these inventions. In 2009, out of 100 solar PV firms operating in the United States, at least 73 were start-ups working on the development of next-generation solar technologies that lacked in-house production capabilities.[31] Few manufacturers existed in the United States with the exception of GE, a multinational producer of wind turbines that also relied on global suppliers for a large share of its components. By contrast, small and medium-sized businesses with skills in the development of componentry and complex production equipment made up the majority of German wind and solar firms. Rather than invest in novel wind and solar technologies, these firms focused on what I call *customization*: the development and small-batch production of equipment and early-stage components to produce new renewable energy technologies. In 2010, more than 70 German firms were offering manufacturing lines for the PV industry, and more than 170 firms developed and produced componentry for the wind energy sector, compared to less than a handful of manufacturers of solar panels and wind turbines.[32] In China,

---

[29] Nemet 2009.
[30] See, for instance, Hiscox 2002; Lake 2009.
[31] Knight 2011, 176.
[32] Arbeitsgemeinschaft Windenergie-Zulieferindustrie 2012; Germany Trade & Invest 2010, 2011b.

meanwhile, large wind and solar manufacturers focused on the R&D required for commercializing and scaling novel technologies—which I refer to as *innovative manufacturing* in this book. As a result of such investments, Chinese firms became the first to bring wind and solar technologies to mass production. Far fewer firms prioritized the production of manufacturing equipment or the invention of new technologies.[33]

As the example of the Shanghai solar PV manufacturer emphasizes, it was the collaboration among firms with such distinct technological capabilities that made each individual specialization functionally viable and economically successful. Although policymakers aspired to create broad and diversified domestic renewable energy industries, the wind and solar sectors in China, Germany, and the United States established distinct constellations of firms with starkly different technical capabilities. With American strengths in invention, German specialization in complex components and production equipment, and Chinese mastery of commercialization and mass production, we have an example of an interdependent and mutually reinforcing partnership.

Plan of the Book

The collaboration of American, German, and Chinese firms is deeply connected to broader changes in the global economy. These changes, often summed up simply as economic globalization, made it easier for goods, services, and ideas to travel between national centers of economic activity. They also restructured how new technologies are invented, commercialized, and produced. Yet any explanation for the persistence of distinct national industrial specializations during this period of international economic integration also requires an account of the domestic political economies that structured firms' attempts to build and maintain distinct capabilities. Understanding how firms in different economies have arrived at such distinct specializations in global industries requires an approach that places firms' behavior in the context of both domestic institutions and the broader forces of economic globalization. The firm-centered perspective offered here emphasizes the relationship between such changes, domestic institutions, and firm behavior. This book develops the concept of collaborative advantage to span a causal arch between new opportunities for collaboration in the global economy and the reinforcement of distinct national patterns of industrial specialization in technological innovation.

---

[33] For the concept of innovative manufacturing, I owe a great debt to many conversations with Edward Steinfeld, which led to the publication of a joint article on the subject. See Nahm and Steinfeld 2014.

In Chapter 2, the first of four empirical chapters, I lay out the central empirical phenomenon of this book and show how firms responded to industrial policies targeted at vertically integrated domestic industries in the context of economic globalization. This chapter highlights the similarity of industrial policy frameworks and state goals in the United States, Germany, and China. All three economies combined R&D policy with demand-side subsidies in an attempt to create vertically integrated domestic wind and solar industries. I then show that firms have responded to such similar policies with distinct and far narrower sets of industrial capabilities. I make the case that the domestic links between innovation and production—connections that prompted government policies—are no longer guaranteed in the new global economy. In the United States, the empirical case with the strongest public investments in R&D, firms responded to industrial policy efforts by creating new capabilities in technological invention without linking such skills to domestic capacity in commercialization and production. In Germany, by contrast, small and medium-sized suppliers from the nation's traditional industrial core responded to federal government industrial policy by creating new capabilities in customization. In China, despite the efforts of the central government to encourage the development of upscale R&D capabilities in high-technology sectors, firms responded by building distinct strengths at the intersection of manufacturing and R&D.

Chapter 3 expands on three elements of the central argument and places them in the context of broader literatures on globalization, technological innovation, and institutional change. I posit a theory about how opportunities for collaboration in the global economy have reinforced national patterns of industrial specialization. The chapter develops the concept of *collaborative advantage* to describe the creative process through which firms insert themselves into globalized production systems. It identifies two types of experimental action that allow firms to reap benefits from participating in the global economy. Economically, collaborative advantage captures the ability for firms to specialize as a result of new opportunities for collaboration. Politically, these new possibilities for specialization allow firms to reuprose existing domestic institutions for application in new industries. The ability to enter new industries through specialization shaped firms' responses to national industrial policies. Even where governments aimed at the creation of comprehensive national industries, firms responded with narrow competitive strategies that built on existing skills and prior experience in other industries.

The chapter documents how collaborative advantage made its impact felt through experimentation with institutional legacies across China, Germany, and the United States—a process that led to distinct industrial specializations. Firms chose specializations that were supported by existing economic institutions, most of them established for other purposes before the emergence of renewable energy sectors. These institutions gained value in wind and solar industries precisely because they no longer had to support the full range of activities required to invent and commercialize new technologies within national borders. The chapter then outlines three structural conditions for collaborative advantage: the rise of global supply chains, nonhierarchical patterns of industrial organization, and opportunities for experimentation in response to state industrial policies.

Chapters 4–6 apply the central argument to the three empirical cases covered in this book. The chapters show that the industrial specialization of these firms relied both on the use of domestic legacy institutions and on the ability to collaborate with global partners. Chapter 4 traces how entrants from legacy industries in Germany used public resources originally intended to support technological innovation in traditional sectors, including machine tools and automobile supplies. The story of these entrants explains why even German firms in new sectors such as wind and solar have reproduced historical patterns of flexible specialization, customization, and small-batch production. Chapter 5 turns to the case of China. I argue that wind and solar firms—often in outright defiance of central government goals—relied on local support for large-scale manufacturing in the process of industrial upgrading. Contrary to the ambitions of policymakers seeking to build autonomous domestic industries, these capabilities were brought to bear on product development in collaboration with global partners. Chapter 6 makes the case that in the United States, a growing divide between an advanced R&D infrastructure and a declining manufacturing sector encouraged wind and solar firms to pursue invention largely divorced from production. Most firms lacked the production capabilities to commercialize and manufacture their innovation in-house and relied instead on the complementary strengths of global partners. In the United States, large public investments in renewable energy research have yielded the smallest industrial footprint of the three cases examined here.

Chapter 7 returns to my comparative analysis and asks what can be gleaned from these cases for our broader understanding of the role of government in industrial policy in fragmented, global sectors. I present comparative data from the automobile and electronics industries to show that even in legacy sectors, distinct national patterns of industrial specialization have shifted the nexus of innovation to global collaboration. I conclude with a reminder that global collaboration—and collaboration with China in particular—will continue to be essential to addressing the climate problem, now and in the future. Voices across the political spectrum in Washington have begun to advocate for economic decoupling from China. Beijing, too, has amplified calls for technological self-sufficiency. Few industries have more at stake in these battles than those producing the clean energy technologies urgently needed to reduce global greenhouse gas emissions. The division of labor I outline in this book is not fixed or inevitable, yet, in the short-term, it is highly unlikely that governments will be able to alter the relationships underpinning global renewable energy industries without jeopardizing global climate goals.

2

Varieties of Innovation in Wind and Solar Industries

On October 23, 2009, in a speech celebrating the 150th anniversary of the Massachusetts Institute of Technology (MIT), United States President Barack Obama warned that the United States risked falling behind in the "global clean energy race." "From China to India, from Japan to Germany," he argued, "nations everywhere are racing to develop new ways to produce and use energy. The nation that wins this competition will be the nation that leads the global economy."[1]

A few days after Obama's speech, the *Financial Times* and *Wall Street Journal* both ran articles about the disappointing US competitive position in global renewable energy sectors. Their articles relied in part on a policy report published by an Oakland-based energy think tank, The Breakthrough Institute, which cautioned that in clean energy industries, China was "poised to replicate many of the same successful strategies that Japanese and South Korean governments used to establish a technological lead in electronics and automobiles. Those governments supported nascent companies with low-interest loans, industry-wide R&D, government procurement, and subsidies for private purchase of advanced technologies."[2] President Obama and the *Wall Street Journal* rarely agreed on much, but they were in lockstep on the notion of a global clean energy race. They also drew surprising parallels between the era of rapid economic development in postwar East Asia and the current period of investments in wind and solar power.

Their statements exemplified a view of national competitiveness and technological innovation that was widely held in media and policy circles, both in the United States and internationally. This view sees the world's large economies as engaged in a race to dominate clean energy sectors; in this paradigm, winning such a race would require large government investments to build domestic industry. Nations would have to be proficient both in innovation and production to achieve and maintain their lead. These expectations were neither new nor unique to clean energy sectors. They built on the experiences of the postwar global economy, when large conglomerate firms, capable of inventing,

---

[1] The White House 2009.
[2] Harvey 2009; Johnson 2009.

commercializing, and producing goods, formed the engines of technological innovation and national competitiveness.

As I argued in the previous chapter, the reorganization of the international economy since the 1970s demands a new understanding of how technological innovation is organized across firms and a recasting of state-business relations in the process of creating innovative industries. The growth of global clean energy industries, which I detail in this chapter, provides the empirical context for this argument. The chapter rules out two common explanations for the persistence of distinct national profiles in the global economy: that governments pursued different industrial policy goals, and that they did so using different industrial policy tools.

In the pages that follow I make two central points. First, I show that a common political logic led governments in China, Germany, and the United States to converge on similar policy goals and industrial policy tools. Public investments in renewable energy began as state initiatives to support scientific discovery; the scientific rationale behind such early support for renewable energy technologies was not immediately connected to expectations of economic results. That changed when improvements in wind and solar technologies opened up new prospects of economic growth and industrial development. As policymakers discovered the economic potential of renewable energy sectors, public investments in R&D and subsidies for the deployment of clean energy technologies became easier to justify politically—these investments now promised local economic returns, particularly in the form of manufacturing jobs. Governments subsequently combined policies to support R&D with demand subsidies, often explicitly tied to local content regulations and other means to attract local industrial activity. The need to provide political justification for public investments in renewable energy sectors yielded similar growth and employment-focused industrial policies across the three countries, irrespective of the underlying political system.

Second, I chronicle the central outcome I explain in this book: the persistent and consequential divergence of national industrial specializations in spite of these policy similarities. Even as governments pursued comparable industrial policy goals, their efforts yielded distinct national profiles in global industries. In the early 2000s, just after China's World Trade Organization (WTO) accession accelerated changes in the organization of many global industries, firms in China, Germany, and the United States chose different technological specializations and competitive strategies for participation in emerging wind and solar industries. The ascent of global clean energy was not, in fact, a race: these national profiles in global renewable energy sectors proved, on the whole, to be complementary, as different types of firms entered wind and solar sectors in each location and pursued distinct competitive strategies.

Scholars of globalization and comparative capitalisms have long been concerned with the ability of states to protect distinct political economies from the forces of liberalization in the international political economy. I show here that such concerns are overstated. The persistence of national industrial profiles challenges the notion that government policies alone are the protectors of national differences and shows that global economic pressures do not, in all cases, chip away at the ability to organize distinct domestic industrial practices and competitive strategies. This is especially true when we recognize that cross-national differences in wind and solar sectors endured even as governments hoped to converge on similar industrial profiles in global renewable energy industries.[3]

Renewable Energy Policies in the Postwar Decades

In making the case that renewable energy policy transitioned from a scientific to a growth and employment rationale, I distinguish between policies aimed at scientific exploration and green industrial policies that explicitly targeted growth and structural economic change. I use the phrase "industrial policy" here to refer to state initiatives whose primary goal is to increase economic output through changes to the composition of domestic economic activity. Industrial policies use the strategic allocation of resources to accelerate economic growth and facilitate structural change in the economy.[4] As such, they differ from science and technology policy that prioritizes scientific discovery without short-term economic objectives, as well as from energy policies that focus primarily on the domestic energy mix and do not emphasize the creation of industries engaged in the development and production of new energy technologies.[5]

Before wind and solar technologies reached sufficient maturity for commercial application, public investments in wind and solar technologies primarily pursued scientific discovery. If science and technology funding had an economic objective, it was simply to prevent broader market failures in R&D.[6] In the United

---

[3] Scholars of globalization have long been concerned with the ability of states to protect distinct political economies from the forces of liberalization in the international economy. They have disagreed over whether such competitive pressures lead to the convergence of domestic political economies or yield varieties of economic liberalization. Yet the literature on comparative capitalisms nonetheless pits global economic forces against the ability of states to craft distinct pathways into highly globalized industries. See, for instance, Höpner and Krempel 2004; Hsueh, 2012; Streeck 2009; Streeck and Mertens 2010; Thelen 2014.

[4] Definitions of "industrial policy" have ranged from any policy governing industrial activity to specific forms of public–private collaboration. See, for instance, Dobbin 1994, 1–2; Schneider 2015, 2.

[5] Aklin and Urpelainen, 2018; Ornston 2013.

[6] Government approaches to R&D in the postwar period embodied the common notion of a linear relationship between scientific advances and the broader economy. Basic research was

States, the main engine of scientific discovery in the postwar decades was the federal government, which spent more than any other nation on wind and solar energy research.[7] Many of the technological advances underlying silicon-based solar cells and thin-film photovoltaic (PV) applications emerged from federally funded R&D institutes and enterprise laboratories starting in the 1950s. Publicly funded research conducted in American universities enabled the spread of solar technologies from their initial application in the space industry to the grid-connected solar PV models that are widely available today. In the wind industry, research consortia led by US corporations made early efforts to apply aerospace technologies to the design of large wind turbines. These costly investments were almost entirely funded through federal government programs.[8]

The first solar cell was developed in AT&T's Bell Labs in 1954, the same year that scientists at RCA Laboratories in Princeton, New Jersey, and at the US Air Force Aerospace Research Laboratory in Dayton, Ohio, published evidence showing that semiconductor devices could convert light into electricity.[9] By 1955, solar cells had reached 8 percent conversion efficiency under laboratory conditions, prompting a flood of speculative media reports about possible future uses of "limitless" solar energy.[10] In reality, applications were few and far between. In 1956, Bell Lab scientists calculated that the number of solar cells needed to power a single-family home would cost more than USD 1.4 million, preventing any use of solar energy in large-scale electricity generation.[11]

The high cost of solar cells was less of a concern in the space sector, where solar PV technologies found an early application as a power supply for satellites. In 1955, President Eisenhower announced plans to launch US satellites into space, only to be defeated at the finish line by the Soviet Union, which launched two Sputnik satellites in 1957. In a scramble to find a reliable and lightweight power source for the American satellite—batteries were bulky, heavy, and capable of holding only limited amounts of electricity—Bell Lab's solar cells offered a promising solution. The first US satellite partially powered by solar cells, Vanguard 1, was launched into orbit in 1958 and outlasted the Soviet satellites by several years. Vanguard's battery failed after twenty days, yet the solar cells provided power until 1964.[12] Despite such early successes, the market for solar cells remained

expected to spark applied research, lead to development and commercialization, and eventually give rise to mass production and industrial development. Leyden and Menter 2018, 228. Stokes 1997, 10.

[7] International Energy Agency (IEA) 2008, 31.
[8] On the contributions of European research, see Heymann 1998. The role of US conglomerates is discussed in Righter 1996, 149–69.
[9] Loferski 1993, 67.
[10] Deudney and Flavin 1983, 89.
[11] Perlin 1999, 36.
[12] Bailey, Raffaelle, and Emery 2002, 400.

limited to satellites and other small, highly specialized applications such as solar-powered radios and calculators.[13]

If the 1950s heralded the modest beginnings of the modern solar PV industry, they marked the end of an era in the wind sector. In 1956, Jacobs Electric Wind Company went out of business; and Wincharger, a second large American producer of wind turbines, all but ceased production.[14] Jacobs had manufactured some 30,000 2–3 kilowatt (kW) wind turbines since its founding in 1927; Wincharger, founded in 1935, had sold more than 400,000 small and affordable wind generators that could charge batteries used for lighting and radios.[15] Both companies supplied agricultural communities before electrification, building on a century-long history of small US firms producing wind turbines for rural America. Overall, six million small wind generators are estimated to have operated in the United States between the mid-nineteenth and mid-twentieth century.[16] Their market rapidly eroded when the Rural Electrification Administration started subsidizing the construction of electric grids in agricultural communities in 1935; by 1956, nearly all American communities were electrified, leaving only a niche market for wind energy.[17]

By the time of the first oil embargo in 1973, neither wind nor solar energy technologies had been established as viable options for large-scale electricity generation. The two oil crises of the 1970s added international urgency to the search for alternative energy sources and prompted widespread strengthening of research efforts. In the United States, as in many other large economies, the government responded by swiftly expanding domestic research efforts (Table 2.1). Supported by bipartisan agreement on the need to diversify the US energy supply, federal investment in renewable energy R&D enjoyed a resurgence, peaking in 1980—two years after the second oil shock—at USD 1.3 billion.[18]

In 1974, immediately following the first oil crisis, the federal government established a Solar Energy Research Institute (SERI) within the Energy Research and the Development Administration (ERDA), the predecessor to the Department of Energy (DOE).[19] The federal government also coordinated

---

[13] Perlin 1999, 35–40. The main solar firm at the time, Hoffman Electronics, which produced solar cells for the Vanguard satellite based on a license to Bell Lab's original solar technology, had four competitors in the United States: Heliotek (which also supplied solar power devices for space applications and eventually merged with Hoffman when both were acquired by Textron in 1960), RCA, International Rectifier, and Texas Instruments. In contrast to Hoffman and Heliotek, RCA, International Rectifier, and Texas Instruments were large corporations that had diversified into the solar sector from the radio and semiconductor industries. All three left the sector by the end of the 1960s, discouraged by the limited commercial market for solar PV. See Colatat, Vidican, and Lester 2009.

[14] Righter 1996, 102.

[15] Righter 1996, chapter 4.

[16] Bereny 1977, 167.

[17] Wolman 2007.

[18] Martinot, Wiser, and Hamrin 2005, 3.

[19] Loferski 1993, 74; Strum and Strum 1983, 134–47.

Table 2.1 Select Industrial Policies for Wind and Solar Sectors

	United States	Germany	China
Technology Push	1973–1988 US Wind Research Program 1991–2000 PVMaT R&D Program Since 1990s NREL R&D Grants 2008 American Recovery & Reinvestment Act: Loans Since 2009 ARPE-E Program	Since 1954 Industrial Collaborative Research (ICR) funding Since 1974 Federal Energy Research Programs, renewed six times	Since 1986 R&D funding for applied research through "863 Program" 2008 "Indigenous Innovation" Initiative 2010 "New Energy" included under Strategic Emerging Industries
Market Pull	1978 Public Utility Regulatory Policies Act (PURPA) 1992 Production Tax Credits (since then renewed seven times) Since 1997 Renewable Portfolio Standards (thirty states by 2012)	1990 Electricity Feed-In Law 1998 Renewable Energy Sources Act (EEG) 2004 EEG Renewed (+ 2009, 2012, and 2014)	2003 Wind Power Concession Program 2006 Renewable Energy Law 2007 Feed-In Tariff: Wind 2009 Feed-In Tariff: Solar 2009 Golden Roofs Initiative 2009 Golden Sun Program

a national wind power research program, which allocated USD 380 million for the development of commercial wind turbines between 1973 and 1988.[20] As part of the program, conglomerates from aerospace, energy, and defense industries were paid to design turbine technologies that could reach generation capacities of up to 7 megawatts (MW), larger than any of the turbines in commercial use today.[21] Ultimately, however, the programs failed to yield a single viable turbine design. The original conglomerates closed their wind turbine divisions over the course of the 1980s.[22]

In Germany, as in the United States, the upheaval in global energy markets spurred by the oil crises of the 1970s made securing access to reliable and domestic sources of energy a central government concern. Germany's scarcity of domestic energy resources, together with its reliance on natural gas from the Soviet Union, fueled a particular sense of vulnerability.[23] The state responded

---

[20] Righter 1996, 158.
[21] Gipe 1995, 77; Righter 1996, 158.
[22] Ackermann and Söder 2002.
[23] Bahnsen 2013.

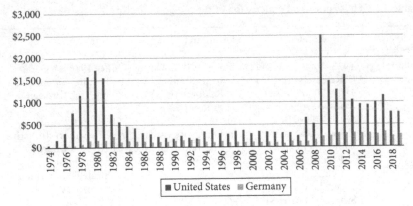

Figure 2.1 Selected Countries' R&D Budgets for Renewable Energy (in Million USD).

Source: IEA Energy Technology RD&D Statistics, 2020

by ramping up R&D efforts, albeit at a smaller scale than the United States had undertaken (Figure 2.1).[24] Starting in 1977, a series of Federal Energy Research Programs (*Energieforschungsprogramme*) supported R&D for specific energy technologies, including wind turbines and solar PV.[25] Despite a focus on manufacturability, these programs failed to yield wind and solar technologies that were ready for mass production. Solar panels produced by participating German firms continued to perform poorly, and many large firms exited the sector in spite of government research funding.[26]

As in the United States, German research funding in the wind industry prioritized the development of large-scale wind turbines and suffered a similar fate. A 3 MW turbine prototype commissioned by the German federal government in 1977 took six years to develop, consuming more than two-thirds of federal funding for wind energy research in the 1970s and 1980s.[27] The turbine encountered a range of technical difficulties before being dismantled in 1987. All in all, the turbine operated for just 320 hours over the course of three years, making it one of the most prominent failures of German science and technology policy to this day.[28] In spite of the research efforts spurred by the 1970s oil crises, commercially viable renewable energy technologies remained elusive.

[24] IEA 2020.
[25] Bundesministerium für Wirtschaft und Technologie 2011.
[26] Lang 2003.
[27] Ohlhorst 2009, 97.
[28] Ohlhorst 2009, 96.

The postwar decades demonstrated that wind turbines and solar panels could be used to generate electricity, not just in remote locations, but also in connection to commercial electricity grids. High production cost and reliability issues, however, confined both industries to a niche existence, leaving them unable to gain traction among commercial players and increasingly cut off from government support.

The Making of Industrial Policies

During the 1980s and 1990s, R&D support for wind and solar technologies was paired with public funding for demonstration projects and deployment. Although production costs declined and some of the technical challenges of early wind turbines and solar panels found solutions, these newer offerings remained uncompetitive with conventional sources of energy. Beginning in the 1980s, governments employed regulatory measures and subsidies to offset some of the cost disadvantages, enabling the first commercial wind and solar installations as demonstration projects for technologies resulting from publicly funded research programs. The combination of ongoing public investments in the development of new technologies and subsidies for their commercial application shifted the goals of government engagement from scientific discovery to economic growth and national competitiveness.[29] By the mid-2000s, China, Germany, and the United States had arrived at remarkably similar industrial policy portfolios to support the creation of new renewable energy technologies and their deployment in domestic markets (Table 2.1).

United States

The transition from R&D as scientific endeavor to R&D as strategic support for industrial development was perhaps the most complicated in the United States, where the federal government had traditionally avoided the impression of economic intervention in favor of particular industries. More generally, plans to support domestic renewable energy industries consistently caused heated debates along partisan lines. Even with these challenges, however, policies that supported the creation of domestic markets gradually took shape, complementing federal investments in renewable energy R&D.

In the wake of the oil crises, the 1978 Public Utilities Regulatory Policy Act (PURPA) required electric utilities to purchase power from third-party generators and to pay for such power at the rate of avoided cost. PURPA was unable to make renewable energy cost-competitive unless state-level policies accompanied it. Wide variation in implementation meant that in some states PURPA

---

[29] Nemet 2009; Nemet 2019, chapters 4 and 6. A similar shift toward growth-driven climate and environmental policy also occurred in international organizations. See Meckling and Allan, 2020.

initially had no effect.[30] When the first Gulf War shone a spotlight on alternative energy sources as a matter of national security, the Bush administration again raised R&D budgets. It also passed a production tax credit (PTC), the first federal attempt to close the cost gap between renewable and conventional sources of electricity through an incentive that rewarded the generation of wind power.[31]

Political conflict between Democrats and Republicans over renewable energy policy continued throughout the 1990s and 2000s, leading to volatility in both federal R&D funding and the availability of tax benefits.[32] Between 1992 and 2006 alone, the PTC for wind energy was renewed in five separate instances, often only for one or two years. On three separate occasions, the PTC expired before it could be renewed, leading to periods of up to nine months during which no federal support was available at all.[33]

The volatility of federal policy prompted state governments to step forward. States became a central force behind the creation of domestic renewable energy sectors and the prioritization of economic benefits in particular. Starting in the 1990s, states began to require electricity retailers to source a percentage of electricity from renewable sources by enacting Renewable Portfolio Standards (RPS). The Massachusetts legislature passed the first RPS in 1997; by 2012, the number of states with RPS had grown to thirty.[34] A second policy measure to encourage renewable energy demand, often used in conjunction with RPS, involved so-called Public Benefit Funds (PBFs). By 2005, 23 states had passed legislation to establish PBFs for renewable energy, collecting some USD 300 million annually to provide low-interest loans, equity investments, and funding for test centers, demonstration projects, and technical support.[35] In addition, a number of states passed so-called net-metering laws. These permitted commercial and individual owners of renewable energy installations to deduct any electricity supplied to the grid from their electric bills. By 2005, 38 states had passed such net-metering laws, and an additional three states passed net-metering legislation between 2005 and 2016.[36]

In contrast to earlier programs aimed at scientific discovery, these state-level demand-side programs prioritized industrial policy objectives that were not hard

[30] Martinot, Wiser, and Hamrin 2005, 3–4; Redlinger, Anderson, and Morthorst 1988, 182–85. An early outlier was California, where PURPA, in combination with a production tax credit, led to lucrative long-term contracts for wind power generation in the early 1980s. More than 15,000 turbines were installed between 1980 and 1986. The elimination of a host of additional tax incentives in 1986 left PURPA as the only remaining support mechanism in California, and new installations came to a halt. See Harborne and Hendry 2009, 3583.

[31] Laird and Stefes 2009, 2625; Martinot, Wiser, and Hamrin 2005, 3–4; Wiser, Bolinger, and Barbose 2007, 78.

[32] Laird and Stefes 2009, 2625.

[33] Karapin 2016, chapter 9; Wiser, Bolinger, and Barbose 2007, 79.

[34] Shrimali et al. 2012, 33.

[35] Bolinger et al. 2001, 84–85; Martinot, Wiser, and Hamrin 2005, 10.

[36] Inskeep et al. 2016; Martinot, Wiser, and Hamrin 2005, 10; Menz 2005, 2404. These regulations were not uncontested, and utility companies in particular mobilized to revert support for renewable energy legislation that they saw threatening to their business model. See Stokes, 2020.

to identify. To build the political coalitions necessary to pass renewable energy legislation, many programs included local content regulations that directly aimed to attract economic activity. Particularly when regulatory measures were insufficient and public funds were required to stimulate the creation of demand, government programs often paired their renewable offerings with the promise of local jobs and economic activity.[37] Measures included, for instance, preferential loans for renewable energy projects that required wind and solar equipment to be manufactured locally. Other states enacted RPS that required a percentage of renewable energy to be generated in-state. In some cases, to meet RPS requirements, utilities had to use locally manufactured solar panels and wind turbines.[38] A 2015 survey found at least forty-four renewable energy programs in twenty-three states that contained local content requirements, often in violation of international trade rules.[39]

Germany

In Germany, the transformation of renewable energy policy into industrial policy took place by accident. Lawmakers fundamentally underestimated the potential of their signature legislation, the 1990 Feed-in Law, in the absence of existing renewable energy industries. Over time, economic justifications for renewable energy policy took center stage as domestic industries grew in response to Germany's initial feed-in tariff. Policymakers took seriously the growth potential of the wind and solar sectors as export industries. The resulting program was more centralized than in the United States. The German federal government controlled all energy sector regulation, thereby avoiding the patchwork of state-level policies seen in the United States.

The 1990 Feed-in Law extended long-term subsidies to producers of renewable energy, combining previous technology-push policies with an attempt to create markets for renewable energy technologies. It required utilities to connect renewable energy generators to the grid, and it mandated the purchase of their electricity at rates between 75 and 90 percent above average end-user tariffs. The federal government estimated that the legislation would at most double renewable energy generation capacity on the grid.[40] Between 1989 and 1995, installed wind generation capacity increased from 20 MW to 1100 MW, more than tripling overall renewable energy generation capacity on the German grid in defiance of original predictions.[41] Yet precisely because the government initially depicted

---

[37] Stokes and Warshaw 2017, 3.
[38] Mack et al. 2011, 11–17.
[39] Meyer 2015, 1959–60.
[40] Deutscher Bundestag 1990, 4.
[41] Advocate General Jacobs 2000; Lauber and Mez 2004, 602. Prior to the Feed-In Law, Germany's renewable energy generation capacity consisted of some 4,000 hydropower plants with a total generation capacity of 470 MW. Deutscher Bundestag 1990, 3.

the Feed-in Law as a small and inconsequential change to electricity sector regulation, an unlikely alliance of environmental progressives and Christian conservatives seeking to support small hydropower plants in their home districts had convinced a majority of the Bundestag to support the legislation.[42]

The German utility sector, which had also missed the initial significance of the legislative changes, came to regard the Feed-in Law as a threat to its business model. Forced to integrate a rapidly growing share of wind energy, utility companies launched a series of legal challenges in parliament and in the courts.[43] These attempts to stop the creation of domestic renewable energy markets were defeated in the courts, and lobbying efforts also failed politically. After sixteen years of conservative government rule, the 1998 federal election awarded victory to a coalition of Social Democrats and the German Green Party, a long-term champion of renewable energy. The new government set ambitious goals to increase the share of renewables on the German electric grid. Acknowledging the development of domestic green energy sectors over the previous decade, government leaders now justified such goals in both environmental *and* economic terms.[44]

The coalition agreement between the two parties listed two key priorities: the creation of jobs through investment in sustainable growth and the "ecological modernization" (*ökologische Modernisierung*) of the domestic economy to marry environmental and economic goals.[45] In late 1999, the new government introduced a new demand-side legislation for renewable energy markets.[46] Replacing the Feed-in Law, the Renewable Energy Sources Act (*Erneuerbare Energien Gesetz*) determined specific rates for each energy source, rather than setting prices as a percentage of end-user tariffs.[47] The introduction of differentiated demand-side subsidies created rapidly growing market demand for solar PV technologies. Particularly after a 2004 amendment that further increased the rates for solar power, the German PV market expanded exponentially, turning Germany into the largest solar market in the world.[48] Cumulative installations of solar panels grew from 370 MW in 2003 to 17,000 MW by 2010. Germany now accounted for nearly half the world's total installed solar energy generation capacity.[49]

---

[42] Berchem 2006. Jacobsson and Lauber 2005; Laird and Stefes 2009. For a history of the German Green Party, see Mair 2001. On environmental politics in Germany more generally, see Hager 1995.

[43] Advocate General Jacobs 2000; Lauber and Mez 2004, 106–8.

[44] Sozialdemokratische Partei Deutschlands and Bündnis 90/Die Grünen, 17–19.

[45] Sozialdemokratische Partei Deutschlands and Bündnis 90/Die Grünen, 2.

[46] Bechberger 2000, 20–26.

[47] For 2000, for instance, the legislation set a price of Euro 0.091/kWh for wind power and 0.506/kWh for solar power. Bechberger, 46–50; Dagger, 73–76; Deutscher Bundestag 2000; Lauber and Mez, 610.

[48] Bruns et al., 208.

[49] Wind and solar data compiled by Earth Policy Institute 2020.

China

The link between state support for renewable energy and economic growth object-ives proved strongest in China, which identified wind and solar sectors from the be-ginning as potential vehicles for industrialization and development. Encouraging the development of an indigenous wind industry, the Chinese government pursued a three-pronged strategy: creating domestic markets, supporting R&D efforts by local enterprises and research institutes, and providing incentives for foreign firms to localize manufacturing and transfer technology to local partners. Throughout the 1990s, Chinese energy policy prioritized the establishment of a domestic wind industry over other emerging renewable energy technologies. Wind turbines had already been tested in large-scale installations in California during the 1980s and remained far more affordable than solar power during this period.[50] In 1994, the Ministry for Electric Power mandated the purchase of wind-generated power from turbines installed on demonstration sites. Under the Ninth Five-Year Plan (1996–2000), part of China's policy practice of setting comprehensive economic goals in five-year increments, government leaders added designated funds for wind turbine R&D to China's 863 Program for applied research, introduced a 40 percent local content requirement for new wind power projects, and created a loan program for wind farm development through the State Development Planning Commission and the Ministry of Science and Technology (MOST).[51] In the early 2000s, the cen-trally funded 863 Program for applied research dispensed RMB 20 billion (roughly USD 3 billion) to research institutes and enterprises, including to startups such as Suntech and Goldwind, which would become some of China's largest producers of wind turbines and solar PV technologies over time.[52] Overall funding for the 863 Program rose nearly fifty-fold between 1991 and 2005.[53]

The creation of large-scale markets for wind turbines subsequently improved China's domestic capabilities. Starting in 2003, through the Wind Power Concession Program, the government provided subsidies for large-scale wind turbine installations through a tender-based bidding system. A clear sign of in-dustrial policy ambitions, the government-run program contained stringent domestic content regulations of up to 70 percent, as well as tax incentives to at-tract foreign turbine manufacturers and their suppliers to China.[54] More than 3,350 MW of turbines—many produced by foreign turbine manufactures in

[50] China had extensive installations in hydropower, which had been used for rural electrification during the Mao years. In 1984, more than half of China's counties had small-scale hydro dams for local power generation. Technically, wind was China's second renewable energy industry. China Yeh and Lewis 2004, 443.

[51] For a detailed timeline of wind power policy, see Lewis 2012, 68–74; 2013. For an in-depth anal-ysis of China's 863 program, see Zhi and Pearson, 2017.

[52] Campbell 2011, 3; Karplus 2007, 23–24.

[53] Osnos 2009.

[54] Ru et al. 2012, 65; Wang Q. 2010, 705–6.

China—were installed between 2003 and 2007. The Wind Power Concession Program rapidly transformed China into one of the largest wind markets in the world.[55]

In 2006, the central government declared "indigenous innovation" (*zizhu chuangxin*) a central goal of the Eleventh Five-Year Plan (2006–2010), after technology was primarily imported throughout the 1990s.[56] In the renewable energy sector, indigenous innovation guidelines triggered the aggressive expansion of renewable energy markets and strengthened support for domestic R&D activities. The central government passed China's first renewable energy law, which provided a framework for introducing feed-in laws similar to those in effect in Germany. The new law also set up the legislative basis for cost-sharing mechanisms to retrieve the cost of renewable energy subsidies through ratepayer surcharges.[57]

In 2009, the central government eliminated individual feed-in laws that had arisen in various provinces in the wake of the renewable energy law, and it instead established China's first national, unified feed-in tariff for wind energy. China was now the world's largest market for wind turbines, having doubled its cumulative wind power capacity from the previous year.[58] At the same time, the first nationwide feed-in tariff for solar energy created a small but growing domestic market for solar PV technologies, with additional subsidy programs available to support both residential customers and developers of utility-scale solar PV installations.[59] These subsidies for a domestic solar PV market went into effect after the global financial crisis had led many European governments to drastically reduce support for local solar installations—a decision that had slowed global market development and caused overcapacity among China's solar producers.[60] After decades of wind turbines dominating the local renewable energy market, solar PV technologies were finally having their moment: cost reductions made these technologies more attractive for domestic use.[61]

By the mid-2000s, China, Germany, and the United States had arrived at remarkably similar industrial policy tools to support the creation of domestic renewable energy industries. In all three economies, governments combined support for renewable energy markets with public funding for R&D activities with the goal of creating domestic wind and solar sectors. As I lay out in the remainder of this chapter, however, firms maintained divergent industrial profiles

[55] Ru et al. 2012, 65.
[56] State Council 2006.
[57] Lewis 2013, 53.
[58] Data compiled by Earth Policy Institute, 2020.
[59] Campbell 2011, 8.
[60] For an overview of the effects of the global financial crisis on the solar PV industry, see Bartlett, Margolis, and Jennings 2009.
[61] Goodrich et al. 2013, figure 1.

in global renewable energy sectors in spite of similar policy environments. The development and persistence of distinct national industrial profiles in wind and solar technologies is surprising, particularly if we consider the similarities in renewable energy industrial policy that these countries shared.

The Political Logic of Green Industrial Policy

By 2009, when President Obama invoked the notion of a clean energy race during his speech at MIT, renewable energy sectors had mushroomed into sizable industries. More than 159 gigawatts (GW) of wind power and 21 GW of solar PV had been installed—equivalent to the generation capacity of roughly 180 nuclear power plants. Such a feat was beyond imagination as recently as the late 1990s, when the high cost of wind turbines and solar panels limited their use to niche applications. Over the early 2000s, however, annual investment in renewable energy installations had steadily climbed, reaching USD 150 billion in 2009. Germany, China, and the United States constituted the world's largest investors at the time. Public subsidies and regulatory incentives made much of this investment possible, helping offset some of the competitive disadvantages of new energy technologies.[62] As governments eagerly eyed the growth trajectory of renewable energy markets and the size of public investments, they began to shift their strategies. They were no longer content to be mere consumers of these resources, nor were they satisfied with attracting individual segments of global renewable energy supply chains. Instead, policymakers hoped to lead the way into a new future: by providing R&D funds and supporting market demand, firms would invest in technological innovation and ultimately co-locate activities to commercialize and produce wind and solar technologies domestically.

The link between renewable energy policy and the promise of material benefits in the form of industrial development (and domestic manufacturing activities) followed a broader political logic. Among state initiatives promoting the reduction of greenhouse gas emissions, policies that pledged to support growth and employment attracted policymakers in part because they allowed for the creation of political coalitions organized around renewable energy by reaching beyond the usual suspects, or core groups of environmental advocates. Mobilizing this broader political support remained particularly important for policies that entailed large public expenditures. The formation of these coalitions also helped justify the additional financial burdens imposed on consumers of electricity, who were being asked to help offset the cost differential between traditional energy sources and higher-priced wind and solar technologies. Simply put, green

---

[62] REN21 2010, 13.

industrial policies that achieved emissions reductions while simultaneously creating new sources of growth were easier to implement politically. They also provided an opportunity to create new interest groups in support of energy sector transformation.[63] Public investments in the creation of industries that could invent, manufacture, and possibly export wind and solar products also followed the goal of strategically positioning domestic economies in sectors with future growth potential.[64]

In his speech at MIT, President Obama gave voice to this ambitious outlook. He delivered his remarks against the backdrop of the global financial crisis of 2009, which had prompted the US government to use stimulus spending to support domestic renewable energy firms in unprecedented ways. The American Recovery and Reinvestment Act (ARRA) included a specific tax credit for clean energy manufacturing, as well as loan guarantees for wind and solar manufacturers and training programs for workers in clean energy sectors.[65] Little about these programs could not be interpreted as targeted industrial policy: government resources were to be deployed with the explicit goal of accelerating growth and facilitating structural change in the economy through the support of select industrial sectors. These national green industrial policy initiatives implemented during the Obama administration followed on the heels of more widespread support for wind and solar industries at the state level. By the time Obama delivered his remarks at MIT, the majority of states had already implemented some form of renewable energy mandates, often directly tied to the promise of employment and growth.[66]

In Germany, the goal to utilize the clean energy transition as a path to broader industrial transformation became apparent in widespread comparisons to the German car industry. Automobiles had historically been developed and assembled by three domestic manufacturers—BMW, Mercedes-Benz, and Volkswagen. Up to three-quarters of domestic vehicle production was destined for export.[67] In the mid-2000s, policymakers argued that wind and solar PV technologies—like cars before them—could create domestic industries with

[63] Breetz, Mildenberger, and Stokes 2018, 500; Meckling et al. 2015, 1170; Nahm 2017a, 711–13.

[64] Additional considerations have led policymakers to consider manufacturing a sector of the economy worthy of political support. In addition to the role of manufacturing businesses in creating (unionized) employment and investing in R&D, policymakers and academics alike have questioned whether, in the long run, domestic strengths in innovation can be sustained without proximity to production capabilities. Particularly in the early stages of technology development, such views have assumed that geographical proximity between R&D and production activities helps commercialization and offers opportunities for learning that fuel further innovation. See, for instance, Ezell and Atkinson 2011a; Helper, Krueger, and Wial 2012; Pisano and Shih 2012; President's Council of Advisors on Science and Technology 2012; Ramaswarmy et al. 2018; Sivaram et. al, 2020; Tassey 2010.

[65] Mundaca and Richter 2015, 1177.

[66] Stokes and Warshaw 2017, 1–2.

[67] Ulrich 2017, 1.

substantial export potential, justifying large public investments in domestic renewable energy markets. A 2005 cabinet decision on Germany's sustainability strategy openly justified continued support for wind and solar sectors by appealing to the "tremendous export market that will permanently secure growth and employment."[68] In 2008, the Federal Ministry for the Environment predicted that green industries—renewable energy but also recycling and energy efficiency technologies—would surpass the German auto sector in their contribution to GDP by 2020. The notion of green industrial policy (ökologische Industriepolitik) became an established concept in Berlin policymaking circles.[69]

Industrial development objectives behind public support for wind and solar were perhaps most obvious in China, where renewable energy sectors were treated as potential export industries in the broader context of the nation's economic development strategy. In 2010, renewable energy sectors were included on a list of designated "Strategic Emerging Industries" (SEIs). The SEI initiative aimed to use a range of preferential policy treatments—including low-interest loans, tax breaks, and R&D support—to forge the development of industrial sectors critical to future national competitiveness. The central government in Beijing encouraged firms to reduce dependence on international technology transfers and to fill remaining gaps in domestic supply chains, including in the production of advanced manufacturing equipment for renewable energy technologies.[70] The Twelfth Five-Year Plan for the solar PV industry called for 80 percent of solar production equipment to be manufactured domestically by 2015.[71] Up until then, the domestic deployment of these technologies had been secondary, particularly in the solar industry, as the vast majority of solar production was destined for export. The central government in Beijing hoped to use the window of opportunity provided by the emergence of new clean energy technologies to establish a strategic foothold in the industries of the future.

Innovation in Global Networks

Burgeoning global markets in China, Germany, and the United States—created as a result of government policies outlined earlier—provided incentives for firms to enter renewable energy sectors, leading the modern wind and solar sectors to emerge virtually simultaneously in all three economies. At the time, a recognition of the links between innovation and national competitiveness—and the related material benefits of growth and employment—prompted governments

---

[68] Bundesregierung 2005, 19.
[69] Bundesministerium für Umwelt 2008, 6.
[70] State Council 2010; US-China Business Council 2013.
[71] Ministry of Industry and Information Technology 2012; National Energy Administration 2011.

to advocate for the domestic establishment of virtually all economic activities related to wind and solar innovation. China, Germany, and the United States, the three largest investors in renewable energy in the early 2000s, were locked in a tight race for leadership in renewable energy. The image of the three nations going head-to-head to attract and build domestic renewable industries dovetailed with a broader narrative, one that described nations in the global economy as locked into a zero-sum competition for global market share and technological leadership. This latter view made a resurgence beginning in 2015 as the US–China economic relationship deteriorated amid mercantilist sentiments and widespread calls for economic decoupling.[72] The idea that national systems competed for leadership in innovative industries also pervaded business school literatures, which portrayed innovative firms as the result of unique conditions attributable to states. From this perspective, the pursuit of innovative firms, the ultimate source of national competitiveness, placed states in direct competition with one another.[73]

Historically, however, the development of global clean energy sectors does not conform to such views. Despite similar government goals and industrial policy tools—firms in each geographical location established distinct industry structures and national patterns of industrial specialization. These national profiles in global renewable energy industries differed in the kinds of innovation and technological challenges they addressed, the type and size of firms that made up the majority of industrial activities, and the relationship between technological innovation and manufacturing (Table 2.2). I distinguish in this book between these three types of R&D capabilities in the transition of new technologies from inception to market application. Underlying this categorization is a definition of innovation as consisting of both invention and deployment. Innovation encompasses *both* the development of new technologies *and* the subsequent changes and modifications required to bring such new developments to market. From this perspective, all three national specializations can be seen as constituent elements of innovation, yet no single specialization can single-handedly complete the innovation process without reliance on external capabilities.

I use the term "invention" to refer to the development of new technologies and the early stages between the laboratory and prototyping before commercial

---

[72] Nahm, 2020.

[73] See, for instance, Porter 1990. Scholarship on innovation has shared the notion that nations remained capable of undertaking technological innovation fully within the domestic economy, even if they have differed in the types of innovation they were able to engage. Scholars of national innovation systems, for instance, have long emphasized the influence of different constellations of domestic actors on the types of innovation that domestic firms can undertake. Institutional scholars, including in the tradition of research on the varieties of capitalism, instead proposed that domestic institutions lock economies into different types of innovation, sharply limiting the kinds of industries that can thrive in different institutional settings governing the domestic economy. Fagerberg and Sapprasert 2011; Hall and Soskice 2001, 41; Vernon 1966.

Table 2.2 Varieties of Innovation

	Germany	China	United States
Type of Innovation	*Customization*	*Innovative Manufacturing*	*Invention*
Challenge addressed	Automation, production equipment, complex components	Commercialization, scale-up of new technologies	Development of new technology
Firm Type	Suppliers	Manufacturers	Start-ups
Predominant Firm Size	< 2000 Employees	> 2000 Employees	< 500 Employees
Production Scale	Medium/Low	High	Low/None

application. In fact, many inventions, including new types of printable solar cell technologies and novel wind turbine designs, never make it beyond the prototyping stage because they lack commercial application. "Customization" describes the R&D skills required for the development of production equipment and components that are not part of the process of invention, but instead constitute necessary inputs into the commercialization of these novel technologies. Automated production equipment and early-stage components for novel technologies share at least two common traits: they are generally not mass-produced, and they require substantial customization and iterative adjustments. Examples of customization include automated production lines for new technologies or novel components that cannot be readily purchased as standardized equipment. "Innovative manufacturing" refers to the engineering skills required to scale and design these technologies for mass production, operating at the intersection of traditional R&D and manufacturing. Such innovation includes, for instance, the substitution of materials, redesign of particular components, and the reorganization of internal product architecture.[74]

Literatures on technological innovation have treated this third set of capabilities residing in the manufacturing process as primarily related to process innovation, describing changes and improvements in the manufacturing process and the method of product delivery.[75] Scholars of product innovation, in contrast,

---

[74] For a detailed discussion of innovative manufacturing and its relationship to broader theories of innovation, see Nahm and Steinfeld 2014.

[75] OECD 2005, para. 163.

have focused on differences between radical and incremental innovation, the former introducing new concepts and technologies that depart significantly from past practice, and the latter improving gradually on existing designs.[76] More recent work has added the concept of architectural innovation, referring to changes in the overall architecture of a product that do not alter its underlying components.[77] Yet the commercialization and production of new products in high-technology industries often face challenges in the scale-up to mass manufacturing. These challenges cannot be met through process innovation alone— they require changes to product design. When it comes to new technologies that lack standardized manufacturing processes, innovative manufacturing serves as an integral part of the innovation process.

Although China, Germany, and the United States each incorporated a mixture of firms with a range of industrial specializations, renewable energy sectors in each economy predominately focused on one of the three constituent elements of innovation noted previously. As Chapters 4–6 discuss in detail, a number of large multinational firms operated in multiple locations, often entering wind and solar industries through acquisitions of smaller start-ups as new energy technologies became promising fields of economic activity. Some manufacturers continued to exist in both Germany and the United States; China, too, was home to select firms focused on invention and customization. But the majority of industrial activity in the United States, Germany, and China revolved around invention, customization, and innovative manufacturing, respectively. Far from the notion of a clean energy race, firms in the three economies settled into complementary evolutionary niches in global wind and solar industries, despite their governments' similar industrial policy goals and broadly comparable policy tools.

In the United States, start-up firms with capabilities in the *invention* of new technologies dominated wind and solar industries in the early 2000s. A number of multinational energy and defense firms had maintained wind and solar divisions in the 1970s and 1980s, but lack of market demand had prompted most to shut their renewable energy divisions.[78] The majority of new firms entering US wind and solar sectors in the late 1990s and early 2000s were start-ups seeking to lower the cost of renewable energy through the invention of new technologies. Many amounted to spin-offs from universities and research institutes, often founded by university faculty or research affiliates seeking to commercialize technological breakthroughs. Patent counts reflect this focus on invention: US firms and research institutes account for approximately 25 percent of cumulative wind and solar energy patents until 2009, roughly twice the number of patents

---

[76] Abernathy and Clark 1985; Abernathy and Utterback 1978.
[77] Henderson and Clark 1990. For an application of these concepts to the case of China, see Ernst and Naughton 2008.
[78] Colatat, Vidican, and Lester 2009; Heymann 1995, 349–54.

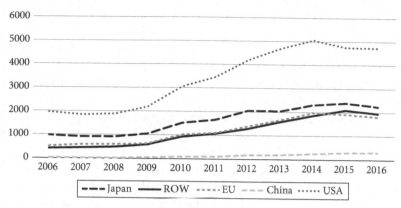

Figure 2.2 Annual USPTO Patents in Clean Energy Technologies
Source: US National Science Foundation Science and Engineering Indicators

filed by China or the European Union.[79] Clean energy patenting in the United
States continually outpaced other large economies (Figure 2.2).

In the solar sector, many of the new US firms focused on the development of
thin film technologies, which promised to lower prices by replacing silicon, an
expensive raw material, with cheaper alternatives.[80] Other firms experimented
with new manufacturing processes and new types of solar technologies, including cells that could be printed on paper and plastic.[81] The Massachusetts-
based company Evergreen had its beginnings in a radically new production
technology developed at MIT that would allow wafers to be produced in one
continuous piece, eliminating the silicon waste incurred in traditional production methods that used a silicon block to saw off wafers.[82] By 2009, out of
100 solar companies operating in the United States, at least 73 were start-ups.[83]
Although fewer in number than in the solar sector, US wind start-ups also sought
to decrease the cost of wind energy with radically different designs. For example,
Clipper Windpower proposed replacing a single turbine generator with several
smaller generators to increase efficiency.[84] Boulder Wind attempted to make
obsolete gearboxes in turbine designs, and firms like Ogin borrowed principles

---

[79] Bettencourt, Trancik, and Kaur 2013, 3.

[80] A particular concern among US scholars of China's rise in renewable energy manufacturing
has been the possibility of technology lock-in. Declining prices for solar technologies as a result of
China's investments in manufacturing have made it increasingly difficult for new technologies to
break into the market, even if they in principle offer better performance potential in the long run. See
Hart, 2020.

[81] Morton 2006.

[82] Renewable Energy World 2000.

[83] Knight 2011, 176.

[84] Goudarzi and Zhu 2013, 199.

from jet engines to develop alternatives to the traditional three-blade design.[85] Others, such as a start-up named Vortex, tried to eliminate blades altogether.[86] If these companies thought about manufacturing at all, they did so to demonstrate the commercial feasibility of their designs through proof-of-concepts and proto- typing. They did not focus on the production of mass manufacturing facilities dedicated to cost efficiency and scale (see Table 2.3).

In Germany, large numbers of small and medium-sized suppliers from ex- isting industrial sectors diversified into renewable energy sectors by zeroing in on *customization*, the development of complex componentry and production equipment. Interview data reveal that the absence of specialized suppliers in re- newable energy industries had previously required wind and solar firms to re- sort to improvisation, repurposing equipment and modifying components from other industrial sectors for application in wind turbines and solar PV modules.[87] Germany's existing manufacturing firms possessed a rich fabric of capabilities applicable to the development of wind turbine components and production lines for the solar industry that could address these needs. German firms sub- sequently responded to this opportunity by applying their niche capabilities to global renewable energy sectors. Firms entered from a variety of industries, in- cluding machine building, automation and laser processing equipment, metal fabrication, and shipbuilding.

In one of my interviews, for example, I met the second-generation head of a German machine tool manufacturer who wanted to diversify the business be- yond the automobile sector. He explained that he was actively looking for an industry where the firm could use 70 percent of what it already knew and com- plement it with 30 percent newly acquired skills to produce innovative technol- ogies. Realizing that little automation equipment existed for the production and assembly of solar modules, where demand was rapidly growing, the tool manu- facturing company entered the solar industry by building on its experience in the auto sector with new technologies in infrared and laser welding.[88] The ma- jority of renewable energy producers in Germany were much like this man. They represented firms from adjacent industrial sectors, and they were looking for new applications of the core skills and capabilities that they already possessed.

By 2011, VDMA, the German Engineering Federation, had listed more than 170 member firms active in the wind industry, only 10 of which were manufacturers of wind turbines. The vast majority of firms developed towers,

[85] Boulder Wind Power 1999; Gertner 2013.
[86] McKenna 2015.
[87] Author interviews: CTO, German solar PV manufacturer, May 17, 2011; head of German oper- ations, global equipment manufacturer, May 18, 2011; CEO, German equipment manufacturer, May 10, 2011; CTO, German solar PV manufacturer, May 23, 2011; plant manager of German gearbox manufacturer, May 16, 2011; plant manager of German generator manufacturer, May 17, 2011.
[88] Berger 2013b, 135. Author interview, October 15, 2019.

Table 2.3 R&D Activities, Select Wind and Solar Firms

Firm	Background	R&D Focus
USA		
Innovalight (Solar)	Silicon Valley start-up, founded 2003.	- R&D on *silicon ink nanomaterial* to increase cell efficiency, funded by DOE and NREL. Research with JA Solar (China), acquired by DuPont (2011).
MiaSolé (Solar)	Silicon Valley start-up, founded 2004.	- VC-funded ($550 million) development of *flexible thin-film cell* on stainless steel substrate. Experimental production line. Acquired by Hanergy, China (2012).
Ogin (Wind)	Aerospace spin-off, founded 2008.	- VC and ARPA-E funding to develop *jet-engine-based high-efficiency wind turbines.* Some R&D and component development in China.
Makani (Wind)	California-based start-up, founded 2006.	- Google-backed R&D on *kite-based flying wind turbines* to increase generation efficiency. Acquired by Google X in 2013 while still prototyping.
Germany		
Schmid Group (Solar)	Family-owned. Founded as foundry in 1864.	- Background in circuit board printers, develops turnkey solar production lines (2001). R&D on *selective emitter cell lines* with Chinese partner (2009).
RENA (Solar)	Private, founded in 1993.	- Applies R&D on semiconductor equipment to wet bench chemical *processing equipment* for solar. Currently work on passivated emitter and PERC cells.
Eickhoff (Wind)	Founded 1864, equipment for mining sector.	- Uses in-house foundry and background in gearboxes for mining to develop *wind turbine gearboxes.* Small-batch production of ultra-large, offshore gearboxes.
VEM Sachsenw. (Wind)	Family-owned machine builder, founded 1903.	- Background in generators, engines for streetcars. R&D on *wind turbine generators* beginning in 1998. Small-batch production of ultra-large, off-shore generators.
China		
JA Solar (Solar)	PV producer, founded 2005.	- Founded by returning overseas Chinese scientists, focus on commercialization of *high efficiency multi-SI cells.* First to apply silicon ink technology (with Innovalight)
CSUN (Solar)	PV producer, founded 2004.	- Founded by returning overseas Chinese scientists, focus on commercialization of *high efficiency mono- and poly-SI cells.* First to commercialize selective emitter cells.

Continued

Table 2.3 *Continued*

Firm	Background	R&D Focus
Goldwind (Wind)	1998 Spin-off from state-owned firm.	- R&D on commercialization of *gearless wind turbines* to avoid maintenance associated with traditional gearbox designs. Collaboration with Vensys (Germany).
Mingyang (Wind)	2006 spin-off from electrical equipment firm.	- R&D on commercialization of *super compact drive turbines* to lower maintenance cost, especially offshore. Collaboration with Aerodyn (Germany).

Source: Information compiled from company websites and public financial filings.

blades, mechanical components, hydraulics systems, and production equipment for the wind industry.[89] Similarly, in the PV sector, more than seventy firms offered production lines, automation equipment, coatings, and laser processing machines. With roughly 41,000 employees in 2010, employment in solar PV equipment and component firms far surpassed the 12,000 jobs in Germany's solar module manufacturers in the same year.[90] Of the four vertically-integrated solar manufacturers operating in Germany in 2011, only two remained in existence by 2014. Their combined annual production capacity amounted to less than a single Chinese PV manufacturing plant.[91] The small number of domestic wind turbine and solar PV manufacturers made Germany's renewable energy suppliers highly dependent on global markets. Export quotas of more than 50 percent in the solar sector and up to 80 percent in the wind industry underscore the tight integration of Germany's wind and solar firms into global renewable energy supply chains.[92]

Chinese wind and solar firms, by contrast, focused on technical capabilities in commercialization and scale-up—what I call skills in *innovative manufacturing*—that neither US start-ups nor German suppliers had established in-house.[93] The majority of wind turbine producers spun off from state-owned or formerly state-owned manufacturing firms. In the solar industry, firms were frequently founded by Chinese scientists educated in solar PV research laboratories abroad.[94] When these firms entered wind and solar PV sectors in the late 1990s and early 2000s, few manufacturers of wind turbines and solar panels were

---

[89] Germany Trade & Invest 2010; Arbeitsgemeinschaft Windenergie-Zulieferindustrie 2012.
[90] Germany Trade & Invest 2011b, c.
[91] Germany Trade & Invest 2011a, 2014.
[92] Fischedick and Bechberger 2009, 26.
[93] Nahm and Steinfeld, 2014.
[94] See Alexander 2013.

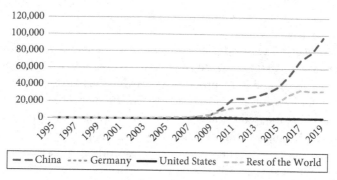

Figure 2.3 Annual Solar Photovoltaics Cell Production by Country, 1995–2019 (in Megawatts).

Source: Earth Policy Institute 2020, Jäger-Waldau 2020.

producing at scale. While technology could be accessed in global networks, mass manufacturing knowledge was simply not available. According to Wu Gang, the founder of Goldwind, one of China's first wind turbine firms: "Whole blades dropped off. The main shafts broke. It was really very dangerous."[95] Chinese firms subsequently concentrated their efforts on building R&D skills around the commercialization and rapid scale-up of complex wind and solar technologies.

By 2012, China's renewable energy firms accounted for over 60 percent of the global production of solar PV modules and nearly half of the world's wind turbines (Figure 2.3).[96] Seven of the ten largest solar manufacturers and four of the ten largest wind turbine producers in the world were Chinese firms.[97] The majority of these producers continued to license technology and source components and production equipment abroad.[98] Site visits revealed designated engineering teams with advanced capacity to rapidly translate complex technologies into mass-manufacturable products.[99] Such tasks required improvements to process designs long associated with manufacturing innovation, but they also entailed changes to product designs—to accommodate manufacturing

[95] Osnos 2009.

[96] Earth Policy Institute 2020.

[97] Bebon 2013; IHS Solar 2013.

[98] Lewis 2013, 136–37.

[99] Author interviews: Senior VP global supply chains, Chinese solar manufacturer, March 13, 2011; CTO and director of R&D at Chinese solar manufacturer, August 26, 2011; head of China operations, European wind turbine engineering firm, January 13, 2011; CEO, European wind turbine engineering firm, May 20, 2011; CTO, Chinese wind turbine manufacturer, August 29, 2011; CEO, Chinese solar cell manufacturer, August 10, 2011; president, Chinese wafer manufacturer, August 26, 2011. CEO, Chinese cell and module manufacturer, interviewed June 28, 2013. Nahm and Steinfeld 2014.

requirements, to incorporate new materials and components, and to meet cost targets for final products.

The engineering teams devoted to innovative manufacturing frequently operated in a separate R&D division that looked solely at the challenges posed by scale-up and mass production. At the wind turbine manufacturer Mingyang, for instance, out of 300 R&D staff in 2010, approximately one-third of the engineers focused on developing new technologies, while two-thirds worked on bringing existing technologies to mass production.[100] Similarly, Trina Solar reported that out of 425 employees working in its R&D division in 2012, just 79 focused on technology development; the remaining 346 engineers devised solutions to the challenges of commercialization in a designated test facility with production lines solely dedicated to R&D.[101] Even as the wage gap widened between urban workers in coastal and interior provinces, wind and solar firms maintained such knowledge-intensive innovative manufacturing strategies in high-wage coastal locations.[102] For instance, Chinese solar PV manufacturers were among the first firms to employ fully automated production lines in response to such changes.[103] Such feats, of course, would be hard to conceive without the makers of production equipment, predominately from Germany, who provided the basic machinery on which such innovative manufacturing capabilities could be applied.

Collaboration *and* Competition

While wind and solar sectors in China, Germany, and the United States developed rapidly and simultaneously throughout the early 2000s, the majority of firms in each location did not compete directly. Firms established distinct—and often complementary—technological skills to carve out unique competitive niches in global renewable energy sectors. In contrast to the notion of a clean energy race, these distinct national industrial specializations remained interdependent: none of the states examined in this book established all the technological capabilities required to invent, commercialize, and produce new energy technologies domestically. The capabilities required to bring new technologies from lab to market spanned the organizational boundaries of the firm, and the resources required to establish such capabilities cut across

---

[100] China Ming Yang Wind Power Group Limited 2011, 54.
[101] Trina Solar 2012, 64–65.
[102] Li et al. 2012, 62.
[103] Author interviews: CTO and director of R&D at Chinese solar manufacturer, August 26, 2011; CEO, Chinese cell and module manufacturer, interviewed June 28, 2013. See also Nahm and Steinfeld 2014.

national borders. Wind and solar industries were not nationally self-sufficient in a particular type of innovation, nor did they distinguish themselves according to each nation's tier in the global economy. Rather, firms specialized in different activities that at one point might have all occurred under the roof of one enterprise, but now required collaboration across firms. In doing so, firms circumvented the traditional division of labor between industrialized and developing economies and transcended the national innovation systems expected to support them.

Before the reorganization of the global economy began in the 1980s, firms tended to have the capacity to translate between complex designs and manufacturing requirements within the four walls of their own company. In the postwar decades, this all-in-one-approach had favored large enterprises as the primary drivers of economic growth and competitiveness. The core competitive advantage of large enterprises had been precisely the ability to establish a broad range of engineering capabilities required for technological innovation and the commercialization of new technologies. Such skills were either established within the four walls of the firm or, at the minimum, located in local clusters of third-party suppliers that could provide such capabilities in close proximity. Moreover, large enterprises could make the capital, human, and financial investments required to establish this broad range of engineering capabilities in ways that smaller firms could not. By organizing manufacturing and R&D in close proximity to one another, these firms coordinated and established critical linkages between innovation and production capabilities in the early stages of product development, more efficiently transitioning new products from lab to mass production.[104] Only after products were reliable, manufacturing processes standardized, and price premiums from technological advantage depleted did production activities shift to developing economies—countries with fewer technical capabilities, lower degrees of vertical integration, and less sophisticated market demand.[105]

In many cases, the relocation of manufacturing activity to developing economies through outsourcing and offshoring has removed the demand or need for such skills in advanced economies. It has created opportunities for manufacturing firms in developing economies to specialize in precisely the type of engineering capabilities that are required to prepare advanced products for mass manufacturing. Throughout the 1970s, US car manufacturers, competing with challengers from Japan and Germany, made more than 70 percent of their

---

[104] Where scholars of East Asian economic development saw a need for the state to encourage the creation of such business in late-developing economies, Chandler, in a study of the origins of large business in the United States, argued that the dominance of conglomerates in the US economy was a result of their competitive success. See Chandler 1977, chapters 3 and 9.

[105] Vernon 1966. For dynamic versions of product cycle theory, see Antràs 2003; Grossman and Helpman 1991; Krugman 1979.

components in-house, tightly integrating the development of new car models and the supply chains required to produce them. Reliance on external suppliers for the remaining parts was primarily an exercise in benchmarking internal production costs and provided a means to respond to rapid fluctuations of demand that could not be met internally. Even as shifts in the global economy prompted outsourcing and offshoring, the lead firms in global auto supply chains firmly controlled the invention and commercialization of new technologies and the growing number of suppliers involved in producing them.[106] In contrast to modern renewable energy sectors, national automobile industries remained firmly anchored in domestic political economies. They competed with firms from other countries that possessed a similar capacity to invent, commercialize, and produce new cars domestically.

Compare the integrated US auto sector of the 1970s to contemporary electronics firms such as Apple. Not only has Apple entrusted virtually all of its production to third-party suppliers in Asia, but it also relies on these suppliers, most importantly Foxconn, to help prepare its novel product designs for mass production. While Apple stands out among its competitors for its ability to conduct product design activities in the United States, its ability to do so largely stems from its active involvement in the commercialization process in Asia. This involvement includes industrial design, the selection of components, changes to product design to meet manufacturing needs, and the ability to translate between the design and manufacturing process and a customer base in the United States.[107] Like Apple, innovators in advanced economies not only rely on manufacturers for the production of their products but also, increasingly, depend on their R&D capabilities to prepare product designs for mass production.

The idea of a clean energy race that I referenced at the beginning of this chapter is also based on such a template of technological innovation and national competitiveness that Apple and others like it have revealed to be inaccurate. This template assumes the need for co-location of activities related to the invention, commercialization, and manufacturing for novel technologies. In contrast to the system of collaboration and specialization in wind and solar industries, governments often presumed that success in any particular sector required the full range of economic activities related to that particular sector to be located within national borders. The varieties of innovation that exist today in the wind and solar industries are therefore not novel in and of themselves, but relate to engineering skills that have long been required to invent new technologies and prepare them for commercialization and deployment. What *is* new in the empirical cases that I describe is the

---

[106] Sabel and Herrigel 2018, 235–36.
[107] Pisano and Shih 2009, 119.

fact that such skills are no longer all located in the same firm or region. What once occurred in a single enterprise or a domestic cluster of firms has now manifested in distinct national specializations in global industries that depend on one another to develop new technologies.[108]

Conclusion

This chapter rules out two common explanations for the persistence of distinct national profiles in the global economy: that governments pursued different industrial policy goals, and that they did so using different policy tools. Instead, a common political logic led governments in China, Germany, and the United States to converge on similar policy goals and industrial tools: after policymakers discovered the economic potential of renewable energy sectors, they justified public investments in R&D and subsidies for renewable energy markets with the promise of economic growth and employment. This led governments to combine long-standing policies to support R&D with subsidies to create renewable energy markets, often explicitly tied to local content regulations and other means to attract local industrial activity and manufacturing jobs in particular. State efforts nonetheless yielded distinct national profiles in global industries. In the early 2000s, just after China's WTO accession accelerated changes in the organization of the global economy, firms in China, Germany, and the United States chose different technological specializations and competitive strategies to enter emerging wind and solar industries.

Three broader implications follow from this phenomenon. First, as I have chronicled in this chapter, the national specializations in different types of R&D show that innovation no longer occurs entirely within national borders. Invention, customization, and innovative manufacturing, the three specializations highlighted in this book, constitute different elements of a single innovation process from lab to market that now spans national borders and the boundaries of the firm. Second, the complementarity of these national specializations in renewable energy industries belies the very notion of a clean energy race and the mercantilist approaches to green industrial policy that spring from such reasoning. Since firms in large part competed with other firms within the same economy but had competitive strategies that complemented those of firms in other countries, collaboration, not competition, lay at the heart

---

[108] A growing literature on global innovation systems has examined the expanding spatial complexity of technological innovation, including in renewable energy sectors. See, for instance, Binz and Truffer 2017, 1286; Markard and Truffer 2008; Wieczorek, Raven, and Berkhout 2015.

of the development of global renewable energy sectors. Third and most important, the phenomenon I describe in this chapter raises a central question to be examined in the chapters that follow: what mechanism explains the distinct national specializations of renewable energy industries in China, Germany, and the United States?

3

Collaborative Advantage and National Patterns of Innovation

In the last chapter I showed that governments in China, Germany, and the United States supported the development of renewable energy technologies—and domestic markets for their use and deployment—not solely for environmental reasons, but also to encourage the growth of domestic industries. The economic motivations behind renewable energy policies were particularly pronounced in the three economies at the core of this book, by far the world's largest investors in wind and solar energy in the early 2000s. Yet the aspiration to combine climate and economic objectives was not unique to the countries examined here. Governments from Brazil to Turkey made clean energy policies contingent on local industrial development, using local content regulations, tariffs, and government procurement programs to ensure that energy policies yielded local economic results.[1] Policies that pursued the dual objective of achieving emissions reductions while creating new sources of growth were easier to implement politically, and public expenses for such programs could be more readily justified.[2] The prospect of growing export markets for renewable energy technologies—part of the broader global shift away from fossil energy sources—further prompted governments to prepare their domestic economies to seize the day, taking advantage of potential opportunities.

Earlier I also dispelled the myth that a clean energy race emerged from such competing government goals. Despite a common political logic that led policymakers to pursue similar aspirations in their support for renewable energy technologies, firms entered wind and solar industries with different industrial specializations. In contrast to the competitive dynamic that pervaded political rhetoric, firms in China, Germany, and the United States tackled different and ultimately complementary types of technical challenges as they sought to bring new energy technologies to market. Manufacturers of wind turbines and solar PV modules certainly competed with one another, as did suppliers for components and production equipment. But they also collaborated: within the global networks that enabled the commercialization of renewable energy

---

[1] Kuntze and Moerenhout 2013, 30–31; Lewis 2014, 14; Meyer 2015, 1957.
[2] Breetz, Mildenberger, and Stokes 2018, 500; Meckling et al. 2015, 1170; Nahm 2017a, 711–13.

technologies, no one national industry approximated the kind of self-sufficiency that policymakers aspired to.

In this chapter I expand on the explanation for these outcomes. Why did Germany, China, and the United States arrive at distinct national profiles in global wind and solar industries? In accounting for the responses of firms to the policies of the state, I pay particular attention to firms' choices about how to participate in the global economy and their repurposing and adaptation of domestic institutions in that process. I describe two constituent elements of collaborative advantage that explain the persistence of distinct national industrial profiles in the global economy. First, because of new opportunities for collaboration, firms can participate in a global division of labor that allows them to specialize. Rather than having to maintain in-house all the skills required to develop, commercialize, and manufacture wind turbines and solar panels, specialization allows firms to focus on distinct and narrow sets of capabilities. Second, as a result of new possibilities for specialization, firms can repurpose existing institutions for application in new industries. Such institutional repurposing drives the persistence of legacy institutions within the domestic economy and propels their iterative reorientation toward new, global industrial sectors.

As a first step in this explanation, I examine two alternate conceptions of globalization, contrasting those that primarily focus on the role of competition with those that emphasize the role of comparative advantage. I then offer my own view of globalization—based on the concept of collaborative advantage—and show why this explanation, centered on the role of collaboration, is particularly suitable to explain patterns of industrial development and institutional endurance in emerging industries. I show how the impact of collaborative advantage was refracted through experimentation and repurposing of industrial legacies and divergent economic institutions in China, Germany, and the United States, leading to distinct national profiles in global renewable energy industries. The final section in the chapter sets the boundaries of the argument and outlines three structural conditions for collaborative advantage: the rise of global supply chains, nonhierarchical patterns of industrial organization, and opportunities for experimentation in response to state industrial policies.

Two Perspectives on Globalization

Over the past three decades, explaining the consequences of globalization has become a central area of inquiry for scholars of political economy. Broadly defined as a process of greater international economic integration driven by technological advances in transportation and the transmission of information, research in this field has examined the impact of increasing cross-border trade in products, international capital flows, and technological diffusion on matters of domestic politics ranging from development and economic policymaking to welfare policy and inequality.[3] Perhaps not surprisingly, such scholarship on increasing economic interdependence—irrespective of its substantive focus—has offered vastly different perspectives on the fundamental nature of globalization itself.

One avenue of research has understood globalization primarily as a process of reaping gains from international trade based on comparative advantage. Grounded in the notion that factor endowments shape nations' relative opportunity costs for specializing in the production of some goods over others, research in this tradition has focused on the circumstances that allow and prevent nations from realizing the benefits of greater economic integration.[4] In its most elemental approach, this view of globalization as the realization of comparative advantage assumes that nations trade in finished products, finding their niche in the global economy based on preexisting factor endowments. Relative factor intensities for final products determine the connections between national economies in the global economy. In this view, globalization is primarily an opportunity to benefit from trade.

This view of the global economy has been challenged on its assumption that products continue to have clear national identities. Products now contain multiple components and production stages—each with different factor intensities—that originate in multiple locations around the world.[5] The final assembly location of a product offers little analytical explanation of how globalization connects different production locations, who is likely to benefit, or how exposure to the global economy shapes domestic interests.

Subsequent literatures on global value chains have offered a more nuanced perspective, examining globalization from the vantage point of global production systems. In this view, globalization is primarily a process of progressive outsourcing, in which firms in advanced industrialized economies have shifted low-value manufacturing and design activities to lower-cost locations in developing economies.[6] As the state features only peripherally in research on global value chains, globalization is primarily conceived of as a phenomenon structured and organized through the activities of firms, in particular by lead firms in advanced economies that control global chains hierarchically.[7] This is not to say that states no longer matter: all global value chains connect at some point to the domestic contexts within which firms operate on the ground. The benefits

[3] Baldwin 2016, 5–6. Hall and Soskice 2001, 55. Kaplinsky 2013, chapter 6; Swank 2002, chapter 2; Zysman and Newman 2006, 5–6.
[4] Samuelson 1938, 265.
[5] Frieden and Rogowski 1996, 36–41.
[6] Gereffi 1994, 43.
[7] For a discussion of different modes of governance in global chains, see Gereffi 2018, 1–39; Gereffi, Humphrey, and Sturgeon 2005, 83–84.

of globalization materialize within links among firms, and those firms that can respond flexibly to changing circumstances on the ground shape the structure of the international economic system. Nonetheless, the domestic environment holds secondary importance, even if globalization has important consequences for domestic growth and economic development.

A second view of globalization, one centered on increasing competition, has approached international economic integration from a domestic perspective. Without necessarily refuting potential gains from trade, research in this tradition has pinpointed the constraints imposed on states by the international economy.[8] Globalization limits the resources available to national governments, for example, as taxes cannot be raised without affecting the competitive position of domestic firms. These constraints, in turn, are likely to lower taxes on mobile capital, causing immobile labor to shoulder a higher fiscal burden over time.[9] Capital mobility similarly shapes the possibilities for industrial policy, as investors become unwilling to fund domestic firms if returns are higher elsewhere.[10] An open international economy also places labor, environmental, and other regulations under scrutiny that might affect the competitive position of domestic firms.[11]

A central question emerging from this body of research is the degree to which competitive pressures from the global economy have led nations to liberalize previously distinct institutions and economic practices. Thirty years after these debates first took shape, it has become clear that globalization has not leveled variation across national political economies. States have neither fully converged in the institutions that govern their economies nor come together in the patterns of industrial capabilities possessed by domestic firms.[12] Far from a race to the bottom, in some cases international trade itself has caused a diffusion of stricter labor and environmental standards to developing economies that previously lacked such regulations.[13]

A large body of literature has examined the degree to which domestic institutions have slowed the impact of this competition. Focusing on advanced industrialized economies, Hall and Soskice, among others, have suggested that mutually reinforcing institutional arrangements lent stability to distinct varieties of domestic capitalisms in spite of global pressures to liberalize.[14]

---

[8] At the core, this perspective argues that technological changes that underpin globalization and the fragmentation of global production have undermined state attempts to bolster national competitiveness by denationalizing comparative advantage. See Baldwin 2016, 222–79.

[9] Rodrik 1998, 87.

[10] Berger 2000, 54–55.

[11] Locke 2013, 10.

[12] See, for instance, Breznitz 2007, 3.

[13] Distelhorst and Locke 2018; Vogel 1995, 5–8.

[14] Hall and Soskice 2001, 38–44. For an empirical critique of this argument, see Taylor 2004.

Complementary institutions preserved distinct political economies, each suitable for different types of production and innovation activities. In "coordinated market economies," such as Germany, the institutions that govern labor markets, financing, and employee participation in corporate governance created an environment best suited to industries that are based on slow-paced incremental innovation. In "liberal market economies" such as the United States, where domestic institutions foster labor market flexibility, well-developed equity markets, and short-term profit expectations, firms based their strategies on radical innovation. Where changes in the international economy have created pressures for reform, distinct national political economies have nonetheless persisted through a process of economic liberalization—a result of sticky institutions that are difficult to change against the opposition from vested interests and self-reinforcing complementarities of domestic economic arrangements.[15]

Yet even if responses to the pressures emanating from the international economy did not level differences among national political economies and the industrial capabilities of domestic firms, historical institutionalists nonetheless pit global economic forces against legacy institutions and the political coalitions that support them.[16] In Europe, for instance, economic competition and the growing reach of global finance has in some places triggered reform. In other economies, such as Germany, competitive pressures have led to a new institutional dualism: an industrial core of legacy sectors invested in existing institutions that suit the nation's competitive strategies, and a rapid shift of remaining economic activity into spheres with fewer institutional constraints, such as services.[17] Globalization, from this perspective, forges long-term and consequential changes in the politics and possibilities of organizing domestic economies within the international system.

Rethinking Globalization

These theories of globalization as either competition or comparative advantage offer little guidance for understanding the industries at the core of this book. Consider the case of two manufacturers of wind turbine generators, one from Germany and one from China. In the spring of 2011, in an industrial park in East Germany, I asked the plant manager of the German manufacturer about competition from China. In the decade before our first meeting, China had become the largest manufacturer of wind turbines in the world, and Chinese firms were now

---

[15] Thelen 2014, 14.
[16] Höpner and Krempel 2004; Hsueh, 2012; Streeck 2009; Streeck and Mertens 2010.
[17] Thelen 2014, 24.

producing nearly all the major components required to make a turbine domestically, including the generators that constituted a core technology of the German
manufacturer. To my surprise, the German plant manager did not appear particularly troubled by China's growing wind industry, even as his German firm could
not compete with Chinese suppliers on price. The plant in Germany, he said, had
always been too small to mass-produce turbine components, and trying to do
so would have proven too expensive. The firm had begun to specialize instead
in prototyping and early-stage production of novel generator technologies, including for offshore wind turbines. It then licensed these technologies to China
when customization—the core skill of the German producer—was no longer
needed.

During our conversation, I learned that a Chinese generator firm had recently
bought such a license when the demand for a particular model exceeded the production capacity of the German plant. For all their experience in customization,
the German team had long dismissed as unworkable the use of the most cost-
effective cooling technology in the generator design they licensed to the Chinese
supplier. As I confirmed in China during a conversation with the licensee a few
months later, the Chinese firm subsequently changed the production architecture of the original model to accommodate the cheaper fan as it scaled up the
model for mass production. The changes prompted a group of German engineers to travel to China, and, eventually, to pay for this proprietary information
through reverse licensing. The German firm also began sourcing fans from
China.[18]

The traditional views of globalization outlined earlier do not adequately
capture the relationship between these two manufacturers, one in a mid-
sized German city with a similarly mid-sized production facility, the other in
a sprawling Chinese metropolis with the capacity to manufacture more than
1,000 generators annually. The two firms were certainly not locked into the kind
of cutthroat competition that some have come to expect from China's integration into the global economy. Both firms held distinct roles and expertise in a
division of labor that allowed the German manufacturer to build on core skills
in customization and investment in new, cutting-edge generator technologies,
while the Chinese firm concentrated on the design changes required to lower
cost and bring products to mass production. During my conversation with the
German plant manager, I came to understand that the firm possessed neither the
ambition nor the access—to financing, infrastructure, training institutions, and
broader technological skills—that would be needed to compete with the Chinese
supplier on scale. Still, their business model required that someone bring their

[18] Interviews: plant manager, German generator manufacturer, May 17, 2011; executive, Chinese
generator manufacturer, August 26, 2011.

products to mass production after demand exceeded capacity at the plant. Licensing enabled the continued focus on customization in Germany.

Yet the two firms were not locked into a licensing relationship invoked in descriptions of globalization as progressive outsourcing, either.[19] The German firm did not have a monopoly on value-added design activities, nor did it enjoy full control over the supply chain. Instead, knowledge traveled both ways, including from China to Germany. The German firm sent engineers to China to observe the performance of their product under conditions of mass production. Their newly acquired knowledge helped these German engineers design new generator models. Simultaneously, the Chinese firm benefited from new technologies developed in Germany. The connection between the two suppliers was neither arm's-length nor unidirectional.

Collaborative Advantage

To explain this phenomenon, I propose a third view of globalization based on the understanding that international economic integration has opened new ways for firms to collaborate. I employ the concept *collaborative advantage* to capture the connection between changes in the global economy and the endurance of distinct national industrial specializations. "Collaborative advantage" is shorthand for two types of experimental action that enable firms to reap benefits from participating in the global economy: because of new opportunities for collaboration, firms can engage in a division of labor that allows them to specialize; and firms can choose competitive strategies for participating in global networks that allow them to repurpose domestic institutions and public resources.

Economically, collaborative advantage describes the importance of specialization in the global economy. Thanks to advances in transportation, the digital transmission of information, and more general acceleration of human mobility, globalization has made it easier for firms to find partners in the development and commercialization of new technologies. The existence of other specialized firms has made it possible to access key skills and capacities necessary for the development of new technologies through collaboration in global supply chains, whether such collaboration occurs through licensing, joint development agreements, or relationships with global suppliers. These new possibilities for collaboration in the global economy have relieved firms of the need to establish in-house the full range of production and innovation skills required to invent and commercialize new technologies.

---

[19] Petersen and Welch 2002, 160–61.

Historically, national borders defined clear boundaries for industries and collaboration between firms. Over time, innovation in transportation technologies, including the invention of steam engines and modern railways, put new markets within reach; the products generated by such national systems of production increasingly found global customers. A third wave of economic integration subsequently moved many of the activities that now make up the global economy beyond the territorial reach of states. It dispersed individual stages of innovation and production beyond national borders, it began shifting know-how to developing nations that had previously been confined to the periphery of the global economy, and it allowed firms in advanced and developing economies to focus on a set of core capabilities.[20] These changes coincided with the emergence of global supply chain networks as central vehicles for international economic integration, binding individual firms and national economies to the global economy and sparking the collaboration that is central to this argument.[21]

The forces that prompted much concern about exposure to heightened competition also made accessible a far greater range of collaborators with diverse sets of skills and capabilities. As I detail in my empirical chapters, German makers of production equipment were able to rely on Chinese wind and solar manufacturers not just as potential customers but also as partners, with research and development teams devoted to mass manufacturing—expertise that was not available to the German producers domestically. Chinese manufacturers, in turn, found themselves freed up to prioritize research and development related to commercialization of new technologies, in part because they could access such technologies through global networks, including American start-ups and German suppliers of production equipment. In the United States, where start-up firms excelled at creating new technologies but possessed few resources for—and little prior experience with—commercialization and production, global networks offered novel opportunities to bring products to market through collaboration. Quite simply, the distinct and highly specialized competitive strategies of the two generator suppliers proved viable because these firms had found a way to work together.

Politically, collaborative advantage opens up new options for participation in the global economy, including those that repurpose existing domestic institutions and public resources. Faced with multiple opportunities for participating in innovation in global networks, specialization allows firms to build on existing industrial capabilities. Although such skills undergo significant transformation and augmentation in their application to new industries, they shape how firms take advantage of new prospects in emerging industrial sectors.

---

[20] For a summary of the evolution of globalization over time, see Baldwin 2016, 5–10.
[21] Henderson et al. 2002, 445.

Globalization allows firms to match existing strengths and competencies with competitive niches in global industries. It enables them to choose among different specializations that present trade-offs between skills and resources that firms already have or need to establish. Even when governments intervene to encourage the development of particular skills and industrial sectors—for instance, by emphasizing the importance of manufacturing jobs in renewable energy sectors—firms can pursue alternative trajectories for participation in ways that would be impossible if the full range of innovative abilities had to be established within an individual firm or even within a single domestic economy.

In choosing a strategy to join the global supply chains that now make up the global economy, firms are able to pick sets of technical skills that are well-supported in the domestic economy. Specialization enables experimentation with familiar public resources at the domestic level, many of which were originally established for legacy, not emerging, sectors. Such institutions include the domestic financial sector, the labor market and vocational training institutions, and government programs to support research and development. While industrial legacies and the presence of different types of institutions constrain what types of activities are supported in different economies, institutions are not determinative: globalization allows firms to repurpose elements of existing industrial legacies for new industrial contexts, presenting resources for experimentation and adaptation that can support firms in taking advantage of new prospects without fully prescribing their path. Specialization creates opportunities for creativity and experimentation because it has opened up new possibilities for participation in new industries. By forging an opening for collaboration in global networks, globalization allows firms to sustain and adapt existing skills and domestic economic institutions as they seek competitive niches in emerging sectors. As I showcase in the wind and solar sectors, existing domestic institutions retain their value precisely because they no longer have to support the full range of activities required to invent and commercialize new technologies within national borders.

Political economy literatures have commonly described institutions as the main agents of path dependence. According to such research, institutions often obstruct the realization of private sector interests and are threatened by the competitive pressures of the global economy.[22] The argument advanced in this book reverses this causal logic. Collaborative advantage allows firms to choose industrial competencies that draw on existing economic institutions at the domestic level, because specialization enables firms to craft new paths for participation in global industries. Even when national industrial policies explicitly tried to establish far broader sets of domestic capabilities, collaborative advantage still

---

[22] Pierson 1994, 2000; Steinfeld 2010; Streeck and Thelen 2005.

enabled wind and solar firms to revive domestic industrial specializations. To put it simply, new options for specialization reinforce existing local institutions.

Such a global division of labor is also self-reinforcing. The incremental development of industrial specializations creates more demand for collaboration: as a result of rapid economic and technological change, even the most capable firms struggle to supply all the skills required to remain competitive in the development of new technologies.[23] Not everything can be accomplished internally. The presence of specialized firms focused entirely on mastering individual steps along the trajectory from lab to market makes it harder for others to compete as generalists, and it thus creates incentives for firms to specialize and focus on core skills. Where firms and nations once prided themselves on being self-sufficient, or islands unto themselves, globalization has challenged that outlook. It has hampered firms' ability to maintain comprehensive competitiveness, but it has also offered an array of bold new opportunities to rely on external actors as needed.

Wu Gang, the founder of Goldwind, one of China's largest wind turbine manufacturers, explained things this way: There "was little reason to start from zero. Technology could be licensed, but manufacturing was not as simple. Early attempts were a terrible failure. Whole blades dropped off and the main shafts broke. It was really very dangerous."[24] Like many renewable energy firms in China, Goldwind had little ambition to reproduce capabilities that could be accessed through collaboration, particularly not if such duplicate skills entailed head-on competition with firms in the United States and Europe. So Goldwind chose to focus its R&D efforts on commercialization and scale-up to mass production. Such skills were scarce in global networks and dovetailed with existing public support for mass production in China.

Because collaborative advantage freed up options for industrial specialization, renewable energy firms in Germany stepped forward to build on existing strengths in customization and automation. For the same reason, Chinese firms broke into global supply chains with skills in commercialization that responded to China's domestic manufacturing strength but also added new competencies in innovation to improve scale-up and mass production. The concept of collaborative advantage reverses the logic that has portrayed distinct national political economies as fundamentally threatened by the competitive pressures resulting from the reorganization of the global economy over the past thirty years. By providing new opportunities for collaboration, globalization causes persistent and consequential divergence of such institutions and national industrial specializations over time.

[23] Sabel and Herrigel 2018, 231–32.
[24] Osnos 2009, 55.

Persistent Divergence of Domestic Institutions

Analyzing domestic institutions to explain cross-national differences is a common practice within research on comparative capitalisms. Here I build on a long history of social science research that has explained the slow pace of institutional change at least partly as a result of institutional interdependence. The institutions considered in this book build on those arrangements that institutional literatures have long held responsible for preserving distinct national capitalisms.[25] My framework departs from such analyses by showing that these institutions continue to be relevant in new, highly globalized industries because they provide utility to firms, not because institutional complementarities lock them into place. In its focus on new and emerging industrial sectors, the concept of collaborative advantage offers a different view of globalization's impact on the distribution of firm capabilities across global supply chains, and its relationship to distinct domestic political economies. The political manifestation of collaborative advantage is that firms are able to choose much more freely which domestic institutions to rely on and support. Scholarship on comparative capitalisms has often described labor market institutions, institutions for social protection, and state-industrial relations as locked into reinforcing complementarities. I show, however, that even if firms choose to work with and repurpose resources at the domestic level, the ability to engage in global collaboration allows them to engage with domestic institutions far more selectively than in the past.

While this argument shares with other literatures an emphasis on the importance of legacies—the outcomes I describe cannot be fully explained through causes that are contemporaneous with that outcome—I offer a different mechanism that links the antecedent and the current phenomenon.[26] Firms from legacy industries and extant economic institutions find pathways into new sectors not because of path dependence resulting from slow-to-change institutions, but because globalization has lent existing institutions new utility in different industrial contexts. Collaborative advantage allows firms to maintain a set of skills that are in keeping with traditional industrial strengths of their countries of origin, but it is the collaboration between them that makes each individual specialization functionally viable and economically successful. In applying themselves to new economic sectors through specialization, firms can repurpose domestic resources, institutions, and networks familiar to them from past industrial activities.[27]

---

[25] For an overview, see Hall and Soskice 2001, 1–68.

[26] For a comprehensive discussion of the use of legacy-based explanations, see Wittenberg 2015, 367–70.

[27] This view differs both from neoliberal and institutionalist accounts and builds heavily on Herrigel's notion that industrial change is essentially a firm-driven, creative process of adapting to changing circumstances while experimenting with existing resources. See Herrigel, 2010.

The impact of collaborative advantage on the competitive strategies of firms is shaped by economic institutions that differ across national economies: different sets of domestic institutions are of course not equally suitable for all types of industrial specializations. The presence of distinct sets of domestic institutions therefore offers both constraints and new opportunities for the types of production activities that are supported domestically. But because they can specialize and collaborate, firms are no longer fully constrained by domestic institutions; they do not have to let those institutions define their strategies for entering new industries. Instead, collaborative advantage lends utility to domestic institutions in new industrial contexts and presents a set of resources that do not have to be used together, at the same time, or even for the purposes for which they were initially intended. Institutions structuring domestic labor markets, training and education, financing, and research and development might have originated as part of interlocking domestic arrangements where institutional complementarities reinforce one another, but now they can function instrumentally, used by firms to enter new industries without necessarily adhering to their original purpose.

As I showed in the previous chapter, modern renewable energy industries emerged virtually simultaneously in China, Germany, and the United States. By the end of the 2000s, governments in all three economies had converged on the goal of developing comprehensive wind and solar industries that could invent, commercialize, and manufacture strategic energy technologies domestically. They also employed similar policy tools to achieve these objectives. Benefiting from the presence of collaborative advantage in wind and solar industries, firms responded with narrow industrial specializations that built on existing skills by repurposing existing institutions within the domestic economy. In the United States, start-ups maintained capabilities in the *invention* of new technologies but rarely developed skills in commercialization and mass production.[28] In Germany, wind and solar firms clustered around the development of production equipment and customized components, offering what I call capabilities in *customization*.[29] In China, large wind and solar manufacturers prioritized the R&D required for commercializing and scaling-up of novel technologies, which I refer to as *innovative manufacturing* in this book.[30] Only in the context of institutions that existed before the rise of wind and solar industries can one understand the effect of industrial policies on the development of distinct renewable energy sectors in China, Germany, and the United States.[31]

---

[28] Knight 2011, 176.

[29] Arbeitsgemeinschaft Windenergie-Zulieferindustrie 2012; Germany Trade & Invest 2010, 2011b.

[30] See Nahm and Steinfeld 2014, 294–98.

[31] On institutions and the political economy of energy transitions more broadly, see Hochstetler, 2020.

The persistent and consequential divergence of national patterns of industrial specialization resulted from aggregate firm decisions to compete by augmenting existing industrial strengths, actively renewing and repurposing different legacy institutions and public resources in each country. In Chapters 4–6, I showcase three types of institutions that became central to the R&D activities of firms but are not usually considered part of the state's repertoire for industrial policy intervention regarding energy or innovation (see Table 3.1): the role of legacy institutions in supporting innovation and production outside renewable energy policy, the role of ownership patterns and financial systems in driving technological specialization, and the role of skills and training institutions in shaping firm practices in wind and solar sectors. The main takeaway is not that these institutions differed across the three economies examined here, but that they maintained relevance as firms learned to repurpose them for application in novel industries, the result of new opportunities to specialize.

First, the case chapters highlight the role of legacy institutions in supporting innovation and production outside the realm of renewable energy policy. These institutions, founded to bolster domestic firms in the existing industrial core, included government programs to promote inter-firm collaboration, public test centers for private sector research, legislation to help firms access technologies developed in research institutes (through licensing and other legal arrangements for technology commercialization), and subsidies for manufacturing. Collectively, such legacy institutions offered an impressive array of resources for different firm strategies, including innovation centered on manufacturing activities and more traditional R&D in laboratory settings.

Firms in all three economies used legacy institutions to support their R&D activities, but they applied them in new industrial sectors and reoriented them to

Table 3.1 Institutional Resources for Specialization

	Germany	China	United States
Innovation, Production	Collaborative research institutions for small and medium-sized enterprises	Institutions for mass production	Technology transfer from university to private sector
Financial institutions	House banks & credit unions, small loans, patient capital	Development banks, large manufacturing loans	Venture capital, early-stage funding
Skills, training, employment	Vocational training for production workers, long job tenures	Manufacturing engineering schools, migrant labor	University training, short job tenures

operate beyond the parameters of whatever problem they had initially intended to address. In an environment of collaborative advantage, China's institutions for mass manufacturing became the basis for R&D initiatives to support commercialization and cost reduction—they did not constrain or limit domestic firms to more traditional low-value manufacturing activities. In Germany, institutions to support R&D in small and medium-sized family businesses fueled far-reaching transformations of products and competitive strategies as they entered the wind and solar sectors. US government support for technology spin-offs from universities and research institutes, originally set up to support domestic commercialization and the production of federally funded technologies, spurred a proliferation of start-ups that increasingly looked to global partners to bring their technologies to market.

Second, the empirical chapters underline the role of ownership patterns and financial systems in driving patterns of technological specialization. Financial systems differ in their expectations about rates of return, the time frame within which investments must generate a profit, and the willingness to invest in novel technologies and practices. Ownership patterns reinforce such differences, as family-owned firms, for instance, tend to have longer planning horizons than publicly traded firms with short-term shareholder responsibilities. Financial institutions set clear limits on what types of activities can be funded domestically.

In renewable energy sectors, large-scale manufacturing investments and long-term research and development programs lay beyond the scope of US venture capital funds and clashed with the financial incentives of publicly listed companies. Federal research funding became a central revenue source, instead, for firms trying to commercialize early-stage technologies. In Germany, family-owned businesses with access to capital from local house banks found ways to revive traditional strengths in automation: such endeavors entailed long development horizons and uncertain future payoffs that local banks were nonetheless willing to fund. Firms in Germany used the financial institutions of the preglobalization economy to fund their entry into postglobalization renewable energy sectors. In China, manufacturing firms repurposed large loans from state-owned banks for the expansion of manufacturing capacity to set up research and development facilities dedicated to the rapid scale-up and mass production of new energy technologies.

Finally, the empirical chapters to follow examine the role of skills and training institutions in shaping firm practices in wind and solar sectors. The development of new technologies, together with the type of technological problems that industries chose to tackle, related directly to the types of proficiencies supplied by education systems and on-the-job training. While some training was organized internally, firms relied extensively on external institutions to meet training needs.[32] The original intent behind the creation of such training institutions, however, offered only limited information about what kinds of industrial specialization could be supported in an environment of collaborative advantage. For example, since manufacturing was not simply the execution of product design but also a site of critical research and development, vocational training for manufacturing assumed a new and weightier significance in a global system of cooperation.

The analysis of such domestic institutions to explain cross-national differences is not unique to my work, of course. I am fortunate to build on a long history of social science research that has, at least partially, explained the slow pace of institutional change as a result of institutional interdependence. In particular, the comparative capitalism literature has described labor market institutions, institutions for social protection, and state-industrial relations as locked into reinforcing complementarities. But by attending to new and emerging industrial sectors, my theory offers a different view of globalization's impact—one that pays special attention to the distribution of firm capabilities across global supply chains, as well as to the relationship between firms and legacy institutions unfolding across distinct domestic political economies. While the institutions considered in this book build on those older arrangements that have long been viewed as responsible for the preservation of distinct national capitalisms, my framework departs from traditional analyses by showing how these institutions continue to find relevance in new industries, precisely *because* globalization has allowed firms to repurpose them in support of narrow industrial specializations.[33] Thanks to new opportunities for specialization in global supply chains, firms learned to choose for themselves which domestic institutions to rely on and support. Even if they opted to repurpose resources that were once part of a larger domestic whole, this ability to collaborate globally allowed firms to engage with domestic institutions far more selectively than in the past. Simply put, firms could now pick and choose.

Structural Conditions for Collaborative Advantage

If we think about globalization as primarily a collaborative phenomenon, we begin to see in a new way how firms respond to domestic industrial legacies and institutions, and we also begin to rethink or challenge existing views about the relationship between advanced industrial and developing economies. Consider the difference between the development of new technologies under conditions of

[32] Berger 2000, 182.
[33] For an overview, see Hall and Soskice 2001, 1–68.

collaborative advantage and the vertically integrated company of the Fordist era, when even the rubber plantations for auto tires formed part of the same firm.[34] Creating new technologies requires invention and imagination, of course, but it has also always required improving product designs and production processes along the entire trajectory from lab to market, including in commercialization and manufacturing. The fragmentation of global production, the concomitant rise of global chains, and new opportunities for cooperation have distributed such capabilities across numerous firms in different economies. These firms are not necessarily located near one another, nor do local strengths in a particular activity necessarily draw related industrial activities into the local economy.

As firms in China and other middle-income economies have attracted mass manufacturing, firms in advanced economies have in many cases lost the infrastructure on which skills related to commercialization can be established.[35] When different types of innovation are geographically and organizationally separated, R&D staff dedicated to inventing new technologies often lack the experience to anticipate what the production process will need. These teams rely instead on engineering capabilities residing in the manufacturer or supplier. What such firms have in common, however, is their increasing specialization in narrow sets of activities: they exhibit capabilities in different varieties of innovation on the trajectory from lab to market.

Three factors distinguish an environment of collaborative advantage from the conventional characterization of innovation and manufacturing activities as sequential in timing, distinct, and hierarchical in skill requirements.[36] First, under conditions of collaborative advantage, innovation and manufacturing activities are not sequentially organized. In contrast to product innovation in modular production networks, for instance, in which products are handed off to manufacturers only once they are fully standardized, collaborative innovation requires sustained interaction between different firms specializing in different steps of the innovation process.[37] As my empirical chapters outline in detail, even licensing agreements, typically conceived as transactional interactions between innovative firms in advanced economies and manufacturers in developing economies, often require in-depth interactions between engineers working in quite different fields.

---

[34]   Galey 1979, 262.

[35]   Pisano and Shih, in a variation on this argument, propose that the decline of manufacturing in the United States prevents firms from realizing their innovative potential in areas where manufacturing skills are essential to product innovation. Restoring competitiveness for US firms, in their view, requires a revitalization of the American manufacturing sector. Pisano and Shih 2012.

[36]   This view has been particularly prominent in discussions of industrial upgrading, which describe a stepwise of progression of late developing economies into ever more complex activities through the strategic imitation of advanced industrial economies. Amsden 2001; Johnson 1982; Kim 1997; Wade 1990.

[37]   Sturgeon 2002; Whittaker et al. 2020, 21–88.

Second, when complex products and firm-level specialization in different types of production and R&D activities require collaboration to bring a product to market, innovation and production activities no longer remain separate. Innovative ideas travel in multiple directions, from manufacturers to firms that invent new technologies, and from firms in middle-income economies to firms in advanced industrialized economies.[38] Within global networks, different specializations are interdependent to succeed economically, but these networks also require that teams learn from one another to remain viable in the long term.

Third, under conditions of collaborative advantage, no single link in the chain of production can be identified as the lead position. Consequently, economies and the firms within them cannot be easily grouped into global technological leaders versus those attempting to catch up. Fundamentally, a theory of collaborative advantage calls into question the notion that industrial activities are structured along a single hierarchy of complexity and value from manufacturing to advanced innovation. While firms in advanced economies are still more likely to possess expertise in basic research and early-stage R&D, the importance of innovation in manufacturing challenges those who would portray production merely as the execution of product design. Thanks to the dependence of highly specialized firms on external partners with complementary skills, engineering capabilities can no longer be organized or ranked hierarchically.[39]

Three structural conditions enable collaborative advantage, including in the renewable energy sectors at the core of this book (Table 3.2). In addition to the presence of potential partners for collaboration in *global supply chains*, firms' ability to benefit from collaborative advantage relies on a form of *industrial organization* based on flat hierarchies and a lack of incumbent firms, as well *flexible government policies* that tolerate these firms' divergence from industrial policy goals. The following paragraphs examine these conditions in detail.

At the most fundamental level, collaborative advantage was made possible by changes in the organization of the global economy that predated the emergence of wind and solar industries. The decline of vertical integration, the fragmentation of production, and the rise of firms organized in *global supply chains* created partners for collaboration. In the postwar decades, the core competitive advantage of vertically integrated firms in advanced economies consisted in the ability to establish the full range of engineering capabilities required for technological innovation within the four walls of the firm, thereby making collaboration redundant. Large enterprises made the capital, human, and financial investments required to establish this broad range of engineering capabilities in ways that smaller firms

---

[38] Helveston and Nahm 2019, 295; Nahm and Steinfeld 2014, 289; Sabel and Herrigel 2018, 231–33.
[39] Binz and Truffer 2017, 1286.

Table 3.2 Structural Conditions for Collaborative Advantage

Structural Condition	Opportunities for Firms	Impact on Renewable Energy Sectors
Global supply chains	New partners for collaboration Ability to specialize	Near simultaneous development of wind and solar industry in China, Germany, and the United States
Nonhierarchical industrial organization	Lack of incumbents and legacy production structures Ability to readily enter global networks	Low/no tariffs, open economy Globalization did not prompt structural adjustment
Flexible government policies	Ability to diverge from official goals	Use of existing institutions and skills Distinct national profiles

could not. By housing manufacturing and R&D capabilities under one roof, such enterprises coordinated and established critical linkages between innovation and production capabilities in the early stages of product development, effectively transitioning new products from lab to mass production.[40] Only after products proved reliable, manufacturing processes achieved standardization, and price premiums from technological advantage were depleted, did production activities shift to developing economies—those with fewer technical capabilities, lower degrees of vertical integration, and less sophisticated market demand.[41]

When President Obama announced in 2009 that the world's nations were in a race for the biggest share of the clean energy economy, these traditional arrangements were under significant pressure—and had been so for some time. Beginning in the 1990s, the rise of the internet suddenly allowed complex design blueprints to be electronically transmitted to faraway production locations, permitting firms to break the connection that had long required R&D and manufacturing to occur in close proximity during the early stages of product development. In subsequent years, new digital technologies made it increasingly possible to standardize interfaces between different components. This improvement allowed firms to introduce modular product architectures where manufacturing was no longer the only outsourced activity: now the design and

[40] Where scholars of East Asian economic development saw a need for the state to encourage the creation of such business in late-developing economies, Chandler, in a study on the origins of large business in the United States, argued that the dominance of conglomerates in the US economy was a result of their competitive success. See Chandler 1977, chapters 3 and 9.
[41] Antràs 2003; Grossman and Helpman 1991; Krugman 1979; Vernon 1966.

fabrication of entire components could be entrusted to third-party suppliers without concerns about how these parts would eventually fit together.[42]

These new options for the organization of production and innovation challenged the primacy of large firms and opened new avenues for collaboration.[43] At a time when the capital investments required for the construction of new manufacturing facilities increased rapidly, firms in advanced economies began to concentrate on research and development; and many moved production activities abroad. They spread their investment risk to suppliers and third-party manufacturers located in developing countries with low production costs.[44] As new digital technologies encouraged firms in advanced economies to reorganize their production strategies, financial markets rewarded such restructuring.[45] For firms in developing economies, meanwhile, global supply chains lowered barriers to entry, permitting them to enter these supply chains for high-technology products through the manufacture of foreign product designs, or through hosting foreign-invested manufacturing facilities. By the time renewable energy sectors began mass manufacturing wind turbines and solar panels in the late 1990s and early 2000s, the global system of production had shifted to global networks of firms, creating opportunities for collaboration that had not existed previously.

Collaborative advantage also required a form of *industrial organization* that allowed firms to freely enter such global networks. Literatures on global value chains have examined how technological complexity and the replaceability of suppliers shape hierarchy in global networks.[46] I argue, however, that the degree to which industries benefited from collaborative advantage depended on their existing footprint and the role of incumbent firms. Research on economic globalization has paid much attention to the role of competition and hierarchy in structuring the international economic order in legacy industries. Incumbent firms in such sectors often responded to economic globalization by defending existing production arrangements against global competition, raising barriers to entry for new competitors, and using their economic and political clout to govern global supply chains in their own best interest.[47] Lead firms subsequently controlled supply chains, becoming powerful organizations that orchestrated the

---

[42] Although the possibility of separating manufacturing and innovation (through offshoring and outsourcing) and the option to develop modular production architectures are separate developments, they are mutually influencing and driven by the same underlying technological developments. See Camuffo 2004; Langlois 2002.

[43] This paragraph draws heavily on Berger 2005a, chapter 4.

[44] Berger 2005b, 73; Ezell and Atkinson 2011b, 22.

[45] Davis 2009, chapters 1–4.

[46] Scholars of global value chains have identified multiple governance forms with varying degrees of hierarchy and control by lead firms. See Gereffi, Humphrey, and Sturgeon 2005, 86–87.

[47] Opportunities for collaboration are in general greater in sectors where incumbents are not organizing to resist the emergence of global chains. For a discussion of political strategies employed by firms confronting economic change, see Uriu 1996, 12–15.

complex task of coordinating activities among a growing number of firms across national boundaries. The presence of brick-and-mortar manufacturing plants, R&D facilities, and existing supplier relationships of lead firms thus determined when and how new firms were allowed to enter. Investments in existing production arrangements structured whether and how firms were able to exploit the benefits of collaboration.

Collaboration was more readily accessible for firms in new industrial sectors. Wind and solar sectors, like other emerging industries, did not respond to the forces of globalization through economic restructuring and adjustment. From the beginning, renewable energy sectors developed within a new global economic order: they lacked incumbent firms and production arrangements that predated economic globalization. Wind and solar industries, in particular, emerged beyond the influence that incumbent firms with existing assets held over the global division of labor in legacy sectors. Firms could insert themselves into global networks as collaboration lowered barriers to entry and invited the development of narrow, specialized skills. Collaborative advantage is not limited to emerging industrial sectors, of course, but perhaps it achieves its greatest visibility and use here—in industries not weighted down by the legacies of a world before globalization.[48]

In renewable energy industries, the relationships through which firms engaged collaborative advantage took a variety of legal and organizational forms. In some cases, firms with complementary engineering capabilities signed research agreements that anchored the nonhierarchical, mutually beneficial collaboration firmly in a legal contract. In other cases, collaboration took place in supplier relationships between firms with complementary skills. Even contract manufacturing and licensing agreements—supply chain relationships that are seen as far more hierarchical—allowed for collaboration, multidirectional learning, and the participation of multiple firms in joint processes of product development.[49] Frequently, a single technological development required many such relationships at once.

The physical requirements of wind and solar production chains informed the organizational structure of these relationships. In the solar industry, the need for a limited number of production steps, a small number of suppliers, and components that could be moved in standard shipping containers catalyzed the emergence of transnational supply chains. Here, regional clusters of firms specialized in individual stages of the production process. In the wind industry,

---

[48] I return to this question in the final chapter of this book, where I examine the application of collaborative advantage to global automotive and electronics industries. While the presence of existing, preglobalization incumbents has limited the ability of new firms to enter global supply chains, patterns of specialization and repurposing have nonetheless begun to emerge in these sectors.

[49] For an overview, see Gereffi, Humphrey, and Sturgeon 2005.

where components were difficult to ship and assembly typically took place in close proximity to the final installation location, suppliers often established secondary manufacturing plants around the world. The development of such globalized clusters—in which firms from diverse global backgrounds convened in a number of settings—nonetheless relied on collaboration, primarily between firms' core research and development operations in their home economies. These varied relationships brought together knowledge and skills from diverse firms and far-flung geographical locations. Despite advances in digital technologies, such expertise could not be fully codified in production equipment or design blueprints. Even if production machines and product designs now traveled more easily to faraway destinations, using, adapting, and improving technologies— let alone inventing new ones and producing them at scale—continued to require tacit skills and close interaction. This knowledge spread across a wide number of firms, and it was coordinated in global networks organized around such collaboration—networks that saw no need to defend or prop up preglobalization production arrangements made by incumbent firms.

A third requirement for collaborative advantage was *space for experimentation* as firms responded to state industrial policy through specialization and repurposing. The presence of collaborative advantage and its attendant opportunities for specialization offered firms new options for making use of industrial policies, many of which did not closely align with state goals. Compare contemporary wind and solar industries to the global auto sector of the 1960s and 1970s. For the late industrializers in Korea and Japan, auto manufacturing was primarily an exercise in emulation and reverse engineering, orchestrated by domestic conglomerates and encouraged by favorable industrial policies. Japanese and Korean auto firms had to compete with European and North American automakers who possessed broad technological skills and rich clusters of domestic suppliers. As East Asian developmental states funneled resources into select industrial sectors and made access to such resources dependent on meeting predetermined development goals, firms found themselves with few options but to establish the same range of technological capabilities as the large industrial clusters in the West. Japanese and Korean car manufacturers in the postwar decades therefore had little choice but to develop the full range of skills required to invent, commercialize, and manufacture new vehicles in the domestic economy: those were the skills that their competitors in Europe and North America possessed. Industrial policies that encouraged domestic firms to compete by integrating vertically and by emulating the technological capabilities of foreign competitors formed the centerpiece of industrialization in Japan and Korea.[50]

---

[50] Johnson 1982, chapters 7 and 8; Kim 1997, chapter 5.

As I showed in Chapter 2, government objectives changed little between the heyday of the East Asian developmental states and the early 2000s, when renewable energy sectors became the target of strategic state intervention. Research on state capacity among the East Asian late developers long emphasized the importance of state autonomy for meeting policy goals, particularly in areas with strong distributional consequences, such as industrial policy, that are prone to capture by outside interests. Building on Weber, scholars have pointed to organizational features of the bureaucracy as predictors of state capacity and effective industrial policy implementation. Hierarchically ranked offices, clearly defined administrative tasks, and meritocratic recruitment stood among the Weberian bureaucratic features that became central to explanations of good government among those East Asian developmental states that extensively employed industrial policy to advance in the global economy.[51]

Governments in China, Germany, and the United States hoped to gain relatively autonomous domestic wind and solar industries in return for large public investments in renewable energy. In one sense, these hopes were not realized: firms responded with specialization and collaboration, not a turn to greater autonomy. Yet at least implicitly, these governments tolerated the creative use of resources they saw unfolding, as firms experimented with strategies to enter global renewable energy sectors. States continued to support wind and solar sectors through industrial policies, even if firms did not meet expectations about traditional trajectories of industrial upgrading. This flexibility of state industrial policies, which is necessary for collaborative advantage to function, contrasts sharply with that of the East Asian developmental states, which rewarded firms only when meeting government-defined upgrading goals and withdrew support from those that failed to comply with official targets. The use of disciplinary mechanisms to encourage firms to meet predetermined upgrading goals, which Alice Amsden identified as an important factor in creating competitive firms in South Korea, likely would have prevented firms from participating in collaboration outside the scope of government plans.[52]

Collaborative advantage thus presented a new set of constraints on the ability of industrial policies to direct domestic industries into particular competitive strategies as the ability to forge autonomous domestic industries came under threat. State industrial policies could encourage firms to enter new industries—and indeed provided critical incentives for doing so—but states enjoyed far less leverage over firms' choices of technological specialization and competitive strategies than before economic globalization. Although governments pursued the goal of creating renewable energy sectors within national boundaries,

[51] See, for instance Amsden 2001, 145–47; Evans 1995, 12–14; Wade 1990, 26–27.
[52] Amsden 2001, 8–12.

industrial policies were unable to achieve these outcomes in the contemporary international economy. Governments in China and Germany failed to replicate the specialization they admired in those American start-ups busily inventing new technologies. Yet the particular institutional resources available to those start-ups prevented the Americans from emulating the R&D capabilities in commercialization common among Chinese manufacturers, as well as the automation skills that German equipment suppliers had mastered.

Political economists have long debated the role of the state in driving domestic industrial outcomes. On the one hand, scholars have pointed to East Asian developmental states to argue that strategic industrial policy interventions can create thriving, innovative firms, even in locations with very little history of industrial activity. Neoclassical economists have instead pointed to market forces and factor accumulation to explain the rise of East Asian firms. The framework I offer here suggests that industrial policy played a more nuanced role in driving industrial outcomes in the three economies under investigation. Under conditions of collaborative advantage, governments were limited in their ability to initiate radical industrial transformation through sectoral intervention; for even in emerging industries, industrial activities took the form of incremental variations on existing strengths, driven by firm experimentation.

I will revisit the role of experimentation in the final chapter of this book, where I show that the discrepancy between government goals and policy outcomes eventually led to a global backlash against collaboration. The trade disputes that have erupted between the European Union, the United States, and Chinese manufacturers of solar panels over the past decade exemplify the expectation that large parts of solar supply chains should locate domestically. They cast light on a growing concern among policymakers about the economic returns on investments in industrial policy.[53] The initial ability of firms to take advantage of collaboration in response to national industrial policies, however, was predicated on their ability to experiment and engage in recursive learning with global partners without government interference.

Empirical Strategy

Before turning to the empirical cases, I need to mention the process of data collection for this project. Sources for the remaining chapters of this book primarily consist of archival documents, public financial filings, and a novel dataset of more than 250 interviews conducted between 2008 and 2019. In China, local government yearbooks provided an important information source on

---

[53] For a summary of trade disputes in renewable energy sectors, see Lewis 2014, 22.

government institutions and served to cross-check interview data. For the vast majority of claims made in this book, I cite documentary sources in addition to interviews. I conducted interviews with executives of wind turbine and solar PV manufacturers operating in China, Germany, and the United States, as well as their suppliers. I held additional interviews with representatives from wind and solar industry associations, both at the national and subnational level, in each of these locations.

In China, I met with civil servants at national and provincial-level developmental agencies, executives in local developmental zones that hosted renewable energy firms, chambers of commerce representing foreign wind and solar firms operating in China, and academics at government research institutes working on renewable energy technologies and wind and solar industry development. A final group of interviews was conducted with state-owned banks, venture capital funds, and private investment firms with stakes in China's renewable energy industries. In Germany, I interviewed government representatives in federal and state (*Länder*) ministries, officials working in funding agencies dispensing federal research funds, and government officials in charge of regional economic development initiatives. A second group of interview subjects included representatives of lending institutions, including local credit unions and economic development banks. Community colleges and other training institutions are included in this category. In the United States, I supplemented industry research with interviews at public utility commissions, regional development organizations, national laboratories, and nongovernmental organizations in support of renewable energy development. Through participation in a broader research collective at MIT, I obtained access to an additional database of 264 interviews with small US manufacturers across a broad range of industrial sectors. I used these to test the application of my argument and the broader empirical patterns beyond the sectors I examine here in detail.[54]

For both wind and solar sectors, I compiled a list of companies from industry publications and official records. I sent interview requests to the fifteen largest wind and solar manufacturers in each location, as well as to suppliers of key components and production equipment. In the United States, I worked off a list of start-ups. With few exceptions, company executives agreed to be interviewed on the condition of confidentiality. In some cases, I was able to conduct multiple interviews within the same firm, meeting with CEOs and heads of technical departments. When companies had close ties with suppliers and other firms in the process of bringing new products to market, I supplemented my list and scheduled additional interviews with their partners to better understand each firm's individual contributions to product development and innovation. For a

[54] See Berger 2013b; Locke and Wellhausen 2014.

number of companies operating globally, I conducted separate interviews in each of these locations. While these subsequent interview subjects were selected according to their relationship with companies I had already visited, I submitted my initial interview requests for manufacturers and suppliers at random, based on lists compiled from industry publications (Table 3.3).

To keep company interviews consistent while also allowing respondents to address the unique characteristics of their firm's manufacturing and product development process, I employed a semistructured interview technique. The core of each interview consisted of a series of questions about the product development process for two products the firm had commercialized within the past five years. After asking interviewees to walk me through the process by which the firms had brought each idea from the R&D stage to large-scale manufacturing, I followed up with specific questions about workforce skills and technical capabilities, partnerships with suppliers and other firms, sources of capital and financing, and, finally, their reasons for choosing particular production locations. A large number of initial interviews were conducted between 2010 and 2012, covering developments in the wind and solar sectors up until that point. I have since made return trips to China and Germany at least once a year, most recently in January 2020; and I have kept in touch with interview subjects to identify potential changes in firm strategies and specialization. Unless drastic changes occurred in firms' strategies and industrial capabilities over time, I cite the first visit to a firm in the text. All interview subjects were promised complete confidentiality if needed, so I have removed identifying characteristics in the footnotes.

Table 3.3 Author Interviews in China, Germany, and the United States

	# of Interviews	# of Firms Interviewed
Wind turbine manufacturers	31	24
Wind turbine component suppliers	25	20
Solar PV manufacturers	37	30
Solar PV component suppliers	39	22
Industry associations	23	n/a
Government interviews	64	n/a
Banks, venture capitals, investment firms	37	n/a
Total	256	96

4

Industrial Legacies and Germany's Specialization in Customization

In 2009, the German Ministry of Education and Research awarded an EUR 40 million research and development (R&D) grant to a group of German solar firms. Comprising twenty-nine solar manufacturers, suppliers, and nineteen research institutes in the *Länder* of Saxony, Saxony-Anhalt, and Thuringia, "Solarvalley Mitteldeutschland" hoped to benefit from the same agglomeration effects as its namesake in California. Federal research funds were intended to support collaborative R&D projects among local firms with the goal of achieving grid parity for solar power by 2013. Subsidies and tax breaks for manufacturing in structurally weak regions in eastern Germany offered additional financial support to firms in the cluster.[1]

A mere year after winning the federal R&D support, observers raised doubts about the viability of manufacturers in Solarvalley. In 2010, Sunfilm, a producer of solar panels with two plants in the region, filed for bankruptcy. Operating losses mounted among other manufacturers.[2] Q-Cells, once Germany's largest producer of solar cells, followed Sunfilm into insolvency during a devastating financial performance in 2012. The German weekly *Der Spiegel* proclaimed that the "bankruptcy of Q-Cells [. . .] shows that the days of German solar cell production are numbered."[3] Meanwhile, the Berlin daily *Der Tagesspiegel* wistfully remembered the days when Solarvalley was "a piece of California in central Germany," referring not to the weather, of course, but to the enviable economic performance of tech firms in Silicon Valley.[4]

Solarvalley's dramatic failure to live up to its Californian namesake distracted observers from another story quietly unfolding during the same period: the striking success of small and medium-sized wind and solar suppliers and their role in the maturation of global renewable energy industries. Hidden in faceless industrial parks, these sectors sprang up around the development and manufacturing of components and production equipment for solar modules and wind

---

[1] Aulich and Frey 2009; Bundesministerium für Bildung und Forschung 2017; Thüringer Allgemeine 2012.
[2] Stafford 2010.
[3] Schultz 2012.
[4] Hoffmann 2012.

turbines. In 2011, the German Engineering Federation (VDMA), the industry association for the German mechanical engineering sector, listed more than 170 member firms active in the wind industry. Only ten were manufacturers of wind turbines. The majority of firms instead developed and produced towers, blades, mechanical components, hydraulics systems, and production equipment for wind turbine manufacturers.[5] By 2019, the number of VDMA member firms supplying parts for wind turbines had increased to 200.[6] Similarly, in the solar photovoltaic (PV) sector, more than seventy firms offered production lines, automation equipment, coatings, and laser processing machines. With roughly 41,000 employees in 2014, employment in solar PV equipment and component firms far surpassed the 12,000 jobs that had once existed in Germany's solar module manufacturers.[7] As of 2019, overall employment in German renewable energy industries reached 290,000, compared to roughly 800,000 workers in the German auto industry.[8]

Germany's wind and solar firms were small, often family-owned, and frequently far from large urban centers, tucked away in small towns ranging from the Baltic Sea to the Black Forest. The transition of firms from Germany's industrial core into the emerging renewable energy sector was therefore far less visible than the highly publicized bankruptcies of prominent solar manufacturers or the ubiquitous wind turbine installations that signaled energy sector change, yet their capabilities in managing complex production processes with high degrees of customization were becoming central to the maturation of global renewable energy sectors. Already in the 1990s, before global renewable energy markets had fully matured, German renewable energy firms began to collaborate with an increasingly international customer base, particularly in China. Firms reached export quotas of more than 50 percent in the solar sector and up to 80 percent in the wind industry over the course of the 2000s.

This chapter chronicles the development of Germany's networks of small and medium-sized enterprises (SMEs) focused on R&D capabilities in *customization*. I use "customization" to refer to R&D skills required for the development of production equipment and components that are not part of the process of invention but are necessary inputs into the commercialization of new technologies. Examples of customization include automated production lines for new technologies and novel components that cannot be readily purchased as standardized equipment.

As I discussed in Chapter 2, renewable energy policies pursued the goal of creating domestic renewable energy sectors capable of inventing, commercializing,

[5] Arbeitsgemeinschaft Windenergie-Zulieferindustrie 2012; Germany Trade & Invest 2010.
[6] Arbeitsgemeinschaft Windenergie 2019, 17.
[7] O'Sullivan, Lehr, and Edler 2015.
[8] IRENA 2018, 30; VDA 2019.

and manufacturing technological breakthroughs flowing out of Germany's R&D institutes—precisely the types of firms that had failed so spectacularly in Solarvalley. I show here that collaboration with global partners—and the resulting opportunities for specialization—actually allowed suppliers of components and production equipment to repurpose local institutions, so that Germany's legacy manufacturing economy could focus on developing complex components and manufacturing equipment for renewable energy sectors. Many SMEs from the traditional core of the German economy, the *Mittelstand*, played a central role in structuring the country's entry into wind and solar sector and the energy transition more broadly. This view is often missed in accounts depicting Germany's framework either as a top-down vision implemented by policymakers over private sector interests or as the result of citizen activism fueled by the environmental catastrophes of the 1980s.[9]

This chapter shows empirically that globalization led to a set of benefits for German wind and solar firms that I refer to as *collaborative advantage*. In particular, when German firms collaborated with Chinese firms, they identified new possibilities for specialization in global supply chains—and began crafting new pathways into the global wind and solar sectors. Relationships with China's manufacturing firms relieved smaller German firms of the burden of mastering all the activities typically required to develop and commercialize new energy technologies, especially those capital-intensive mass manufacturing competencies that proved difficult to finance in Germany. Through partnerships with Chinese firms, German suppliers from a range of existing industrial sectors learned to diversify, entering the renewable energy sectors with niche capabilities in customization and small-batch production.

In the process, Germany's wind and solar suppliers appropriated and repurposed a number of familiar public resources and institutions, many of which were originally established for legacy industries. I chronicle how the existence of this particular set of legacy institutions shaped the impact of collaborative advantage on the Germany economy and supported domestic wind and solar firms focused on customization. Political economists have long expressed concerns that the institutions underlying the German manufacturing economy—including strict labor market regulations, firm ownership patterns, corporate governance structures, and domestic financial markets—stifle industrial change.[10] In fact, these institutions presented a set of tools that were used to support the R&D required to enter the renewable energy industries. Collaborative advantage enabled wind and solar suppliers to sustain the legacy

[9] For a detailed analysis of the politics of Germany's energy transition, see Hager and Stefes 2016.
[10] See Hassel 2014; Thelen 2014.

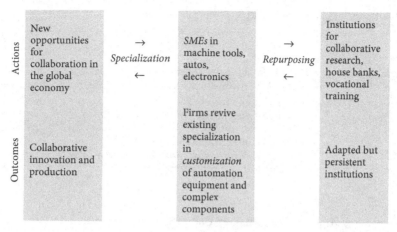

Figure 4.1 Industrial Specialization in Germany

institutions of the manufacturing economy; they became critical resources in support of the development of new industries (Figure 4.1).

This chapter begins with a discussion of industrial origins of Germany's wind and solar firms, focusing in particular on machine tools, automation, and automotive sectors. It then outlines the learning process that firms navigated in pivoting from their existing industries into new industrial sectors. The second half of the chapter focuses on the two key resources that enabled these developments: new opportunities for specialization as a result of collaboration, in particular with China, and the repurposing of institutional legacies. It concludes by highlighting the political implications of this particular industrial composition within Germany's renewable energy sectors, as firms used their membership in established industry associations to defend policy support for wind and solar sectors over time.

Building on Industrial Legacies

In 1990, when the German parliament began to debate the passage of the first Feed-in Law (*Stromeinspeisungsgesetz*) to subsidize power from renewable sources, wind and turbines and solar panels remained niche technologies. Large multinationals, in Germany and elsewhere, had largely closed or sold their wind and solar divisions. In the shadow of federal government R&D programs that had targeted large industrial conglomerates for many years, the renewable energy sectors continued to be the modest domain of passionate environmentalists, who tinkered with new technologies in a makeshift fashion without much

Table 4.1 Select Industrial Policies for German Wind and Solar Sectors

	Germany
Technology Push	Since 1954 Industrial Collaborative Research (ICR) funding
	Since 1974 Federal Energy Research Programs, renewed six times
Market Pull	1990 Electricity Feed-in Law
	1998 Renewable Energy Sources Act (EEG)
	2004 EEG Renewed
	2009, 2012, 2014 EEG Modifications
	2016 EEG reform, switch to auctions, "deployment corridors"

government support. Policymakers only gradually discovered the economic potential of the wind and solar industries; and at least initially, they vastly underestimated the effects of renewable energy legislation. Their lack of adequate information proved to be a blessing in disguise: the inability of lawmakers to predict the rapid development of renewable energy installations—and the concomitant growth of powerful industrial sectors—ushered the ambitious renewable energy law past parliamentary scrutiny. The implementation of the Feed-in Law on January 1, 1991, marked a critical transition from government-supported renewable energy research to long-term demand stimulation through the regulatory framework (Table 4.1).

Initially, the growing domestic markets created as a result of demand-side subsidies saved existing renewable energy manufacturers from bankruptcy. In the wind industry, the Feed-in Law helped a number of small German wind turbine manufacturers find stable financial footing after decades without reliable sources of demand. Experimental wind turbine start-ups founded in the 1980s now found themselves empowered to increase sales and invest in upgraded production facilities after years of makeshift operations.[11] With the exception of the industrial conglomerate MAN, these firms had in common their small size, an experimental approach, and roots in the agricultural machinery sector.

As wind power generation capacity in Germany expanded in the decades after the introduction of the Feed-In Law—increasing between 30 and 50 percent annually through the 1990s and slowing to annual growth rates between 6 and 20 percent in the early 2000s—a few additional manufacturers entered the sector.[12] Jacobs Energie and DeWind emerged in the 1990s in response to new

[11] Among the twelve firms with the most turbine installations in 1992, seven were from Germany, four from Denmark (Vestas, AN Bonus, Nordtank, and Micon), and one from the Netherlands (Lagervey). Company websites; Keuper, Molly, and Stückemann 1992, 21; Ohlhorst 2009; Schlegel 2005, 33; Tacke 2003.

[12] Earth Policy Institute 2020.

market opportunities. Vensys and Bard joined the industry in 2000 and 2003, bringing gearless turbines and offshore wind technologies to the market. On balance, however, the assembly of wind turbines was dominated by firms with origins prior to the Feed-In Law; more than half of wind turbine manufacturers operating in Germany in 2010, for instance, were founded during the 1980s or earlier.[13]

Once the 2000 Renewable Energy Sources Act (EEG) increased electricity rates for solar energy to compensate for the high cost of solar technologies, solar firms, too, could rely on rapidly increasing domestic demand. As in the wind industry, these changes initially benefited existing solar firms. It also encouraged larger manufacturing firms such as Schott Solar and Schüco, founded as glass and window producers during the 1950s, to enter the solar business. After decades of challenging technological trajectories and uncertain market environments—factors that had prompted large conglomerates to divest their solar divisions—the subsidies included in EEG once again made the PV industry desirable for large multinational firms. Firms like Bosch and Siemens, for example, entered the solar sector simply by taking over existing businesses.[14]

Although the wind industry in Germany had been on the upswing since the 1991 Feed-in-Law, standardized production equipment had not been developed; and no supplier industry existed to support small domestic manufacturers. Companies bought components from related industrial sectors and repurposed them for wind turbines as best as they could. Since government R&D projects on large-scale turbines in Germany and the United States had not yielded results, firms relied on an entrepreneurial, do-it-yourself approach as they applied engineering principles to turbines of increasing size. Sönke Siegfriedsen, head of the German wind turbine engineering firm Aerodyn, describes testing new turbines in the absence of standardized measurement equipment as a process of placing increasing numbers of sandbags on the blades; he remembers worrying that the new blade designs would be unable to withstand the required force.[15] In an interview, the head engineer for another German turbine manufacturer explained that he "didn't like coming to the office on Mondays during [the 1990s], because there would always be a message about a failed turbine somewhere. After every storm you would get a call about a failed turbine. We learned a lot from these problems, and it really taught us how to properly adjust specifications and improve turbine designs."[16]

---

[13] For a compilation of wind turbine manufacturers operating in 2010, see Germany Trade & Invest 2010. Founding dates according to company websites.

[14] Germany Trade & Invest 2011c.

[15] Siegfriedsen 2008, 58.

[16] Author interview, CEO of German engineering firm, May 20, 2011.

Growing markets required firms to restructure their manufacturing operations and made such experimental approaches increasingly untenable. As sales volumes increased, firms had to replace the components they had previously borrowed from other industries and repurposed in a makeshift fashion; to do so, they turned to designated, professional solutions. Wind turbine manufacturers began searching for external expertise in the production and design of components such as gearboxes, generators, blades, towers, and control software. In the solar industry, the growing market demand for solar panels necessitated the development of specialized manufacturing equipment for wafer, cell, and module production.

During the early 1990s, small-batch production and the prototyping of new cell technologies had occurred in the absence of specialized equipment suppliers, forcing manufacturers to modify production equipment from other sectors— particularly the microelectronics industry—and to perform many production steps manually.[17] While the production requirements for solar cells were less demanding than integrated circuits when it came to particulate contamination— solar production guidelines permitted the use of scrap silicon from the microelectronics industry—using equipment from other sectors still presented enormous challenges. Wafers twice as thin as those used in semiconductors, for instance, required a redesign of all handling aspects of the production line to prevent breakage; and changing material purity requirements necessitated new production and testing processes to isolate impurities. With the rapidly growing demand for solar modules, repurposed equipment at best presented a stopgap measure. Ultimately, such repurposing could not support the manufacturing volume and the cost reductions that Germany needed to establish solar energy as a competitive source of electricity.[18]

Despite concerns that Germany's high-wage manufacturing economy would be unable to compete in the long run against fierce competition in increasingly globalized industries, it was precisely SMEs from Germany's core manufacturing sectors that stepped forward to take advantage of opportunities in global renewable energy sectors.[19] Germany's *Mittelstand* possessed a rich fabric of firms with an array of expertise—these firms proved well-suited to support wind and solar manufacturers. They offered skills both in the production of components required in the wind sector and in the manufacture of production lines and automation equipment necessary in the solar industry.

Initially, the small size and ownership structure of German manufacturing firms left many of them reluctant to place bets on emerging renewable energy

---

[17] Author interview, CTO, German solar PV manufacturer, May 17, 2011.
[18] See Crane, Verlinden, and Swanson 1996; Green 2001.
[19] Berghoff 2006; Seliger 2000.

industries. For some firms, limited R&D resources precluded complicated development projects unless commercial prospects were relatively certain; for others, a history of custom orders had established a practice of developing new products only after a customer had been identified. By establishing long-term demand-side subsidies through the regulatory system, the 1990 Feed-in Law and the 2000 EEG provided the necessary investment stability and customer base to attract small and medium-sized firms.[20]

The managing partner of a family-owned supplier of automation equipment explained the reasoning behind the decision of many SMEs to enter the solar sector. His firm was heavily exposed to the auto industry, with 90 percent of their business coming from domestic automotive manufacturers. "We thought this kind of exposure to one sector in one market was very dangerous, so our team started thinking about sectors that we could diversify into," he said.[21] The firm hoped to find an industry where its core capabilities could be supplemented with additional skills to develop an innovative, competitive product. In early 2004, thanks to stable government policies and rapidly growing markets, the solar PV sector promised a significant demand for industrialization and low levels of automation. "Only a few firms were offering automated production solutions, and their processes were slow. We looked at what they were doing and thought we could do a lot better."[22]

Germany retained a large manufacturing sector of similar SMEs, particularly compared to other advanced industrialized economies, where the relative importance of manufacturing was rapidly declining. Between 1995 and 2005, the share of manufacturing value-added increased slightly in Germany, from 22.6 percent to 22.7 percent; in the United States, it dropped from 16.8 percent to 13.6 percent over the same period.[23] A significant share of German manufacturing remained concentrated in the production of machine tools, automotive supplies, and automation and process equipment. In 1995, for example, the production of machinery and equipment constituted 28 percent of manufacturing activity in Germany, making it the largest manufacturing subsector, ahead of fabricated metal products, chemicals, and food products. Overall, 6.3 percent of value-added in Germany came from machinery and equipment manufacturing firms, compared to 3.5 percent in the United States. Metal products, machinery, and equipment together accounted for more than half of manufactured output.[24]

---

[20] On policy stability and the development of German renewable energy sectors, see Grünhagen and Berg 2011; Lipp 2007; Mitchell, Bauknecht, and Connor 2006; Vasseur and Kemp 2011. For a discussion of policy stability and renewable energy sector development more broadly, see Butler and Neuhoff 2008; Couture and Gagnon 2010; Nemet 2009.

[21] Author interview, managing partner, Solar PV supplier, May 20, 2011; October 15, 2019.

[22] Author interview, managing partner, Solar PV supplier, May 20, 2011; October 15, 2019.

[23] OECD STAN Indicators, "Manufacturing Share of Value-Added 1970–2009," 2013.

[24] Author calculations based on OECD STAN database, 2020. Machinery and equipment figures calculated using ISIC code C29T33.

Small and medium-sized enterprises played a significant role in these industries. In 2002, enterprises with fewer than 500 employees made up 98.2 percent of businesses and 38.2 of revenue in machinery and equipment manufacturing. In metal fabrication, 99.6 percent of firms and 38.1 percent of turnover came from small and medium-sized firms.[25]

The vast majority of suppliers entered from these sectors that had long formed the heart of the German economy. In the wind energy arena, demand created by the 1990 Feed-in Law attracted the first wave of component suppliers to develop designated products for the wind industry, initially in collaboration with domestic manufacturers. These new suppliers included tower manufacturers, blade producers, manufacturers of mechanical components, and firms offering electrical components and control systems. Starting in 2004, after a EEG revision provided greater subsidies for offshore installations, firms began providing solutions specifically for wind turbine installations at sea.[26] Most suppliers carried decades of manufacturing experience from multiple industrial sectors. EEW Special Pipe Construction was founded in 1974 as a producer of steel pipes for refineries before it began specializing in towers and foundations for offshore wind turbines in 2003.[27] Back in 1926, SGL supplied wooden rotor blades for agricultural machines; decades later, the company began building expertise in fiber-reinforced plastics, eventually becoming a blade manufacturer for modern wind turbines.[28] Hansa-Flex, HAWE, and HYDAC were producing hydraulics and lubrication machinery for a wide range of industrial sectors before developing designated applications for the wind industry.[29] Stromag, founded in 1932 as a manufacturer of conductor rails and electric rail material, specialized in the production of clutches and breaks for textile machines before shifting to offer pitch controls, break systems, and gearbox components to the wind energy sector.[30]

After the domestic solar market expanded in the early 2000s, the solar industry, too, witnessed an influx of supplier firms from existing industries. Centrotherm, Roth & Rau, Schmid, and Singulus began producing turnkey production lines for crystalline solar cells; others targeted the manufacture of wet chemical benches, equipment for antireflective coating, and screen printers, as well as stringers and laminators for module manufacturing. Bürkle and Leybold

---

[25] Günterberg and Kayser 2004, 8. In Germany, SMEs (Mittelstandsunternehmen) were traditionally defined as enterprises with fewer than 500 employees and less than EUR 50 million in revenue. More recently, Germany has converted to the general EU definition, which defines SMEs as firms with fewer than 250 employees and less than EURO 50 million in revenue.

[26] Ohlhorst 2009, 196. Years of industry entry compiled from company websites.

[27] EEW 2013.

[28] SGL 2013.

[29] Flex 2013; HYDAC 2013.

[30] Stromag 2016.

started offering thin film production lines; and firms like Reis Robotics, Schmalz, and Rofin began the production of automation and laser processing equipment for solar firms.[31]

As in the wind industry, these firms had previous experience in the machinery and equipment sectors. Founded in 1948, Centrotherm initially specialized in the manufacture of production equipment for microelectronics and semiconductor firm.[32] Bürkle supplied machinery to furniture, automotive, electronics, and glass firms for more than eighty years before supplying production equipment to thin film solar firms.[33] Schmid, founded in 1864, began the production of manufacturing equipment for furniture businesses in 1926, started manufacturing printers for electronic circuit boards in 1965, and entered the solar industry in 2001. In 2008, Schmid developed the first automated production process for higher-efficiency selective emitter cells in collaboration with a Chinese solar manufacturer. In 2011, Schmid's production lines set the record for conversion efficiency for monocrystalline solar cells.[34] Schmid was representative of Germany's renewable energy suppliers not just for its rich manufacturing history across successive industrial sectors but also for its location. Headquartered in Freudenstadt, a small town of red-roofed houses dating to the sixteenth century on a high plateau above the Black Forest, the firm was far removed from both urban centers and the designated wind and solar clusters established by ambitious regional governments.

Entering Wind and Solar Sectors

Germany's wind and solar firms had direct roots in legacy manufacturing industries long at the core of the German economy. Technically, these were emerging industrial sectors that only became commercially viable as a result of regulatory policies in the 1990s and 2000s. Yet they were populated by firms with deep roots in existing industries, including the German auto sector, which policymakers had held out as an example. The profiles of Germany's wind and solar suppliers therefore broadly resembled the overall industrial specialization of Germany's manufacturing economy, which had historically prioritized customization, small-batch production, and the complex manufacturing of components and production equipment.

Although their backgrounds in traditional industrial sectors provided many of these firms with the type of tacit knowledge they needed to produce intricate

---

[31] Timing of industry entry compiled from company websites.
[32] Centrotherm 2016.
[33] Bürkle 2013.
[34] Schmid Group 2013.

machines and components, applying these existing skills to the emerging wind and solar industries entailed a steep learning curve. To enter the wind and solar sectors and successfully develop new generations of products required these firms to be adaptable and flexible, as they learned to substantially modify their existing product lines and technological capabilities. R&D engineers described three main modes of learning among wind and solar suppliers.

A first group of firms entered wind and solar supply chains through what I call *reengineering*, essentially a process of modifying and repurposing existing technologies for new applications. Customers played an active role in the reengineering process by encouraging industry entry, providing product specifications, and often participating in the design process through collaborative R&D. Reengineering existing technologies occurred in the wind industry, for instance, when Hedrich Vacuum Systems, a firm with decades of experience in the production of casting equipment, modified its cast resin technology for application in the manufacture of wind turbine blades from epoxy resins.[35] Similarly, SHW Werkzeugmaschinen, a firm with seventy years of experience in the manufacture of production equipment for large engines, reused its core technology, a milling head, in machines for the production of turbine housing and nacelles.[36]

Reengineering was particularly prevalent in the solar sector, where the similarity between microelectronics (semiconductors) and crystalline PV cells encouraged numerous firms to use their capacities in semiconductor manufacturing as a platform to enter the solar sector. The resulting production machines shared many technological principles with their ancestors in the semiconductor industry but applied them dynamically and creatively to new product applications.

In many cases, the initial entry of suppliers into renewable energy sectors was prompted by domestic manufacturers who had borrowed production equipment from the semiconductor industry. While these improvised production lines were adequate as long as production volumes remained low, manufacturing quality sometimes varied; and experimental lines were unsuitable for mass production—many of the steps had to be performed manually.[37] An integrated solar manufacturer originally began development and production in the facility of a previously state-owned East German semiconductor firm that had been divided and sold off in separate pieces after German unification. As the firm's chief technology officer (CTO) explained, in the late 1990s there simply was no commercial equipment available for the large-scale production of PV cells.[38]

35 Hedrich Group 2013.
36 de Vries 2011.
37 Palz 2011.
38 Author interview, CTO, German solar PV manufacturer, May 17, 2011.

In order to bring the technology from lab to mass production, the firm decided to use its local microelectronics industrial base—which already boasted a history of large-scale production—by repurposing the existing knowledge and machinery within that arena for the budding solar industry. While the production requirements for solar cells were less demanding than integrated circuits, in other ways using equipment from the microelectronics industry presented challenges. Thinner wafers required a redesign of all handling aspects of the production line to prevent breakage, and different material purity requirements necessitated the introduction of new production and testing processes to isolate impurities. After successfully experimenting with production lines retained from the semiconductor plant, the solar firm contacted some of the original equipment manufacturers and persuaded them to formally collaborate on the development of specialized solar production equipment.[39]

Although many manufacturers of production equipment initially resisted investing in product development for such young and emerging industries, the need for professional automation and manufacturing machinery in the solar industry presented a market opportunity too good to pass up. A manufacturer of wet benches for the semiconductor industry described how maintenance calls from solar firms whose teams were experimenting with semiconductor wet benches ultimately convinced the company to develop a product line specifically for the solar sector. This process not only entailed the design of a new product based on principles borrowed from the microelectronics industry but also necessitated new manufacturing strategies that would increase production speed while simultaneously allowing a greater degree of customization than was common in the semiconductor sector. The company eventually developed a modular production system that permitted higher manufacturing volumes while offering customers individual options for cell size and wafer thickness. It took the firm a year to design the first prototype to enter the solar sector, and an additional seven years to improve the product so that it could be mass produced. As the work progressed, the firm collaborated with solar cell manufacturers in Germany and, increasingly, with mass producers in China. Team members also worked closely with the Fraunhofer Institute for Solar Energy Systems (ISE) to further improve the firm's technology.[40]

A second group of firms developed wind and solar components through a process of *integration*: firms borrowed principles from different industrial sectors and applied them in an original way to new products and industries. Integration often occurred through collaboration among firms with different

---

[39] On the differences between microelectronics and solar PV in early mass production, see Crane, Verlinden, and Swanson 1996; Green 2001; Morris 2012, VI.

[40] Author interview, CEO, solar PV equipment manufacturer, May 10, 2011.

core skills and capabilities. Occasionally, however, it took place within the same firm, through the integration of technologies and skills internally. Although principles from the original application of technologies and processes were here repurposed, the combination of different technologies resulted in the development of new product designs.

In a fairly typical example, a small supplier of automation equipment used strategic learning and hiring to combine its core skills in the production of automation and testing machines for the auto sector with proficiencies from other industries. Trying to reduce its exposure to a single sector, the firm decided to diversify into solar module assembly, since very little automation technology for that activity was on the market; and much of the existing automation technology originally developed for the auto sector could be reapplied. While the firm reused about 70 percent of the technologies it had previously applied in the auto industry, it also integrated novel infrared and laser welding processes, as well as laser drilling technology originally used in dental offices. These dynamic additions allowed the firm to process cells contact-free, an improvement that increased speed, reliability, and production efficiency, particularly in the handling of ever-thinner wafers that were prone to breakage.[41]

In addition to hiring engineers with skills in laser welding and setting up training programs for existing R&D staff, the firm worked closely with laser and robotics suppliers during product development. The head of R&D pointed out the following:

> A lot of these suppliers are just down the road. In that sense, we benefit from being in the Silicon Valley of the machine tool industry. They send engineering teams that can come for days, weeks, or months, and work on site with our engineers until the product works. It's very different from working with global software firms, for instance, from whom we purchase testing and measuring software. If we have a problem there, we can call a call center, but those people don't really know any more than our own staff.[42]

All in all, the firm took two years to develop a prototype and another two years to start delivering the first products to customers—a lengthy process that occupied almost all of the firm's R&D sources.

A third mode of industry entry, *resizing*, pervaded the German wind power sector. Resizing occurred when the application of an existing technology to a new industry required a radically different scale not just of production but also

---

[41] Author interview, managing partner, solar PV equipment manufacturer, May 10, 2011; October 15, 2019.
[42] Author interview, head of R&D, solar PV equipment manufacturer, May 11, 2011.

of the product itself. Especially with mechanical parts, resizing often dictated a complete redesign of the product and the production process: structural loads and forces changed exponentially as the size of the product increased. As a consequence, computer models had difficulty developing adequate specifications for new components, and trial-and-error approaches dominated product development, as they do to this day.[43]

A manufacturer of gearboxes for wind turbines originally produced gearboxes for tunnel drilling machines in the mining sector. Although the core principles shared similarities—both types of gearboxes needed to withstand strong forces, high operating temperatures, and, unlike cars, needed to maintain almost continuous operation for years or even decades—gearboxes for large wind turbines required a completely new design. This remake needed to accommodate the structural requirements of the new size, new control software, a new logistics system to run operations, and new measuring and testing procedures; what's more, it also needed to use different materials to prevent corrosion in off-shore applications. Since gearboxes needed to meet the particular requirements of a wind turbine design, they almost always were developed in close cooperation with a future customer. Accordingly, for the firms' initial gearbox and subsequent product generations, a wind turbine manufacturer supplied specifications for interfaces, noise levels, vibration tolerances, and other parameters. The gearbox manufacturer then developed a prototype in close consultation with the customer, who was also involved in testing and ramping up to volume production. Although the firm possessed decades of experience in the gearbox industry, the development process for the first wind turbine generation lasted more than four years, with slightly shorter development times for subsequent product generations.[44]

A generator manufacturer described a similar process of bringing generator technologies from the shipbuilding and railways industries into the wind energy sector. In this case, space constraints and more stringent weight requirements inside the turbine prompted a redesign of the product and production line, a process repeated every time a larger turbine generation required exponentially larger components. The plant manager explained that for some components, the firm found ways to reuse parts from its railway and industrial engine business; but for others, the need for smaller and lighter-weight structures and the reality of different climate conditions in wind turbine applications mandated the use of alternative materials and construction methods. In adapting existing technologies to the requirements of the wind turbine industry, the firm benefited greatly

---

[43] Author interview, plant manager, gearbox manufacturer, May 16, 2011.
[44] Author interview, plant manager, gearbox manufacturer, May 16, 2011.

from its proximity to local suppliers, who worked closely with the firm's engineers to adapt parts and components. As the plant manager explained:

> We work with a local iron caster on making a part. Even with something as simple as iron casting we have to be careful. These firms make parts for all sorts of machines, so they don't know what's relevant and important in our business. For the first 100 parts or so we have to have an engineer work on site with them to make sure the part is optimized. For a small company like us, it's much easier if the supplier is around the corner, because we can jump in the car and meet with them to discuss tolerances and fits.[45]

Collaboration and the Mittelstand

These unlikely entrants into Germany's wind and solar industries succeeded in finding their customization niche because of collaborative advantage. Collaboration freed up options for specialization, allowing renewable energy firms in Germany to pick competitive strategies that built on their existing strengths in customization. If conventional wisdom predicted that small and medium-sized manufacturing firms in a high-wage economy would be threatened by competition with China, the reality on the ground subverted this assumption: precisely *because* of their engagement in China, these firms were able to survive. Relationships with Chinese firms allowed these companies to enter renewable energy sectors without having to set up mass manufacturing facilities, allowing highly specialized German firms to enter the marketplace.

In both the wind and solar power sectors, the development of new technologies necessitated large investments in time and capital, even if they allowed firms to draw on existing knowledge. Product development times of two to four years were standard among the majority of firms interviewed for this project, with an almost equal length of time recorded for each new product generation. For small and medium-sized suppliers, the move into wind and solar sectors commandeered the vast majority of their R&D resources, preventing firms from working on product alternatives for different industrial sectors.[46] In this context, Germany's small and medium-sized supply firms were attracted to the wind and solar sectors as much by the stability of Germany's renewable energy legislation as by growing market demand. In both sectors, suppliers entered after

---

[45] Author interview, plant manager, German generator manufacturer, May 17, 2011. I also visited the Chinese partner of the German firm and interviewed the lead R&D engineer, December 6, 2016.
[46] Author interview, engineer, robotics manufacturer, May 13, 2011.

government support had switched to long-term demand stimulation by passing the 1990 Feed-in Law and the 2000 EEG.

In the solar sector, the availability of off-the-shelf manufacturing equipment for solar cell production—attributable to the growing number of designated supply firms—lowered barriers for entry for manufacturers both in Germany and abroad. In previous decades, field tests had struggled to replicate laboratory results. Manufacturing difficulties often led to large variances and degradation of solar cell performance over time. Before the development of designated production equipment, assembling a solar production line comprised a makeshift combination of chemical baths, screen printers, furnaces, and other equipment borrowed from various industries.[47] Advanced manufacturing equipment now permitted manufacturers to more reliably translate their R&D efforts into mass production and made it easier to reach scale economies. The greater consistency and standardization of manufacturing output—including the development of industry norms for wafer and cell sizes—further supported firm specialization in discrete steps of the supply chain, since the interfaces between different production steps now enjoyed compatibility across producers.

In the 1980s and 1990s, wafers had to be cut from silicon ingots one at a time. In the early 2000s, the introduction of wire-saws by equipment producers allowed 4,000 wafers to be cut simultaneously, reducing cost, time, and capital expenses.[48] In the early 1990s, a single manufacturer was at best able to produce solar panels with a few kilowatts capacity annually. A mere decade later, a single production line could churn out solar panels with 66 MW of generation capacity a year. Although R&D efforts by universities, research institutes, and industry improved the conversion efficiency for multicrystalline cells by 15 percent between 1995 and 2005, advances in manufacturing technology allowed the price of solar PV systems to drop by more than 40 percent over the same period, far exceeding gains from increased conversion efficiency.[49]

In theory, the availability of off-the-shelf production equipment permitted anyone to produce solar cells with the flick of a switch. In practice, producers relied on extensive collaboration among solar firms, equipment producers, and research institutes. To embed new technologies in production equipment, research institutes and solar firms shared the results of internal R&D efforts with equipment producers. These firms had experience with automation technology and equipment manufacturing but, in return, often lacked knowledge of new solar

---

[47] Morris 2012, vi.

[48] Swanson 2011, 543.

[49] Cell efficiencies over time gathered by NREL. See https://www.nrel.gov/pv/cell-efficiency.html (accessed November 12, 2020). Prices of solar PV systems over time compiled by Grau, Huo, and Neuhoff 2012, 23, figure 4.

PV technologies. Solar manufacturers and equipment suppliers generally collaborated on extensive field-testing of new equipment.

For solar firms, participating in R&D joint projects meant walking a tightrope between protecting proprietary technologies and accessing advanced automation equipment to commercialize these technologies. Investments in new production technologies made little commercial sense to equipment manufacturers if they could not be marketed to other customers, so few were willing to build equipment exclusively for a particular solar firm. Additionally, through their collaboration with equipment suppliers, solar manufacturers could access technological contributions made by competitors and research institutes, a benefit many believed outweighed the disadvantages of making proprietary technologies available to the competitors. In interviews, solar firms emphasized the risk of missing out on important technological innovations when not collaborating with equipment suppliers, a possibility that deterred them from trying to manufacture equipment in-house.[50] The CTO of a producer of thin-film solar modules summarized this point: "we often have internal debates over whether we want to be like Apple and follow a closed innovation concept, or whether we want to be more like IBM and use an open platform."[51] In the end, the firm decided to follow the IBM model in order to benefit from knowledge sharing through equipment suppliers.

Of course, once production lines had been installed in manufacturing facilities, solar firms continued to improve and alter purchased equipment in ways they did not always share with equipment suppliers. Yet at the core of technological innovation and the development of mature production technologies was a highly collaborative process in which equipment producers acted as a focal point for contributions made by a wide range of firms.

In Germany, such collaboration initially occurred domestically. As Germany's domestic wind and solar manufacturers stagnated in size and were quickly surpassed in production capacity by large-scale manufacturing facilities in China, demand for the latest wind turbine components and solar PV production equipment increasingly came from abroad. Small and medium-sized German manufacturers of production equipment possessed neither the financial support nor the technological capacities to establish large solar PV manufacturing operations. At the same time, suppliers' ability to develop manufacturing equipment required that they have access to engineering knowledge about mass production. Although German manufacturers had initially triggered the rise of domestic wind and solar suppliers, partners with complementary skills in mass

[50] Author interviews: CTO, German solar PV manufacturer, May 17, 2011; head of German operations, global equipment manufacturer, May 18, 2011; CEO, German equipment manufacturer, May 10, 2011; CTO, German solar PV manufacturer, May 23, 2011.
[51] Author interview, CTO, German solar PV manufacturer, May 23, 2011.

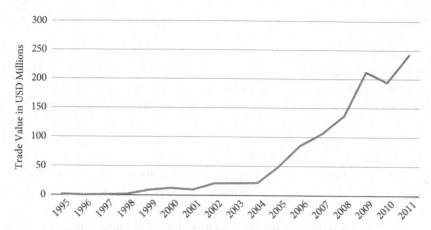

Figure 4.2 Germany's Exports of PV Equipment to China, 1995–2011
Source: UN Comtrade Database (no designated HS Code exists for PV equipment. As an approximation, I am using HS Code 854140 for "Photosensitive/photovoltaic/LED semiconductor devices" to track the growth in export value).

production—those with a need for the customization and small-batch production supplied by German SMEs—were increasingly located abroad. For German suppliers, the most important sources of such complementary skills were Chinese manufacturers (Figure 4.2).[52]

In the solar sector, the German manufacturer of solar production lines Centrotherm had already begun selling its products to Chinese customers by 2000. Similar partnerships quickly followed.[53] Between 2000 and 2007, the export quota for German PV equipment producers rose from 10 to 51 percent, most of it destined for Chinese factories.[54] In interviews, German equipment suppliers reported that the scale of production activities and access to large-scale financing for manufacturing plants afforded their Chinese partners the option of setting aside considerable resources to test new production equipment. Several Chinese firms constructed demonstration facilities with full test production lines—so-called Golden Lines—on which new technologies could be developed in collaboration with German equipment suppliers.[55] An analysis of 178 Sino-German technology collaborations between 2010 and 2012 conducted by the German Ministry for Research and Technology revealed more than a dozen such

[52] Rothgang, Peistrup, and Lageman 2011; Rheinisch-Westfälisches Institut für Wirtschaftsforschung and WSF Wirtschafts- und Sozialforschung Kerpen 2010; Seemann 2012.
[53] Nussbaumer et al. 2007, 109.
[54] EuPD Research data cited in Fischedick and Bechberger 2009, 26.
[55] Author interviews: CEO, Chinese solar manufacturer, August 10, 2011; CEO, Chinese solar manufacturer, August 26, 2011; chief engineer, Chinese solar manufacturer, March 31, 2015; head of research and development, Chinese solar manufacturer, January 7, 2019.

interactions between German machine builders and Chinese renewable energy firms.[56]

More than mere customers, Chinese manufacturers became long-term partners in the development of production equipment for new solar PV technologies. In bringing new solar technologies from lab to market, China's producers willingly assumed considerable risks in the development and application of new production technologies and materials. The rapidly growing demand for new production lines often allowed equipment manufacturers to apply new production technologies first in China, relying on mass-manufacturing skills of Chinese solar firms throughout the commercialization process. Centrotherm and Schmid, the two German equipment suppliers, experimented with the development of production equipment for selective emitter cells but were unable to find German producers willing to partner on the commercialization of this new technology. In 2009, it was Chinese cell manufacturers who proved willing to collaborate with German suppliers on developing production equipment for elective emitter cells, adjusting their own production processes to test and optimize the new equipment with German engineers.[57] In 2010, Roth & Rau, another German equipment supplier, entered a similar agreement with a Chinese solar manufacturer to develop production equipment for a new thin-film technology.[58] Although Chinese manufacturers sourced basic production equipment from domestic suppliers, production lines for the latest PV technologies continued to be developed in Sino-German collaborations.[59]

China differed from other markets both in its aggregate demand for production equipment and because the scale of manufacturing activities in individual solar firms far exceeded those elsewhere. In 2010, Suntech, a single Chinese manufacturer, produced more solar modules than the top five German manufacturers combined.[60] Finding new ways to manufacture cheaper, faster, and at greater scale dominated the value proposition of China's solar firms. Working with equipment producers to achieve cost reductions on new production equipment constituted standard practice. In the words of the CEO of one of China's major solar cell manufacturers, "Solar PV is not so much a technology as it is a manufacturing business."[61] As China's solar firms took the lead in fully automating the production of wafers, cells, and modules, they continuously demanded new

[56] Grune and Heilmann 2012.

[57] Neuhoff 2012, 156.

[58] Roth & Rau 2010.

[59] Author interviews: managing partner, German solar PV equipment manufacturer, May 10, 2011; head of R&D, German solar PV equipment manufacturer, May 11, 2011; CEO of German solar equipment manufacturer, May 20, 2011.

[60] Germany Trade & Invest 2012, 26; Christopher Martin, 2010, "Suntech Boosts 2010 Solar Panel Shipments, Production Capacity on Demand," *Bloomberg*, August 18.

[61] Author interview, CEO, Chinese solar manufacturer, August 10, 2011.

production equipment and retrofits to existing manufacturing lines. Over time, Chinese solar producers thus became important partners to German equipment suppliers in the commercialization of new production technologies.[62]

In the wind industry, global turbine producers also partnered with German supplies in the commercialization of new technologies. As I mentioned earlier, entrants to the wind sector came from a variety of industries and included manufacturers of control systems and software, producers of manufacturing equipment and machine tools, and steel and composite materials firms. Many of the new supplier firms possessed technical expertise and production experience that could be applied to the manufacture of wind turbine components. For example, a firm that for decades had supplied gearboxes for large tunnel-drilling machines in the mining sector wanted to reduce its exposure to a declining mining industry in Germany. In 1992, the firm decided to develop the capabilities to produce gearboxes for wind turbines. In 1996, after four years of R&D, it was ready to enter mass production.[63] Similarly, a generator supplier for trains and industrial motors decided to diversify its product portfolio, and in 1998 began the development of a generator for the wind market.[64]

The growing wind industry supply chain permitted firms to restructure their manufacturing operations and to devote attention to core strengths. With the exception of Enercon, which to this day manufactures major components in-house in order to protect proprietary technologies, wind turbine manufacturers began to rely on the expertise of outside firms for the production and design of components such as gearboxes, generators, blades, towers, and control software. Turbine design and component specification remained with the turbine manufacturer. The production experience that supply firms had gathered in other industries contrasted sharply with that of younger, smaller, and less experienced wind turbine manufacturers. The introduction of new production technologies by supplier firms—including lean production practices borrowed from the automotive sector—reduced cost, permitted increased production scale, and enabled the fabrication of ever larger turbine designs without the technical failures that had plagued large-scale turbines in previous decades. In interviews, suppliers—particularly in the generator and gearbox sector—frequently pointed to lean production concepts such as just-in-time-production, continuous improvement (Kaizen), six sigma, and the Toyota production model in explaining their contribution to the wind energy sector.[65]

---

[62] Author interviews: CEO, Chinese solar manufacturer, August 10, 2011, CEO, Chinese solar manufacturer, August 26, 2011.

[63] Author interview, plant manager of German gearbox manufacturer, May 16, 2011.

[64] Author interview, plant manager of German generator manufacturer, May 17, 2011.

[65] Author interviews: plant manager of German gearbox manufacturer, May 16, 2011; plant manager of German generator manufacturer, May 17, 2011; head of European operations of global turbine manufacturer, May 19, 2011.

Over the course of the 1980s, the majority of debates within the wind industry on wind turbine design had been settled; and almost all manufacturers
had converted to the Danish model: they built turbines with three blades posi-
tioned upwind that could be rotated along their own axis to adjust for variable
wind speeds.[66] Aside from improving aerodynamics, the main remaining challenge was scale. Increasing the size of turbines meant exponentially larger loads
and stresses on components, many of which could not be simulated well on
computers. By combining the results of ongoing R&D efforts with new production methods and technical expertise contributed by third-party suppliers, turbine manufacturers successfully increased the average rotor diameter from 30
meters to 70 meters over the course of the 1990s, enlarging the area swept by the
rotor blades by a factor of five and improving average generating capacity from
250 kW to 1500 kW by the year 2000.[67]

German suppliers became a resource for an expanding global network of wind
turbine manufacturers, increasingly seeking collaboration with foreign partners
and competing with supply firms elsewhere. Aside from Denmark, which had
long played a pioneering role in wind energy development, and Spain, which
began subsidizing the large-scale installation of wind turbines in the late 1990s,
the most important foreign partners of German supply firms heralded from the
United States and China.

In October 1997, Enron Corporation, an American electricity and natural gas
company, purchased Tacke Windtechnik of Salzbergen. Enron had previously
bought Zond, one of the few American wind turbine manufacturers remaining
from the California wind boom in the 1980s, but experienced technical problems
with the Zond turbine technology. The purchase of Tacke, which kept operating
under its own name until GE took over Enron's wind business in the wake of
Enron's accounting fraud scandal in 2001, gave Enron access to Tacke's turbine
technology and supplier network. Enron retired the Zond turbine technology,
and Tacke's 1.5 MW turbine became Enron's workhorse wind energy product.[68]
GE retained its relationships with German suppliers, in particular with Eickhoff,
which had manufactured the gearboxes for the 1.5 MW Tacke turbine, but also
with Winergy and Bosch Rexroth, the other large German gearbox suppliers,
and VEM Sachsenwerke, a generator firm. It remained an active member of the
VDMA's wind chapter, participating in collaborative research activities to advance wind turbine designs.[69] Over time, GE began sourcing components from

[66] Musgrove 2010, chapter 6.
[67] Data from Bundesverband Windenergie. See http://www.wind-energie.de/infocenter/Technik.
(accessed March 25, 2019.)
[68] Lewis 2013, 95; Windpower Monthly 1997. For additional details on GE's path into the wind
energy sector, see Chapter 6.
[69] VDMA website, http://wind.vdma.org/en/article/-/articleview/599526 (accessed March
15, 2019).

other locations, adding suppliers from China (gearboxes and metal castings) and Brazil (blades).

The early model of collaborative relationships that originated in the German wind sector during the 1990s was now being applied globally and maintained through successive product generations. At the core, it brought together specialized expertise residing in companies around the world to develop and manufacture ever-larger turbine designs. According to GE's chief wind engineer at the time, Vincent Schelling, GE has to "put the knowledge in the gearbox manufacturers' hands. It would be better if we designed the gearbox and they built it, but we don't have all the knowledge." Likewise, Thomas Narath of Eickhoff stated, "Gearbox design is always a close cooperation between the turbine OEM (original equipment manufacturer) and the gearbox suppliers. OEMs usually deliver the main product specifications and a conceptual design which our engineering team further develops into a final product design." Narath added, it "also happens that gearbox development advancement points to a need for main chassis [i.e., wind turbine] design changes. This underlines the great value attached to regular exchange of ideas."[70] Cross-border collaboration of the kind described here between GE and Eickhoff was singularly important to the maturation of wind energy technologies starting in the late 1990s.

Around the time that the United States became an important market for German wind turbine suppliers, Chinese firms also made their first foray into the wind energy industry. From the beginning, Chinese producers relied on a global supply chain for wind turbine components and entered collaborative relationships with specialized suppliers. Just as German gearbox manufacturers worked with GE to improve gearbox and turbine designs without co-locating production, so Chinese firms also drew on expertise from abroad.[71] Global sourcing lowered the level of local content for China-assembled wind turbines to as low as 12 percent in 2002, though this percentage increased significantly as foreign suppliers set up manufacturing facilities in China and as domestic firms entered the industry over the course of the decade.[72]

Much as in the United States and Europe, these relationships with supply firms, joint venture partners, and license grantors were not a case of one-directional technology transfer. Although market access considerations and the complex regulatory environment in China certainly contributed to the willingness of foreign firms to enter joint development agreements, such relationships frequently resulted in multidirectional learning that benefited the foreign partner. According to an engineer working for a German wind turbine design

[70] de Vri es 2013; Windpower Monthly 2005a.
[71] Wang Z. 2010, 197–203.
[72] Wang Z. 2010, 68.

firm, the ability to learn from Chinese engineering teams as they reconfigured a product design for mass manufacturing constituted a key motivator for the German firm to jointly develop and commercialize a wind turbine, rather than simply selling a license.[73] Even under licensing agreements, however, foreign firms found avenues to learn from Chinese wind turbine manufacturers. In the case of one generator licensed from a German supplier, for instance, the Chinese firm improved the original design through reconfiguration of the product architecture, so much so that it licensed the improved generator design back to the German firm.[74] In other cases, foreign firms tried to replicate capabilities in scale-up and mass manufacturing outside of formal relationships with Chinese partners, setting up their own manufacturing facilities in China and poaching engineers from their Chinese competitors.[75]

For Chinese wind turbine manufacturers, an expanding Chinese domestic supply chain frequently complemented relationships with suppliers from Germany and elsewhere. While Chinese suppliers developed capabilities focused on cost, scale, and ease of manufacturability, German suppliers retained expertise in producing components for prototyping, small-batch production, and commercialization. Engineers for wind turbine manufacturers indicated that they were relying on German suppliers in early stages of product development. For large scale production, however, they switched to local partners, as innovation in the scale-up to mass production does not center around technological improvement, but rather on changing product designs to accommodate lower-cost manufacturing processes and materials.[76]

A long-term collaborative relationship between the German turbine firm Vensys and the Chinese wind manufacturer Goldwind illustrates this dovetailing of skills. Lacking capabilities in mass production, Vensys entered into a partnership with Goldwind to commercialize a novel direct-drive technology that Vensys had developed. Direct-drive technology eliminates the need for a gearbox, which is one of the costliest turbine components and notoriously prone to technical problems. Vensys first licensed its technology to Goldwind in 2003, having previously only manufactured a small number of prototypes. From that point on, commercialization and the preparation for mass manufacturing took place in China. This was the case for a first 1.5 MW model as well as

[73] Author interview, CEO of German engineering firm, May 20, 2011.

[74] Author interview, plant manager of German generator manufacturer, May 17, 2011.

[75] Author interview, head of China operations, European wind turbine manufacturer, September 22, 2011.

[76] Author interviews: plant manager of German generator manufacturer, May 17, 2011; head of China operations, global wind turbine manufacturer, January 21, 2011; head of China operations, European turbine manufacturer, October 28, 2010; head of China, German wind turbine design firm; March 27, 2017; head of R&D, Chinese generator manufacturer, January 4, 2016.

subsequent product generations.[77] By 2008, the relationship between German and Chinese engineers had become so central to the development of the technology that Vensys sold a 70 percent stake to Goldwind over a number of other bidders. According to Vensys, Goldwind was chosen as a partner precisely for its capabilities in commercialization and large-scale production. Upstream R&D for Vensys's new turbine generations has remained in Germany, but the design changes to improve cost and manufacturability take place at the Goldwind facilities in China.[78] The two firms have maintained this division of labor nearly fifteen years after first establishing a relationship.[79]

Manufacturing Institutions and Green Energy Innovation

If collaboration allowed firms from Germany's Mittelstand to apply their existing skills in customization, it also allowed them to repurpose existing institutions of the domestic economy. These legacy institutions of the German manufacturing economy retained value in wind and solar industries precisely because they no longer had to support the full range of activities required to invent and commercialize new technologies domestically. It is important to note here that these domestic institutions formed a particularly good fit for the strategies of those small and medium-sized German firms that had found ways to collaborate with Chinese manufacturers. In the solar industry, German manufacturers that tried to compete with China directly struggled like their American counterparts to raise the financial capital to build manufacturing plants that could reach the necessary scale economies. Collaboration with Chinese firms was also difficult for German manufacturers of wind turbines such as Nordex, which established relationships with local partners but were, over time, largely driven out of the Chinese market. Local competitors both underbid German firms on price, but local procurement rules also created additional obstacles for foreign manufacturers of wind turbines in China. Domestic institutions of the German economy offered little protection against these broader obstacles to competing in the Chinese wind power market.

Despite the eventual success of small and medium-sized firms, Germany's renewable energy legislation contained few provisions specifically targeting the development of dense supplier networks for wind and solar sectors. Initial renewable energy laws were not expected to lead to the development of large domestic industrial sectors. Subsequent changes to the Feed-in Law and its successor, the

---

[77] Vensys sold similar licenses to manufacturers in other markets but was not as closely involved in production and scale-up with its other licensees.

[78] See Peters 2009; Vensys 2012.

[79] Vensys 2017. Author interview, Beijing, March 23, 2015.

EEG, adjusted tariffs for different sources of energy to account for technology improvements. Specific provisions for small and medium-sized firms were absent from later generations of renewable energy legislation, as well. Neither the original Feed-in Law nor the EEG included local content requirements or loan programs for German wind and solar suppliers. For manufacturers of solar panels and wind turbines, grants of up to 50 percent of investment costs for capital-intensive manufacturing plants were available as part of special development policies for eastern Germany. Most solar PV manufacturers subsequently chose to locate in Berlin, Brandenburg, Mecklenburg-Vorpommern, Saxony, Saxony-Anhalt, and Thuringia.[80] Such programs were of little use to existing small and medium-sized producers of components and production equipment—they remained deeply anchored in local supplier networks and needed to retool extant production facilities.

Just as demand-side legislation provided little concrete assistance for firms seeking to enter renewable energy sectors, federal R&D funding for energy technologies also bypassed small and medium-sized firms. A series of federally funded energy research programs (*Energieforschungs-programme*), each of which offered a specific substantive theme within the field of energy technologies, and which ran between three and ten years' duration, dispensed EUR 1.81 billion for renewable energy research between 1990 and 2005.[81] Though they promoted advanced wind and solar research in Germany, these programs primarily targeted large firms and research institutes such as the Fraunhofer centers. An evaluation of research funded through the third Federal Energy Research Program, for example, which ran from 1990 until 1996, included projects conducted by industrial laboratories at Siemens, Bayer, Wacker Chemical, and Deutsche Aerospace, but revealed little participation from smaller firms.[82]

The situation improved by the time the 2000 EEG created large-scale demand for solar energy products. The firms carrying out these research activities now began to reflect the diversity of suppliers in wind and solar sectors. Among manufacturing firms that received federal R&D funding for renewable energy research, machine tool producers and manufacturers of electrical equipment (*Elektrotechnik*) constituted the two largest groups; they made up 13 percent and 11 percent of firms, respectively.[83] Despite the shift in federal research programs

---

[80]   Grants comprised incentives available through two separate programs: the Joint Task Program for the Promotion of Industry and Trade (*Gemeinschaftsaufgabe*), available in all of Germany depending on local economic conditions, and the Investment Allowance (*Investitionszulage*), designed specifically as part of the economic recovery program for Eastern Germany. See Germany Trade & Invest 2013.

[81]   Bundesministerium für Wirtschaft und Arbeit 2005, 22; Prognos AG et al. 2007, 14; Sandtner, Geipel, and Lawitzka 1997, 260.

[82]   Forschungszentrum Jülich 1993.

[83]   Prognos AG et al. 2007, 204–6.

to include small and medium-sized suppliers, federal R&D funds played only a small role in helping firms enter and compete in wind and solar industries. More than 70 percent of firms receiving federal funds for renewable energy R&D stated that they were already active in renewable energy sectors prior to participating in the programs. Forty percent of firms indicated that federal R&D funds were used to bolster existing R&D activities or had no influence on firm strategy at all. Fewer than 30 percent of firms used federal funds to enter new industries and markets.[84] For the majority of firms, federal R&D support thus at best supplemented existing R&D infrastructures and resources.

Instead, supply firms made extensive use of resources, networks, and industrial practices familiar to them from prior activities. Broad macroeconomic institutions, established long before the emergence of wind and solar industries, shaped firms' strategies as they entered global renewable energy supply chains. The development of wind and solar supply chains contrasts with expectations that economic competition in highly globalized sectors would threaten the survival of such institutions.[85] The ability of firms to insert themselves into global chains depended on their reliance on, and repurposing of, legacy institutions. This self-insertion also made firms in emerging industries part of broader political coalitions in support of such institutions. Firms participated in these existing institutional arrangements not because they lacked alternatives, but because these institutions provided resources for the specialized learning strategies they chose to pursue. Three sets of institutions in particular were repurposed by renewable energy firms.

First, wind and solar suppliers highlighted the importance of collaboration between their R&D engineers and their manufacturing workforce in developing technologies for wind and solar industries. For many products, such collaboration and bidirectional exchanges were not just critical to improving the manufacturability of new designs, but they also formed the core of trial-and-error based development processes that could not easily be modeled using computer-aided design (CAD) technologies. To foster collaboration between R&D and manufacturing staff, firms located their R&D teams inside or in close proximity to manufacturing operations. Almost all German wind and solar supply firms retained production activities close to their headquarters.[86]

In the opinion of executives, the skills and training of their employees—R&D engineers as well as manufacturing staff—was as important to product development as the co-location of such activities (if not more so). The recruitment of highly skilled production workers and their continuous professional

[84] Prognos AG et al. 2007, 262.
[85] Hassel 2014; Thelen 2014.
[86] Germany Trade & Invest 2010, 2011c.

development remained essential to the overall success of the operation. Without the appropriate skills and training opportunities, workers would be unable to identify problems within the product development process, suggest appropriate technical solutions, and implement these solutions together with R&D engineers. The production and research activities in many small firms were so closely linked that some did not formally differentiate between R&D teams and their manufacturing staff. According to the director of R&D for one solar equipment supplier, all production staff had gone through industry-specific training in Germany's vocational training system, and most engineers had also completed an apprenticeship before entering university. Despite such rigorous practical training for production workers and R&D engineers, tacit knowledge acquired on the job was also considered critically important. "CAD and similar programs are unable to simulate the conditions that we find in our machines," the R&D director said. "So what we do instead is to build the machine and then test it, tweak the parameters, and then test it again. A lot of this process is tacit knowledge. Our capital is the experience of our staff, and they didn't gain this [experience] in university, they learned it on the job."[87]

In finding, training, and retaining skilled workers, firms reaped the benefits of broader labor market institutions. Firms collaborated through interfirm networks and industry associations, maintaining programs for highly industry-specific vocational training in the form of apprenticeships and, increasingly, dual degree programs (*duales Studium*). The latter offered joint practical training and a university education at vocational universities (*Berufsakademie*). Together, firms ensured that individual companies continued to contribute to such programs by offering traineeships and extracted financial support from Länder and federal governments.[88] These skills and training institutions did face challenges: firm participation in collaborative efforts declined over time, leading to calls for an "apprenticeship tax" (*Ausbildungsplatzabgabe*) for firms unwilling to contribute; and growing numbers of high-school graduates were shut out of the vocational training system altogether as demand for apprenticeships continued to outstrip supply. From the perspective of manufacturing firms, however, the vocational training system continued to work well.[89] In a 2012 survey of more than 14,000 firms conducted by the Association of German Chambers of Commerce and Industry (DIHK), manufacturers in machinery and equipment sectors planned to offer permanent positions to 80 percent of their apprentices;

---

[87] Author interview, head of R&D, solar PV equipment manufacturer, May 11, 2011.

[88] Culpepper 1999; Ebner, Graf, and Nikolai 2013; Minks, Netz, and Völk 2011, iii–v. On dual degree programs, see Ebner, Graf, and Nikolai 2013; Graf 2013; Streeck 1989, 37–38. For a history of the vocational training system with examples specifically from the metal-working industry, see OECD 1994.

[89] On changes in collaborative institutions, see Streeck 2009, esp. chapter 4.

84 percent of firms indicated that ensuring access to skilled labor was their principal motivation for contributing to the vocational training system.[90]

At the same time, strong worker representation and employment protection legislation slowed employment turnover, even as a series of labor market reforms permitted more flexible employment contracts.[91] Barred from organizational restructuring through large-scale hiring and firing, German manufacturers instead invested in training their existing workforce, taking the onus on themselves to meet the skill requirements of new R&D and production activities.[92] To retain experienced production staff during recessions and seasonal downturns, federal short-time labor policies (*Kurzarbeit*) subsidized wages through policies akin to part-time unemployment support.[93] During the 2008–2009 economic crisis, a survey conducted by the VDMA showed that despite a 25 percent drop in orders, employment among VDMA member firms only shrank 5 percent, in large part due to short-time labor subsidies.[94] In 2009 alone, the federal government spent EUR 5 billion on short-time wage subsidies for more than one million employees.[95] In short: by offering resources for sector-specific training and by ensuring long employment tenures, labor market institutions established well before the rise of large-scale renewable energy industries had a lasting impact on the type of R&D activities that firms entering the wind and solar sectors could—and did—pursue.

Second, existing *financial institutions and legacy firm ownership patterns* allowed firms to compete in the wind and solar industries. Germany's bank-based financial system offered few opportunities to fund the commercialization of new technologies through venture capital. Government attempts to create a venture capital sector had failed repeatedly, as funds suffered losses and financiers shied away from investing in new firms and technologies.[96] Of venture capital invested in Germany in 1996, for instance, only 7 percent supported seed and start-up funding; more than 60 percent went to investments in large, established firms.[97] Even though the federal government injected nearly EUR 1.5 billion in venture capital funds between 2005 and 2006, overall venture capital activity remained at 0.06 percent of GDP, compared to 0.8 percent in the United States.[98] In 2011, a little more than one-third of venture capital financing came from (mostly

[90] Deutscher Industrie- und Handelskammertag 2012, 29–30. For similar results reported in a broader survey across industries, see Wenzelmann, Schönfeld, and Dionisius 2009.

[91] OECD 2012, 43.

[92] Culpepper 2001; Estevez-Abe, Iversen, and Soskice 2001.

[93] Bosch 2011; Eichhorst and Marx 2009; OECD 2012, 47.

[94] Author interview, VDMA Stuttgart, May 31, 2012.

[95] "Kurzarbeit rettet mehr als 300 000 Arbeitsplätze," *Handelsblatt*, October 1, 2010.

[96] Becker and Hellmann 2003; Mayer, Schoors, and Yafeh 2005.

[97] Giesecke 2000, 215.

[98] Röhl 2010.

government-funded) organizations headquartered in Germany.[99] Not surprisingly, a number of studies identified the financial system as the main obstacle to R&D activities of young, innovative firms in high-technology industries.[100]

The scarcity of venture capital funding presented fewer barriers to existing firms seeking to diversify into wind and solar supply chains. Because, for most firms, developing wind and solar components amounted to a variation of their existing R&D practices, many could rely on funding sources they had used in the past. In doing so, some firms benefited from long-term relationships with local credit unions, which agreed to provide loans after demand-side subsidies had created stable market conditions for renewable energy sectors. Other firms reported either supplementing such loans with retained earnings or completely relying on internal funds for R&D activities. Among the firms interviewed for this project, only one CEO mentioned floating a bond to finance the construction of a new production facility, adding that "financing has never been an issue for us."[101] Wind and solar suppliers reflected broader trends among small and medium-sized businesses: a 2010 survey among German firms that had received federal R&D assistance found that nearly 69 percent of R&D activities were funded through earned income or retained earnings. Only 6 percent of R&D funds came from bank loans, with the rest coming through grants and subsidies.[102]

Although loans and retained income provided relatively modest sums for R&D projects, particularly when compared to the venture capital financing available to high-technology firms in the United States and Israel, these funds had few constraints attached. They allowed firms to pursue long-term development strategies, and this mattered greatly. Taking up to four years to develop a complex equipment or component prototype was not uncommon, and many firms could not generate revenue from investments in renewable energy R&D until years after they made the initial decision to enter the wind and solar supply chains. Local credit unions, familiar with firms' R&D practices, thus provided essential bridge funding. As credit unions stepped forward to finance long-term development projects with firms that they knew, the income that these firms generated from activities in other sectors could be used to cross-subsidize projects in ways that were simply not possible for newly established firms.

The high share of family-controlled firms in Germany, particularly among small and medium-sized businesses, further assisted firms seeking to diversify into new sectors through complex, long-term R&D projects. Over the past

---

[99] Zademach and Baumeister 2013. For 2011, the Zademach and Baumeister report even lower venture capital activity in Germany than Röhl, at 0.028 percent of GDP.

[100] See, for instance, Kreditanstalt für Wiederaufbau 2006; Zimmermann and Hofmann 2007.

[101] Author interview, CEO of solar equipment manufacturer, May 20, 2011.

[102] Belitz, Eickelpasch, and Lejpras 2012, 102.

twenty-five years, the share of family-controlled businesses among Germany's 100 largest firms remained relatively stable at around 20 percent, with significantly more family control among smaller businesses.[103] In 2002, more than two-thirds of firms with fewer than 500 employees were sole proprietorships.[104] In interviews, the managers of wind and solar suppliers repeatedly emphasized how their owners' commitment to preserving the businesses for future generations served to motivate diversification into emerging industrial sectors. That same commitment also made it strategically possible for these firms to reinvest profits in R&D projects. The plant manager at a German generator supplier explained that the family owners had not withdrawn funds from the business since the early 1990s, instead allowing the firm to reinvest its profits into the firm's diversification from ship building into the wind turbine sector.[105] The CEO of an automation equipment manufacturer discussed entering the solar business to reduce overexposure to the automobile industry by investing retained earnings when he took over the family business from his father.[106] Long-term planning horizons created a willingness to forgo immediate profits in favor of future returns, an outlook that sharply differed from short-term strategies driven by the need to maximize shareholder profits.[107]

A third set of legacy institutional tools *helped firms access capabilities and resources outside the firm.* The development of new technologies, components, and production equipment for wind turbine and solar PV industries posed challenges particularly to small and medium-sized firms. Limited R&D resources, which had long prevented smaller firms from absorbing the new technologies generated by publicly funded R&D programs, constrained these smaller firms' ability to develop new technologies, components, and equipment for emerging industrial sectors.[108] For all the skills such firms had historically acquired—proficiencies in the application of core technologies, as well as competencies in managing long-term, complex, and trial-and-error-intensive R&D processes—the development of products for wind turbine and solar PV supply chains required that they adopt new materials, components, production processes, and industry standards. Particularly among smaller, more specialized firms, the capabilities required to master such product development processes could not all be found or maintained within the four walls of the firm.

---

[103] Lubinski 2011, 705.

[104] Günterberg and Kayser 2004, 12.

[105] Author interview, plant manager, generator supply firm, May 17, 2011.

[106] Author interview, CEO, solar equipment manufacturer, May 10, 2011.

[107] For an analysis of the impact of financial markets and shareholder value considerations on American manufacturing firms, see Davis 2009. For a discussion of the long-term planning horizons of German family-owned manufacturing firms, see Berger 2013b, chapter 5.

[108] Belitz, Eickelpasch, and Lejpras 2012, 51; Bruns et al. 2011, 55–56.

The role played by external capabilities is perhaps best observed in the process of integration, in which firms strategically chose new technologies and associated capabilities to complement their existing skills. At the same time, albeit less visibly, other modes of industry entry and subsequent product development processes also required competencies that firms did not possess in-house. Their solution? In order to master specifications for new components, find materials capable of withstanding the stresses of new applications, and use novel production processes, firms turned to external partners. For small and medium-sized suppliers, such partners in many cases were larger wind turbine and solar PV manufacturers, initially domestically and subsequently in global supply chains. Other firms turned to universities, research institutes, and contract researchers for help. In a situation somewhat unique to Germany, however, many small and medium-sized firms also collaborated with one another other, pooling resources and sharing capabilities across sectoral boundaries to meet product development challenges.

In their reliance on external capabilities, small and medium-sized German firms in the wind and solar sectors built on a long tradition of collaborative R&D in German industry. Starting in the late nineteenth century, German manufacturing firms organized themselves in research networks to find suitable partners for joint R&D projects. By 1939, just prior to World War II, nineteen such research networks had been created. By 2011, 101 industrial research associations were facilitating collaborative research activities among member firms.[109] Of the 101 associations active in 2011, 91 focused on a single industry, including machinery and equipment manufacturing; chemicals, plastics, and rubber sectors; and the production of energy generation equipment. Ten research associations had an interdisciplinary focus. By 2011, a total of 50,000 firms had organized themselves into such associations.[110]

Although research associations relied on industry associations to find members, set up collaborative projects, and at least partially fund research through member dues, the state played a critical role in encouraging these joint efforts. In 1954, a Federation of Industrial Research Associations (*Arbeitsgemeinschaft industrieller Forschungsvereinigungen*) was established to facilitate interdisciplinary projects across sectoral boundaries and to represent the interests of research associations to the government. In the same year, the Federal Ministry of Economic Affairs began supporting collaborative research projects through subsidies and research grants.[111] Initially, the main justification for federal support

---

[109] Rothgang, Peistrup, and Lageman 2011, 398.
[110] Rheinisch-Westfälisches Institut für Wirtschaftsforschung and WSF Wirtschafts- und Sozialforschung Kerpen 2010, 79; Rothgang, Peistrup, and Lageman 2011, 400–401.
[111] A number of Länder governments later began to also fund collaborative industrial research, complementing federal policies. Rothgang, Peistrup, and Lageman 2011, 398.

for industrial collaborative research (*Industrielle Gemeinschaftsforschung*) was to level the playing field for SMEs, which were assumed to suffer from competitive disadvantage in an economy increasingly populated by large diversified companies. Over the years, however, as SMEs ceased to be regarded as structurally disadvantaged legacies and came to be understood as integral parts of Germany's innovation economy, the reasoning behind continued support for collaborative research shifted to the creation of spillovers for the broader economy from encouraging R&D in SMEs.[112]

Despite these shifting motivations for state involvement in collaborative research, the policies and institutional resources provided to foster such collaboration remained relatively stable over time. At the core, state support for industrial collaborative research (ICR) meant R&D funding for research projects that included partnerships among several firms and research institutes.[113] Participating research institutes included universities, industry research institutes funded by industry associations, and nonuniversity institutions such as Germany's large number of Fraunhofer and Max Planck Institutes. Funded projects were by definition precompetitive: to qualify for funding, projects needed to focus on technologies and materials with multiple potential applications in a range of future products, rather than targeting the development of commercializable products. The results of ICR projects were shared among all members of participating research associations, although direct involvement in the project was often necessary for firms to be able to use these research findings.[114]

In contrast to other federal R&D funding schemes, firms designed these ICR projects without thematic requirements.[115] As members of research associations, firms could suggest ideas for new projects at association meetings, find partners, and identify research institutes with expertise in solving the particular problem at stake. In finding partners for R&D collaboration, firms explicitly targeted colleagues with different technical capabilities, R&D resources, and priorities in product development.[116] Each project formed a planning group of participating firms, and that group defined the exact scope of the R&D undertaking, jointly submitting

[112] For a full discussion of the motivation behind such programs and changes in the justification of subsidies for collaborative research over time, see Eckl and Engel 2009; Karmann-Proppert 2017; Rothgang et al. 2011.

[113] In addition to the programs for industrial collaborative research, other government R&D programs provided bonus funding for projects involving several partners. For instance, ZIM (Zentrales Innovationsprogramm Mittelstand), which provided R&D funding targeted specifically at SMEs, dispensed R&D grants to individual firms but increased funding for projects that involved multiple partners or entire clusters of firms. Author interview, department head, Federal Ministry of Economics and Technology, May 24, 2016.

[114] Author interview, director of research association in the machinery and equipment sector, May 25, 2016.

[115] Eckl and Engel 2009, 4.

[116] For detailed results of a survey of R&D intensive firms engaged in collaborative projects, see Windolph 2010, 7. For results specifically for the PV industry, see Seemann 2012, 353.

applications for federal funding under one of the ICR programs. In addition to government grants, these associations funded projects through membership fees; and individual firms were expected to contribute funds, R&D staff, and equipment. In some cases, donations by larger firms made more costly R&D projects possible.[117] Industry contributions allowed relatively modest sums of federal government support to initiate much larger R&D efforts. In 2008, for instance, EUR 123 million in federal subsidies went to ICR funding; and a total of EUR 2.6 billion has been dispensed since the inception of ICR programs in 1954. Estimates suggest that as little as 15 percent of funds spent on ICR projects came from government coffers.[118]

As firms from Germany's traditional manufacturing sectors began to create products and components for the rapidly growing wind and solar industries, they relied on ICR programs to solve concrete technical challenges; and they benefited from relationships with other firms and research institutes established through previous participation in collaborative projects. Even in the absence of research associations established specifically for the renewable energy sectors, firms accessed federal ICR funding and entered interdisciplinary research networks through participation in one of the many associations set up for existing industrial sectors. Within this open, bottom-up structure for research collaboration, shaped largely through the input of individual member firms, partnerships in the wind and solar sectors manifested in a wide range of forms.[119]

For some firms, collaboration simply meant working closely with end-customers for products and components.[120] Such relationships initially focused on wind and solar manufacturers in Germany, but increasingly they began to draw in international partners, as sizable renewable energy industries emerged in China and elsewhere. Other firms used ICR networks to fund collaboration with research institutes or used contacts from past joint projects to independently facilitate collaboration with external research centers. The CEO of a manufacturer for production equipment for solar modules, for instance, recalled using such ties to establish a cooperation with the Fraunhofer ISE in Freiburg.[121]

In some cases, firms participated in projects set up by associations from other sectors. For example, the director of a research association for the machinery and equipment sector established by the VDMA described how

---

[117] Author interviews: director of research association in the machinery and equipment sector, May 25, 2016; department heads, Federal Ministry of Economics and Technology, May 24 and June 4, 2016. See also Rheinisch-Westfälisches Institut für Wirtschaftsforschung and WSF Wirtschafts- und Sozialforschung Kerpen 2010, chapter 3.

[118] Rheinisch-Westfälisches Institut für Wirtschaftsforschung and WSF Wirtschafts- und Sozialforschung Kerpen 2010, 399.

[119] Bouncken 2004; Rheinisch-Westfälisches Institut für Wirtschaftsforschung and WSF Wirtschafts- und Sozialforschung Kerpen 2010, 75; Seemann 2012.

[120] Braun 2001.

[121] Author interview, CEO, solar module equipment manufacturer, May 10, 2011.

small suppliers and a multinational wind turbine manufacturer participated in interdisciplinary projects to develop new alloys that none of the partners could have created on their own.[122] In other cases, firms formed still larger clusters, seeking funding both through regional development programs for high-tech clusters (set up by the Federal Ministry of Education and Research) and through traditional ICR programs for individual projects conducted within the group. In Solarvalley Mitteldeutschland, the cluster that included a number of ill-fated solar PV manufacturers, some ninety-eight collaborative projects conducted by members along the entire solar PV supply chain received state research support.[123]

In a survey of 60 firms in the solar PV industry, 72 percent of firms that had received public support for collaborative research stated that they would not have participated in the absence of government subsidies. Seventy-four percent of all respondents reported participating in collaborative R&D efforts.[124] Active research associations for a wide range of industrial sectors and government subsidies for collaborative R&D both encouraged and maintained collaborative practices in Germany's manufacturing industries—practices retained by small and medium-sized firms as they entered the emerging wind and solar sectors.

Small and medium-sized firms from Germany's legacy industries responded to policies for renewable energy industries by building on existing capabilities and by using institutions established in support of sectors that had long lain at the core of the German economy. Rather than abandon such institutions when entering new economic sectors, firms repurposed and applied these institutions to the global wind and solar sectors. In doing so, they used Germany's distinct institutional infrastructure to compete in highly globalized sectors and expanded the political coalitions behind such institutions beyond the areas that had originally backed them. Globalization did not threaten the existing fabric of the German manufacturing economy. Instead, specialization and repurposing explain why globalization enabled Germany's specialization in customization to over time.

Conclusion

In the shadow of the high-profile bankruptcies of a number of German solar manufacturers—precisely the type of firms that government policy had

---

[122] Author interview, director of research association in the machinery and equipment sector, May 25, 2016.

[123] Author interview, CEO, solar PV supplier, May 18, 2011. For information on individual projects conducted within the cluster, see http://www.bmbf.de/en/20870.php (accessed September 10, 2019).

[124] Seemann 2012, 355–59.

supported when it prioritized invention in early R&D funding programs—suppliers of automation equipment and complex components created dense networks of firms focused on customization. The ability to repurpose core strengths for new applications within an environment of collaborative advantage lent specialized suppliers remarkable flexibility.[125] Collaborative advantage in global renewable energy sectors allowed these suppliers to contribute skills to a wide range of product development processes with partners from around the world, making them increasingly independent from the fate of local assemblers.

I have argued in this chapter that collaboration with manufacturers from China enabled firms to pursue competitive strategies that aligned with legacy institutions of Germany's domestic economy. Labor market and training institutions, the German financial system, and state support for collaborative research supported SMEs as they pivoted to new industrial sectors. The trajectory of industrial development I have described points toward an interactive evolution of both firm specialization and institutional change. Firms entered new sectors in response to new opportunities for collaboration in global supply chains and found their competitive niche by repurposing domestic institutions and existing skills for application in new sectors. The fact that their turn to customization mirrored the historic strengths of the German economy obscures the central role of learning and industrial change in this narrative. Firms were not simply borrowing from existing knowledge. They were actively learning and reinventing themselves.

The strong response of Mittelstand firms to state industrial policies shaped the trajectory of renewable energy policy. It underlined the divergent interests of firms that could exploit collaborative advantage and firms seeking to compete with China head-on. Highly dependent on an open economy, wind and solar suppliers used their political connections to maintain support for domestic renewable energy markets while preventing trade barriers and other obstacles to collaboration. Between 2005 and 2009, installed solar capacity doubled every two years. Despite its perpetually gray skies, Germany now accounted for nearly half of the world's installed solar PV modules, most of which they imported from China. This breakneck development speed raised concerns about the increasing cost and long-term sustainability of domestic renewable energy markets.[126]

These networks of wind and solar suppliers, organized in politically well connected industry associations such as the VDMA, were vocal in their support

---

[125] Suppliers were, of course, also not immune to industry crises and suffered during broader downturns in global renewable energy industries, including during the 2009 financial crisis and other periods of overcapacity and stagnation in wind and solar sectors.
[126] Earth Policy Institute 2020.

of continuing policies that favored domestic renewable energy markets. In addition to industry associations and environmental groups, Länder governments in regions with renewable energy manufacturing and deployment now lobbied on behalf of local industries.[127] The decentralized nature of these renewable energy supply chains helped broaden the coalition of subnational governments opposed to drastic subsidy cuts and willing to block such legislation in the Bundesrat, Germany's second chamber.

Because of this widespread policy support, successive government administrations at the federal level struggled to change the legislation. After the 2005 federal election, the Conservative/Social Democratic coalition government left the tariff schedule unchanged. In 2009, when a new Conservative/Liberal coalition attempted to cut subsidies for solar energy in a revision to the EEG, several Länder governments blocked the amendment in the Bundesrat to protect the local economy.[128] The federal government again tried to reduce subsidies in 2012, provoking protests by subnational governments and widespread demonstrations in front of government offices in Berlin.[129] Both instances resulted in a compromise between Länder governments seeking to protect local firms and the federal administration. Feed-in tariff rates were reduced, but not by nearly as much as requested by the federal government.[130] The core principle of the feed-in tariff remained unchallenged until 2014, however, and electricity generated from wind turbines and roof-top solar installations continued to receive above-market compensation.[131]

Despite their successful campaign to protect the feed-in tariff legislation, the interests of original equipment manufacturers and the domestic supply industry increasingly diverged. The Mittelstand had long been instrumental to maintaining and shaping industrial policy for the wind and solar sectors in Germany. Firms' geographical spread and their powerful industry organizations added significant political weight to the broad coalition of renewable energy supporters. As the production of solar panels and wind turbines stagnated in Germany and suppliers increasingly depended on global markets, they used their political clout to defend positions that no longer aligned with domestic OEMs. In 2012, German manufacturers of solar panels called for trade barriers to prevent import competition from Chinese competitors, filing antidumping cases domestically and with the European Union.[132] Protests by Germany's component suppliers and manufacturers of production equipment, who vehemently

---

[127] Grewe 2009.
[128] For a detailed account of the negotiations leading up to the 2009 revision of the Renewable Energy Sources Act, see Dagger 2009.
[129] Ismar 2012; Theile 2012.
[130] Gawel and Klassert 2013.
[131] Schwenn, Rossbach, and Heeg 2012.
[132] Bullis 2012.

and ultimately successfully opposed plans to enact antidumping measures, stemmed from the recognition that their contributions to solar technology development now relied on collaboration with global partners.[133] Not only did wind and solar suppliers from Germany's Mittelstand use their political clout to maintain policy support for domestic renewable energy markets, but they were also instrumental in ensuring that these markets remained open to their Chinese partners.[134]

---

[133] Wessendorf 2013.
[134] Meckling and Hughes 2017.

5

China's Specialization
in Innovative Manufacturing

China has not always been an obvious location for innovation in clean energy technologies. For all the headlines generated by China's ascent in the global economy, technological innovation has—until recently—rarely featured in debates about China's role in global supply chains. Since the early 2000s, its share of global manufacturing output has more than tripled, from 6.9 percent in 2001 to over 25 percent in 2015—surpassing the United States as the world's largest manufacturer starting in 2010. Accordingly, observers focused on China's low-cost production environment to understand its contribution to the global economy.[1] Chinese firms attracted attention not with their research and development (R&D) capabilities, but with the sheer scale at which they manufactured commodities for Western markets. In 2002, Wenzhou, an industrial city in Eastern China, produced 70 percent of the world's cigarette lighters, single-handedly causing a trade dispute with the European Union.[2] Even as Chinese firms quickly became proficient in the production of ever more complicated products—China surpassed the United States as the world's largest assembler of computer hardware in 2004, and in 2006 it became the world's largest exporter of high technology products—China's role in the global division of labor was long understood in terms of its advantages in low-cost production.[3]

China is an unexpected location for clean energy innovation for a second reason. Beginning in the mid-1990s, a combination of rapid economic growth and lax environmental enforcement triggered an air environmental crisis of unprecedented magnitude. Transportation emissions, industrial facilities, and coal power plants built to feed the energy demands of industry and a growing urban middle class spread a problem once confined to industrial centers in Northeast China to most of the coastal and interior provinces. Pollution levels in major cities at times exceeded conventional measurement scales, as official weather

---

[1] Levinson 2017, 3; Marsh 2011; UNIDO 2020.
[2] China Daily 2002.
[3] Meri 2009; Yang 2006. A focus on China's low-cost production environment (and inability to innovate) is prevalent both in academic and popular writing. See, for instance, Fishman 2005; Lardy 2002, 134–76; Nolan 2012; Zhang 2006. For a critical discussion of China's ability to innovate, see Economist 2012; Segal 2010.

reports continued to refer to pollution as "haze." In 2015, an online documentary about smog and its public health effects in China gathered more than 200 million views before being banned from the Chinese internet after 48 hours.[4]

Amid this environmental catastrophe, China nonetheless became the location of the world's largest clean energy industries.[5] Over the past two decades, China's renewable energy firms launched manufacturing facilities capable of producing more wind turbines and solar panels than the rest of the world combined. Between 2000 and 2010, China increased the domestic production of solar modules from 3 MW to 10,852 MW, while wind turbine manufacturing grew from 80 MW to almost 19,000 MW annually.[6] By 2016, China accounted for 81 percent of the world's manufacturing capacity for solar PV. It installed 42 percent of the world's wind turbines that same year, virtually all of them manufactured domestically.[7] The conventional narrative that China is one of the world's largest polluters is thus incomplete, if not misguided: it fails to take into account the dramatic developments in Chinese clean energy industry over the past twenty years.

This chapter chronicles the development of China's renewable energy sectors to make two central claims: First, the chapter demonstrates that China's role in global renewable energy industries was rooted in a set of R&D capabilities that I refer to as *innovative manufacturing*. Challenging views that have portrayed China's rise in the global economy as a function of factor cost advantages, I show that China's wind and solar manufacturers established R&D divisions focused on technical capabilities in commercialization and design for mass production. In the early 2000s, when Chinese wind and solar manufacturers first entered these emerging sectors, wind turbines and solar panels had never truly been mass-produced. The rapid translation of new energy technologies into mass-manufacturable products required changes to product designs to accommodate new manufacturing equipment, the incorporation of new materials and components to improve efficiency, and modifications to product architecture to lower production cost. Because Chinese firms found core technologies accessible through collaboration in global supply chains, they used central government R&D funding to build capabilities that their foreign partners could not provide: specifically, the engineering and design skills required to prepare new technologies for commercialization and to implement mass production in nascent renewable energy industries.

Second, and perhaps counterintuitively, this chapter shows that China's particular variety of innovation relied on the adaptation and repurposing of local

[4] Wong 2015.
[5] Guan et al. 2009.
[6] Earth Policy Institute 2020.
[7] Ball et al. 2017, 18; GWEC 2017, 16.

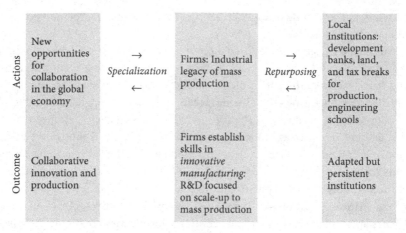

Figure 5.1 Industrial Specialization in China

government support for the manufacturing economy. China's central government in Beijing pursued a vision of industrial upgrading and economic development centered on technological independence and vertical integration in domestic industries through the support of national champions. Yet the presence of collaborative advantage allowed wind and solar manufacturers to respond to such policies with the establishment of R&D skills that took advantage of local government resources for mass production, even when they did not explicitly target such industrial upgrading. Entrepreneurial firms identified opportunities for specialization beyond the scope of central government goals and deployed the tools available in China's industrial ecosystem to advance their skills in commercialization. This ability of Chinese manufacturers to diverge from central government goals was predicated on their close relationships with firms in Germany and the United States: collaboration relieved Chinese firms of the burden of developing the full slate of industrial capabilities required to invent, commercialize, and produce green energy technologies; and it paved the way for China's particular specialization in innovative manufacturing (Figure 5.1).

Earlier I showed how, in Germany, small to medium-sized enterprises (SMEs) from the traditional industrial core that entered renewable energy industries depended on demand from and collaboration with Chinese manufacturers. This chapter discusses the flipside of this partnership. In the presence of collaborative advantage, Chinese firms strategically exploited the divergence between the central governmental goals of technological independence and the local governments that continued to support mass production and that remained wary of investing in long-term innovation strategies. Collaborative advantage allowed Chinese firms to become central nodes in technological innovation in the wind and solar industries while taking advantage of a fragmented domestic industrial policy regime.

This chapter begins with a discussion of the links between China's emerging wind and solar industries and China's broader manufacturing economy. It then uses firm-level data to explain the establishment of Chinese capabilities in innovative manufacturing—R&D skills targeting the commercialization and rapid scale-up to mass production. The second half of this chapter examines the role of collaborative advantage in enabling firms to specialize in innovative manufacturing. It then shows that collaborative advantage allowed renewable energy firms to build on and repurpose local government institutions for mass production that diverged sharply from central governmental goals. The conclusion returns to the implications of China's rise in renewable energy sectors for broader debates about industrial policy and economic development in highly globalized industries.

Scale-Up Nation

In Chapter 2, I showed that a political logic led governments to connect green industrial policies with the expectation of economic co-benefits in the form of growth and employment. These expectations soared the highest in China, which had always regarded renewable energy industries as potential sources of export-oriented development. Differences did occur in the timing of policy support for wind versus solar—the central government had emphasized creating national champions in the wind industry since the late 1990s, while the solar industry in China had initially benefited the most from subnational subsidies for manufacturing and was not included in central government plans until 2009. Nonetheless, the government's treatment of both industries mirrored the broader trajectory of economic development policy in China, which shifted from learning through the attraction of FDI to an emphasis on technological autonomy (Table 5.1).

The release of China's indigenous innovation strategy in 2006 underscored the expectation that the Chinese economy would eventually invent and commercialize homegrown technologies in key industrial sectors without foreign assistance. After technology imports had given way in the 1990s to technology transfers to Chinese firms, the central government declared the pursuit of "indigenous innovation" (*zizhu chuangxin*) a central goal of the Eleventh Five-Year Plan (2006–2010).[8] China's strategy of trading market access for technology had not achieved the desired results among domestic technology firms, and the leadership—informed by a caucus of more than 2,000 scientists, engineers,

---

[8]   State Council 2006.

Table 5.1 Shifting Priorities for Science and Technology Funding

1988–1995 R&D investment, technology imports	1996–2005 First increase, then reduction of FDI dependence	2006– Promotion of indigenous innovation
• Invest in R&D infrastructure • Promote university spin-offs • Promote transformation of R&D into marketable products • Promote establishment of high-technology zones in new localities • Attract research institutes to HTZs • Attract foreign investment to HTZs to increase competitiveness of local tech firms	• Establish production bases for high-tech industries in HTZs • Encourage new technology-based industrial sectors • Since 2001, encourage HTZs to return to original mission, reduce FDI dependence and promote innovation in domestic firms	• Promote "indigenous innovation" • Reduce reliance on technology imports • Preferred government procurement for domestically developed technologies • Encourage SME-based technology clusters • Encourage Chinese scientists and entrepreneurs to return to China from foreign universities and enterprises

Source: Heilmann, Shih, and Hofem 2013.

and corporate executives—decided that the nation was ill-equipped to solve challenges independently in areas critical to China's future development. These included energy, environmental protection, and health.[9] Two documents issued by the State Council in January 2006—the "Medium- and Long-Term Strategic Plan for the Development of Science and Technology" (MLP) and the "Decision on Implementing the MLP and Improving Indigenous Innovation Capability"— laid out the central leadership's intention to place indigenous innovation at the core of China's developmental strategy.[10]

Apart from setting targets to further increase R&D spending to 2.5 percent of GDP and to reduce reliance on foreign technologies, the MLP selected a range of core industrial sectors for special treatment, energy among them.[11] It supplied a list of government instruments for achieving such goals, including the procurement of domestic technologies, the development of domestic

---

[9] Cao, Suttmeier, and Simon 2006, 38–39.

[10] OECD 2008, 389; Schwag Serger and Breidne 2007; State Council 2006. See also: Xinhua, 2006, "China Outlines Strategic Tasks for Building Innovation-Oriented Country," http://english.people.com.cn/200601/09/eng20060109_233919.html (accessed May 10, 2021).

[11] Specifically, the MLP called for a reduction of reliance on imported technology from 50 percent to 30 percent by 2020, measured as spending on technology imports as part of overall spending on domestic R&D and foreign technology purchases. Ernst 2011, 24.

Table 5.2 Select Industrial Policies for China's Wind and Solar Sectors

	China
Technology Push	Since 1986 R&D funding for applied research through "863 Program"
	2008 "Indigenous Innovation" Initiative
	2010 "New Energy" included under Strategic Emerging Industries
	2015 Made in China 2025 Initiative
Market Pull	2003 Wind Power Concession Program
	2006 Renewable Energy Law
	2007 Feed-In Tariff: Wind
	2009 Feed-In Tariff: Solar
	2009 Golden Roofs Initiative
	2009 Golden Sun Program

technology standards, a range of tax benefits and subsidies for R&D, the improvement of intellectual property rights practices, the improved use of technology standards, and international collaborations to accelerate learning among domestic firms.[12] Central science and technology (S&T) programs, including the so-called 863 Program for applied research, received increased funding as a result, and funds for core research areas were adjusted accordingly. The 863 Program now included ten focus areas, including energy technologies, and sought to further increase the proportion of funds supplied to enterprises rather than to universities and research institutes, which had long won the majority of grants (Table 5.1).[13]

In the renewable energy sector, the indigenous innovation guidelines stimulated the aggressive expansion of renewable energy markets and increased support for domestic R&D activities. In 2006, the central government passed China's first renewable energy law, which provided a framework for introducing feed-in laws similar to those in Germany. The law also built the legislative foundation for cost-sharing mechanisms aimed at recovering the cost of renewable energy subsidies through rate-payer surcharges. The Medium- and Long-Term Plan for Renewable Energy Development, issued in 2007, fixed targets for renewable energy markets in China that had been introduced in the renewable energy law: the plan mandated that 15 percent of energy demand must be met from renewable sources by 2020.[14] It also called for the installation of 30 GW of wind turbines as

[12] A short overview of the MLP guidelines for implementation can be found in OECD 2008, 390. Annex F (*China's Policies for Encouraging Indigenous Innovation of Enterprises*) of the same volume lists policies in more detail. OECD 2008, 613–30.

[13] Tan and Gang 2009, 2–4.

[14] Lewis 2013, 53.

well as 1.8 GW of solar photovoltaic (PV), although both 2020 targets have since been revised to 200 GW for wind and 20 GW for solar, respectively.[15] In 2009, the central government eliminated individual feed-in laws set up in various provinces in the wake of the renewable energy law and established China's first national, unified feed-in tariff for wind energy. China was now the world's largest market for wind turbines, having doubled its cumulative wind power capacity from the previous year.[16]

At the same time, a first nationwide feed-in tariff for solar energy created a small but growing domestic market for solar PV technologies, with additional subsidy programs available to support both residential customers and developers of utility-scale solar PV installations. For smaller installations, the Golden Roofs Initiative provided a subsidy of USD 2.63 per watt, covering up to half of the total installation cost. The Golden Sun Program reimbursed up to 70 percent of the installation cost for utility-scale installations.[17] These subsidies for a domestic solar PV market came after the global financial crisis had led many European governments to drastically reduce support for their local solar installations, a decision that had slowed global market development and created overcapacity among China's solar producers.[18] Cost reductions in solar PV technologies made these technologies more attractive for domestic use after decades during which wind turbines had held sway over local renewable energy markets.[19]

As a result of the renewable energy law and its accompanying regulations, the period of the Eleventh Five-Year Plan saw an unprecedented expansion of domestic demand for renewable energy technologies in China. Market opportunities and resources provided by the central government were increasingly restricted to domestic firms. Even though local content requirements for wind turbines were removed in 2009 and China's feed-in tariffs required no formal nationality requirements, foreign wind turbine manufacturers complained about being systematically excluded from government tenders and undercut by local competitors.[20] These manufacturers—many of which had established local manufacturing facilities in China—argued that central and subnational governments were using the government procurement clauses within the indigenous innovation legislation to purchase from domestic firms.[21] Many foreign

[15] Campbell 2011, 6–8; Lewis 2013, 53.
[16] Data compiled by Earth Policy Institute, 2020.
[17] Campbell 2011, 8.
[18] For an overview of the effects of the global financial crisis on the solar PV industry, see Bartlett, Margolis, and Jennings 2009.
[19] Goodrich et al. 2013, figure 1.
[20] See "China Shuts Out Foreign Businesses from Its $14 Billion Plan." *Business Insider*, June 4, 2009; Keith Bradsher, 2010, "On Clean Energy, China Skirts Rules," *New York Times*, September 8.
[21] Liu and Cheng 2011, 25–26.

firms ceased to participate in public tenders and subsequently scaled down their planned investments in China-based manufacturing facilities.[22]

Policies implemented after the release of the indigenous innovation guidelines aimed to close the remaining technology gaps between foreign firms and Chinese suppliers by encouraging the development of domestic capabilities. Government programs for international science and technology collaborations on wind and solar technologies, for instance, increasingly prioritized the academic exchange between universities and research institutes, rather than firms; and they no longer traded access to local markets in exchange for technology transfers.[23] Direct subsidies for renewable firms were now tied to the successful commercialization of new technologies. Starting in 2008, for example, Chinese turbine manufacturers were eligible for significant financial support for the first fifty turbines of 1 MW capacity or more, as long as they were indigenously developed, certified, and connected to the grid.[24] To consolidate the industry and increase technical standards among turbine producers, the Ministry of Industry and Information Technology (MIIT) in 2010 restricted the operation of turbine manufactures that could not produce wind turbines of 2.5 MW or more and that failed to meet a series of R&D and quality requirements.[25]

In the solar sector, which had received direct government subsidies only since the beginning of the Eleventh Five-Year Plan, central government policies now emphasized the domestic manufacture of production equipment, which most Chinese solar firms had previously sourced from Europe and the United States. In 2010, when the State Council released a list of seven "Strategic Emerging Industries" to replace the old pillar industries that had traditionally structured industrial policy, not only were renewable energy technologies included but so also was advanced manufacturing equipment.[26] This new emphasis on equipment manufacturing subsequently pervaded the Twelfth Five-Year Plan for the solar PV industry, released in 2012. That plan called for 80 percent of solar production equipment to be manufactured domestically by 2015, a goal that has not been met and since made its way into numerous subsequent policy documents.[27]

The state goal of achieving technological independence belied both the reality in global renewable energy sectors and China's domestic developmental trajectory as the world's largest manufacturer. By the time China's first domestic

---

[22] Author interviews: head of China operations, foreign wind turbine manufacturer, August 17, 2011; general manager, foreign wind turbine manufacturer, August 30, 2011.

[23] See Zhao et al. 2011. The International Science and Technology Collaboration Program on New and Renewable Energy set up by NDRC and MOST in 2007 resulted in 103 collaboration agreements with institutions in 97 countries. See Tan and Gang 2009, 5.

[24] Lewis 2013, 72.

[25] Kang et al. 2012, 1913; Lewis 2013, 73.

[26] State Council 2010; US-China Business Council 2013.

[27] Ministry of Industry and Information Technology 2012; National Energy Administration 2011; Wübbeke et al. 2016.

producers entered the wind and solar industries in the late 1990s, two decades of economic reform had already turned China into a large manufacturing economy. Between 1978 and 1998, China's per capita GDP had expanded nearly eighteen-fold, from RMB 381 to RMB 6,796, and it would double again within six years.[28] New rules on private ownership had enabled a gradual restructuring of the state-owned sector. In the countryside, economic liberalization and fiscal decentralization in the 1980s had created incentives for rural governments to intervene aggressively on behalf of enterprises.[29] Along the coast, special economic development zones had proliferated, offering tax breaks, land deals, and development assistance to foreign investors and domestic manufacturers.

By 2003, fifty-four national economic and technological development zones (ETDZs), fifty-three national high-technology industrial zones (HTZs), and hundreds of economic development zones managed by local governments were competing to attract investment in manufacturing and, increasingly, in high-technology industries.[30] Manufacturing in China's development zones initially focused on consumer goods, textiles, and shoes—both Nike and Reebok sourced nearly half of their athletic shoes from Chinese factories in the late 1990s. By 2004, China had become the world's largest producer of electronics and communication equipment.[31] Nearly two-thirds of the world's laptop computers were manufactured in China in 2005.[32]

The shift or expansion to high-technology manufacturing occurred primarily at the hands of foreign firms, which had flocked to China's economic development zones in response to favorable investment policies. Between 1979 and 2000, China attracted USD 346 billion in foreign direct investment (FDI). Throughout the 1990s, China was second only to the United States on the list of the largest FDI recipients; 70 percent of FDI targeted the manufacturing industry.[33] By far the largest sources of FDI were manufacturing firms in Taiwan and Hong Kong, which used China's opening to foreign investment during the reform years to move labor-intensive export production to low-cost manufacturing locations in China's coastal development zones. Sixty percent of FDI arriving in China between 1985 and 2005 originated in Hong Kong, Taiwan, and Macau.[34] Eighty-eight percent of high-technology exports during the 1990s were manufactured by foreign-invested enterprises.[35] Although empirical studies found mixed

---

[28] China Statistical Yearbook 2007, chapter 3–1.

[29] Naughton 2007, 271–94; Oi 1995, 1136–38.

[30] Naughton 2007, 304, 409–10.

[31] Tomas Meri, "China Passes the EU in High-Tech Exports," in *Eurostat: Statistics in Focus*, 25/2009. Shoe manufacturing statistics cited in Landrum and Boje 2002, 84.

[32] In 2005, Taiwanese companies produced more than 70 percent of the world's notebook computers, 85 percent of which were manufactured in facilities in mainland China. Yang 2006, 7–12.

[33] Huang 2003, 6; Naughton 2007, 419.

[34] Naughton 2007, 413.

[35] Naughton 2007, 417.

evidence of direct technology transfers to local firms as a result of China's FDI-led development regime, foreign-invested firms provided training opportunities for staff in economic development zones, pushed local governments to continue to provide incentives for mass production, and attracted large supplier industries for materials, production equipment, export logistics, and other complementary capabilities required for large-scale manufacturing.[36]

China's domestic renewable energy firms had their beginnings in this era of manufacturing expansion and functional upgrading in economic development zones. Although central government economic policymaking pursued the goal of creating high-technology start-ups and national champion firms with skills in the *invention* of new technologies, entrants into the renewable energy industries focused largely on building skills in the *manufacturing* of wind turbines and solar PV technologies. Whether firms spun off from state-owned heavy machinery conglomerates, as proved common in the wind energy sector, or were founded by foreign-trained returnees, as was the case in many of China's solar firms, the legacy of mass manufacturing endured: It influenced hiring practices, templates for interaction with global supply chains, and the range of capabilities available to firms among local suppliers. As I lay out in detail in the remainder of this chapter, China's wind and solar firms, instead of building R&D capabilities in the invention of new technologies, emphasized their engineering skills in scale-up and mass manufacturing.

Even before the emergence of domestic wind energy markets and the rise of market demand for solar PV technologies in Europe, China's national S&T policies created incentives for firms to enter these industries. The central government supported technology spin-offs, provided funding for high-tech R&D, and offered start-up support in HTZs created as incubators under the so-called Torch Program. The domestic demand for wind turbines, fueled by China's 2003 Wind Power Concession Program, by subsequent feed-in tariffs, and by the rapidly growing export markets for solar PV technologies, further encouraged industry entry.

New wind and solar firms moved into the renewable energy sectors along different paths. Like Goldwind, China's first domestic wind turbine manufacturer, many wind turbine producers amounted to spin-offs from government research institutes or subsidiaries of state-owned (or formerly state-owned) enterprises. Goldwind began in 1997 as a spin-off from Xinjiang's Wind Energy Research

---

[36] Huang has argued that China's FDI-led development strategy has crowded out local firms by providing investment incentives and favorable tax policies predominately to foreign-invested enterprises. See Huang 2003. For a discussion of training and other benefits provided by foreign-invested firms, see Naughton 2007, chapter 17. Others have found mixed statistical evidence for direct technology transfer from foreign investors to local firms beyond their Chinese subsidiaries. See, for instance, Hu, Jefferson, and Jinchang 2005; Lemoine and Ünal-Kesenci 2004; Liu and Buck 2007.

Institute, after the 863 Program provided funding for the development of small wind turbines with 600 kW capacity.[37] In 2004, after domestic markets expanded, Dongfang Electric began producing wind turbines with a license from German REpower. Dongfang was itself a subsidiary of China Dongfang Electric Corporation, a centrally owned enterprise with a wide product portfolio that included power generation equipment, transformers, railway engines, and power converters.[38] Sinovel, a start-up backed by Dalian Heavy Mechanical and Electrical Equipment Engineering Company, began producing 1.5 MW turbines in 2006 with a license from Germany's Fuhrländer; it began offering a 3 MW turbine a few years later, at a time when European producers were still testing their 3 MW technology.[39] China's 2006 renewable energy law, which introduced feed-in tariffs for the wind industry and created the prospect for long-term growth in domestic markets, prompted other producers to follow. Mingyang, a privately owned supplier of switch-gears, frequency converters, and pitch control equipment for wind turbine manufacturers, began the production of its own 1.5 MW wind turbine in 2007.[40]

In the solar industry, Chinese scientists founded the majority of firms. Many of these scientists had received their training at the School of Photovoltaic and Renewable Energy at the University of New South Wales in Australia.[41] Research funding dispensed by the central government and support for high-technology start-up firms in China's High-Technology Development Zones attracted these scientists back to China. Many returned to their hometowns to open solar PV firms right around the same time that manufacturers were springing up in Europe and the United States. Trina Solar, today one of China's largest producers of solar wafers and modules, began as a solar PV installer for demonstration projects in 1997.[42] Yingli Solar followed in 1998, setting up its first facility in Baoding.[43] Suntech opened its first production plant in Wuxi in 2001.[44] In 2004,

---

[37] Osnos 2009. See also Chen Lei, 2011, "Goldwind: From Follower to Leader [金风科技：从追风到引领]," http://www.goldwind.cn/web/news.do?action=detail&id=201103310223342852 (accessed January 19, 2014).

[38] Dongfang Electric Corporation was originally founded in 1956. See company website at http://www.dongfang.com.cn/index.php/business/ (accessed January 19, 2014).

[39] Qin 2013, 598. See also Pu Jun and Wang Xiaocong, 2011, "Boom, Then Blowdown for Wind Energy's Sinovel," Caixin Online, November 21.

[40] China Ming Yang Wind Power Group Limited 2011. See also http://www.mywind.com.cn/English/about/index.aspx?MenuID=050101 (accessed January 19, 2014).

[41] See Alexander 2013. Other solar firms recruited Chinese citizens from elsewhere in the world. Wan Yuepeng, CTO of Trina Solar, for instance, completed a PhD at Aachen University and worked for New Hampshire–based equipment manufacturer GT Solar prior to returning to China. See http://www.ldksolar.com/com_team.php (accessed March 27, 2013).

[42] Trina Solar, 2013, "TSL: Company Milestones," http://media.corporate-ir.net/media_files/irol/20/206405/milestones.pdf (accessed January 19, 2014).

[43] For a list of all national-level high-tech industrial zones established under the Torch Program, see Cao 2004, 648, http://www.yinglisolar.com/en/about/milestones/ (accessed January 19, 2014).

[44] Ahrens 2013, 2–3.

after global demand for solar panels increased—the result of improvements to Germany's domestic subsidy regime for renewable energy—a number of additional firms entered the industry. CSUN was established in 2004 in Nanjing as a subsidiary of the China Electric Equipment Group, a manufacturer of electrical transformers and advanced composite materials. JA Solar began manufacturing wafers in Shanghai in 2005.[45]

Although the majority of solar PV start-ups did not share the same direct connections to manufacturing conglomerates that were common in the wind industry, executives at China's solar PV firms did bring substantial experience from their time in existing manufacturing industries, in particular in electronics and semiconductor production. The chief technology and financial officers at LDK Solar, for instance, had previously worked for a range of semiconductor, glass, and solar manufacturers, including GT-Solar and Saint Gobain, before joining LDK in 2007 and 2006, respectively. At JA Solar, the CEO and chief technology officer had managed factories for semiconductor firms such as SMIC and NEC before joining JA in 2008 and 2010, respectively. Similarly, the chief technology officer of Yingli had worked in chemical manufacturing before entering the solar industry.[46]

By 2012, China's renewable energy firms accounted for over 60 percent of the global production of solar PV modules and nearly half of the world's wind turbines.[47] Seven of the ten largest solar manufacturers and four of the ten largest wind turbine producers in the world were Chinese firms.[48] Tellingly, the majority did not focus on building capabilities in invention. Instead, they continued to license technology and source components and production equipment abroad, instead emphasizing the establishment of unique capabilities in scale-up and mass production.

Innovative Manufacturing in Wind and Solar Industries

When the first Chinese firms entered the wind and solar sectors in the late 1990s, production technologies for these areas had not fully matured; and low production volumes still allowed for experimentation and manual labor in bringing new technologies to market. Few foreign producers of wind turbines were manufacturing at scale, or if they were, they had begun doing so only recently. Engineering challenges in the commercialization of wind and solar technologies became critical in 2003, when the growing global demand for wind and solar

---

[45] JA Solar Holdings 2007, 6.
[46] Information compiled from company websites and annual reports.
[47] Earth Policy Institute 2020.
[48] Bebon 2013; IHS Solar 2013.

technologies no longer permitted trial-and-error approaches to mass production. Successful commercialization necessitated advanced production capabilities and tacit knowledge around design-for-manufacturing, yet Chinese firms still had to establish these skills in-house.

Those who have studied innovation in mass production have largely looked at process innovation, referring to changes and improvements in the manufacturing process itself.[49] Scholars have distinguished between such process improvements and product innovation, which refers to the introduction of new concepts and technologies that depart significantly from past practice.[50] In emerging industries such as wind and solar, however, the commercialization of new products presented challenges in the scale-up to mass manufacturing that could not be met through process innovation alone: changes to product designs were also needed. In the past, vertically integrated firms had translated between technological blueprints and manufacturing requirements within the four walls of a single company. As the global economy increasingly relocated manufacturing activities away from traditional centers of invention, it removed the need for such skills in firms that no longer possessed in-house manufacturing facilities. For manufacturing firms in developing economies, this removal opened the door to specialization, allowing a concentrated focus on precisely the type of engineering skills that were required to prepare advanced products for mass manufacturing.

The growing importance of capabilities in scale-up and commercialization coincided with an increased emphasis on the development of domestic innovative capabilities in China's national S&T policy framework. Between 2000 and 2006, China's domestic spending on R&D increased from RMB 89.6 billion to RMB 300 billion; R&D intensity, still below the targets set in the Tenth Five-Year Plan, grew from 0.9 to 1.4 percent of GDP over the same period.[51] Both the 863 Program and a second research program, the 973 Program, named after its inception in March 1997, dispensed more funds for technology development; and both offered designated budgets for energy technology research. China's 863 Program budget for energy technology doubled in 2001, providing funding mainly for R&D on low-carbon energy technologies.[52] The 973 Program provided RMB 8.2 billion for basic research between 1998 and 2008, 28 percent of which went to projects that targeted technologies in the fields of energy, resource conservation, and environmental protection.[53] Additionally, centrally funded

---

[49] OECD 2005, para. 163.
[50] Abernathy and Clark 1985; Abernathy and Utterback 1978; Porter 1986; Tushman and Anderson 1986.
[51] Ministry of Science and Technology 2007a, 2–3.
[52] Osnos 2009.
[53] Tan and Gang 2009, 4.

Table 5.3 Goldwind Wind Turbine Collaboration

Year	Program Goal	Technology Source
1998	600 KW turbine	Jacobs Energie, Germany (license)
2001	1.2 MW turbine (direct drive)	Vensys, Germany (license)
2005	1.5 MW turbine (direct drive)	Vensys Germany (license)
2010	2.5/5 MW turbine (direct drive)	Vensys Germany (joint development)
2012	10 MW offshore	Vensys Germany (joint development)

Source: CRESP 2005; Ministry of Science and Technology 2007; Author Interview, Beijing, March 23, 2015.

state key laboratories, which had supported strategic research topics in universities since the early 1980s, could be located within private businesses starting in 2007; and firms were encouraged to seek state key laboratory accreditation for their R&D programs.[54] Overall, central government R&D appropriations for renewable energy research increased from RMB 21.1 billion in 1996 to RMB 104.8 billion in 2008.[55]

From the beginning, producers of wind turbines and solar PV technologies took advantage of public R&D funding. Although such government grants increasingly stipulated the goal of technological independence, wind and solar manufacturers continued to collaborate with global partners. Multiple global pathways made technologies available to them. In the wind industry, Chinese firms enjoyed access to turbine technologies, first, through licensing and joint development agreements with foreign manufacturers. The founder of Goldwind reasoned that there was no need to replicate existing technologies. When government programs encouraged domestic turbine development, Goldwind licensed a design from a German firm and used government R&D funds to build engineering capabilities in commercialization instead (Table 5.3).[56] The vast majority of Chinese wind turbine manufacturers entered similar relationships with foreign partners to access turbine technologies. Among the thirty-one largest wind turbine manufacturers in China, at least sixteen entered license agreements with foreign firms, fourteen signed joint-development contracts, six autonomously developed wind turbine technologies, and three started joint

---

[54] Ministry of Science and Technology 2007b; OECD 2008, 462.
[55] Cao and Groba 2013, 12.
[56] Osnos 2009; Vensys 2017; Author interview, Beijing, March 23, 2015.

venture operations. Seven firms had both joint-development and licensing agreements with foreign firms.[57]

The second source of technology for China's domestic turbine manufacturers involved global suppliers, many of which eventually established local production facilities in response to local content requirements.[58] Foreign firms also began sourcing from Chinese suppliers and, in turn, helped these suppliers meet global technical standards.[59]

In the solar sector, Chinese scientists educated at the world's top solar laboratories founded the majority of firms. Research funding dispensed through the 863 and Torch Programs, together with support for high-technology firms in HTZs, attracted these scientists back to China. The technological skills of foreign-trained returnees obviated the need for licenses and joint development agreements common in the wind industry, but solar firms still tapped into global technology networks, in particular for production equipment. Foreign equipment manufacturers quickly established Chinese sales networks.[60] Foreign partners provided access to key technologies, capabilities, and components that Chinese wind and solar manufacturers could not establish in-house. But they had less ability to help Chinese producers scale new technologies to mass production.

In such collaborations, China's wind and solar firms focused their R&D efforts on building skills that could not be accessed in global supply chains: knowledge-intensive capabilities in scale-up and mass manufacturing that I refer to as *innovative manufacturing*.[61] These proficiencies built on existing manufacturing capabilities in China's economic development zones, yet they traveled far beyond mere fabrication and assembly, utilizing engineering and design knowledge to translate complex technologies into mass-manufacturable products. Innovative manufacturing included improvements to process designs long associated with manufacturing innovation, but also entailed far-reaching changes to product

[57] Compiled from Lewis 2013, 136–37; Wang 2010b, 197–203. Chinese wind and solar firms were generally able to obtain intellectual property through licensing and other legal arrangements with global partners. Perhaps in contrast to other industries, cases of IP theft were rare in China's clean technology sectors. A prominent exception was a case involving the Chinese wind turbine manufacturer Sinovel and the US component supplier AMSC and its Austrian subsidiary Windtec. Initially entering a successful licensing relationship, AMSC discovered the unauthorized use of its software in Sinovel wind turbines after Sinovel refused previously agreed-to purchases. AMSC alleged that Sinovel had stolen software source code to be used in Sinovel turbines, and Sinovel was eventually convicted of IP theft. Both companies suffered commercially as a result of the dispute, with AMSC losing a key customer and the majority of its revenue and Sinovel pulling out of major international markets. See Lewis 2015; Raymond 2018.

[58] Wang 2010b, 197–203.

[59] Information retrieved from company websites; the China Wind Power Center database (http://www.cwpc.cn); Li 2011b; Windpower Monthly 2005a, 2005b, 2006, 2008.

[60] Nussbaumer et al. 2007, 109.

[61] For a detailed discussion of innovative manufacturing in China, see Nahm and Steinfeld 2014.

designs to accommodate manufacturing requirements and meet cost targets for final products. Engineering teams in China's wind and solar firms met their production and cost targets through the substitution of materials, the redesign of particular components, and the reorganization of internal product architectures to allow for better and faster manufacturability at scale.[62]

As executives repeatedly highlighted in interviews, most firms relied on global partners to access new technologies, so what set them apart from one another in the highly competitive wind and solar market was their ability to achieve higher speeds and lower costs in manufacturing.[63] Heads of technical departments in wind turbine and solar PV manufacturing firms frequently discussed the importance of design capabilities for achieving cost and speed targets in the commercialization of renewable energy technologies, even when an external firm had originally developed those technologies. Many reported either significantly redesigning licensed turbine technologies or observing similar improvements in technologies licensed by local partners and competitors.

To specialize in innovative manufacturing was not a monolithic enterprise. Yes, these firms all needed advanced capabilities in product design; yet their work differed from the ideal of autonomous technology development that resided at the heart of Beijing's indigenous innovation strategy. Chinese wind and solar firms engaged in learning and industrial upgrading, but they did so without developing the full range of industrial capabilities required to invent, commercialize, and produce green energy technologies. In spite of government plans to create autonomous local enterprises, China's wind and solar firms developed highly specialized capabilities within collaborative relationships in global supply chains. Simply put, the firms opted for partnership.

China's renewable energy manufacturers established two divisions within their R&D facilities. A first group of engineers targeted applied research on new

[62] Author interviews: senior director manufacturing, Chinese solar PV manufacturer, March 21, 2017; lead engineer, Chinese generator manufacturer, December 6, 2016; director of China office, German turbine supply firm, March 31, 2017; senior VP global supply chains, Chinese solar manufacturer, interviewed March 13, 2011; CTO and director of R&D at Chinese solar manufacturer, both interviewed August 26, 2011; head of China operations, European wind turbine engineering firm, interviewed January 13, 2011; CEO, European wind turbine engineering firm, interviewed May 20, 2011; CTO, Chinese wind turbine manufacturer, interviewed August 29, 2011; CEO, Chinese solar cell manufacturer, interviewed August 10, 2011; president, Chinese wafer manufacturer, interviewed August 26, 2011. CEO, Chinese cell and module manufacturer, interviewed June 28, 2013. See also Nahm and Steinfeld 2014.

[63] Author interviews: R&D engineer, wind turbine manufacturer, March 24, 2015; senior VP global supply chains, Chinese solar manufacturer, March 13, 2011; CTO and director of R&D at Chinese solar manufacturer, August 26, 2011; head of China operations, European wind turbine engineering firm, January 13, 2011; CEO, European wind turbine engineering firm, May 20, 2011; CTO, Chinese wind turbine manufacturer, August 29, 2011; CEO, Chinese solar cell manufacturer, August 10, 2011; president, Chinese wafer manufacturer, August 26, 2011; CEO, Chinese cell and module manufacturer, June 28, 2013; head of R&D, Chinese solar manufacturer, January 7, 2019. See also Nahm and Steinfeld 2014.

wind and solar technologies to meet and surpass the technological standards of foreign competitors, as intended by the central government programs. A second R&D division, by contrast, addressed the challenge of scale-up and mass production. It is in this second division that the most advanced Chinese wind and solar firms developed unique skills in bringing new technologies to market. The wind turbine manufacturer Mingyang in Zhongshan had 300 R&D staff in 2010; of those 300, only about one-third focused on the development of new technologies. The majority of engineers worked on the types of design changes required to bring technologies to mass production.[64] Similarly, Trina Solar, located in one of the manufacturing parks between Shanghai and Nanjing, reported that out of 2,488 employees working in its R&D division in 2015, only 842 focused on technology development. The remaining 1,746 engineers devised solutions to the challenges of commercialization in a designated test facility with so-called golden lines, production lines solely dedicated to R&D.[65]

These two-fold R&D activities explain why Chinese firms built strengths in bringing new technologies to market but were not able to match the early stage R&D activities of firms in other economies and thus remained dependent on foreign partners. Already in 2006, some of the world's most efficient solar PV modules in mass production were being made in Chinese manufacturing facilities, even as China could not match the conversion efficiencies of foreign R&D laboratories in experimental setups.[66] By 2015, the solar cells tested in Chinese laboratories still lagged in conversion efficiency, even if their distance to US and European technology had narrowed. Some of the most efficient solar modules in mass production, however, continued to roll off of Chinese production lines.[67]

Interviews with plant managers, R&D engineers, and chief technology officers in the largest Chinese wind and solar manufacturers revealed differences across firms in the deployment of such capabilities. Innovative manufacturing skills among China's wind and solar firms manifested in three different variants that resembled knowledge-intensive variations of reverse engineering, contract manufacturing, and export processing—manufacturing activities long at the center of economic development.[68] These variations were not mutually exclusive, and wind and solar producers often applied their engineering capabilities in multiple ways to solve the challenges of commercialization.[69]

---

[64] China Ming Yang Wind Power Group Limited 2011, 54.
[65] Trina Solar 2016, 89. Author interview, chief engineer, State Key Laboratory, March 29, 2015.
[66] Marigo 2007, table 1.
[67] Ball et al. 2017, 68–69.
[68] The role of such manufacturing activities in economic development and industrial upgrading is discussed in Ernst and Kim 2002; Gereffi 2009; Lüthje 2002; Minagawa, Trott, and Hoecht 2007.
[69] The discussion of innovative manufacturing over the following pages draws heavily on a collaborative project with Edward Steinfeld. See Nahm and Steinfeld 2014, 294–98.

A first form of innovative manufacturing, here referred to as backward design, resembled traditional processes of reverse engineering. By creating versions of existing products that were simpler and cheaper to manufacture at scale, Chinese entrants outcompeted foreign incumbents by undercutting them on price. In contrast to conventional reverse engineering, however, in which mature technologies are copied and cost advantages stem from differences in factor prices and scale economies, Chinese firms cut costs through changes to product designs.[70] Although backward design led to products that resembled the original archetypes, the new product versions could be scaled at lower cost and faster speed owing to the use of simplified components, cheaper materials, and better design for manufacturability. While backward design thus retained the core features of reverse engineering, it went a step further: firms created *new* products with distinct characteristics, rather than simply attempting to reproduce the original template.

Wind turbine technologies offered the perfect fit for backward design processes. The large number of mechanical components, the importance of product architecture for the manufacturing process, and the sophisticated material needs of advanced wind turbines made these technologies particularly suitable for design improvements. Out of twelve Chinese wind turbine manufacturers interviewed for this project, nine reported having either improved licensed turbine technologies through backward design or observed such improvements in technologies licensed by local partners and competitors. Yet even in the solar sector, where products possess far fewer components and are fabricated using nonmechanical production processes, manufacturers also used backward design strategies. One Chinese manufacturer of solar cells and modules reported buying a foreign equipment manufacturer to access technology and then reengineering parts for its production lines to save costs and time over equipment available domestically.[71] A competitor expressed frustration with the lack of speed exhibited by some foreign suppliers in adapting production lines to changing technology applications, and as a result shifted to local suppliers, who could more quickly—and cheaply—improve equipment designs for new manufacturing needs.[72] Although such instances of backward design in the Chinese solar sector focused on rapid customization rather than scale, they retained the principle's core feature: they improved on existing technologies through knowledge-intensive manufacturing innovation.

[70] For a discussion of reverse engineering in economic development, see Amsden 1989, 2001; Kim 1997; Kim and Nelson 2000.

[71] Author interview, senior VP global supply chains, Chinese solar manufacturer, March 13, 2011.

[72] Author interviews: chief engineer, State Key Laboratory, March 29, 2015; CTO and director of R&D at Chinese solar manufacturer, August 26, 2011.

The ability of Chinese firms to rapidly move complex products toward commercialization also manifested in the commercialization of new technologies. In many cases, such technologies originated from foreign partners who did not possess in-house manufacturing capabilities, who could not manufacture the product at a commercially viable price, or who were deterred by the capital and tooling costs of commercializing new technology. In other cases, Chinese firms used such capabilities to commercialize their own product innovations, birthed in the technology development divisions of their R&D facilities. What these cases held in common was their reliance on production knowledge to replace, redesign, and substitute parts until the product could be manufactured at a commercially viable price. In contrast to contract manufacturing, which relies on firms in developing economies to manage only the production process of foreign-owned designs and technologies, Chinese wind and solar producers improved the product designs themselves in the process of scale-up to mass production.[73]

In a third variant of innovative manufacturing, the presence of production know-how provided a platform for external innovators to integrate their technologies into existing wind and solar technologies already mass-produced in China. But the firms supplying the technology were more than just high-end component vendors who sold a product at arms-length to a Chinese competitor. Instead, vendors commercialized their technology in collaboration with a Chinese partner. The vendor contributed knowledge about a particular technology that might have applications to a product the Chinese manufacturer had already scaled up. The Chinese manufacturer, in turn, provided knowledge about production, about the use of existing production technology to apply the component technology at scale, and about projected improvements to the original product as a result of these innovations.

Manufacturing as a platform for product development became especially common in the interaction between manufacturers and component suppliers who relied on customers not just for demand but also for the engineering skills and product knowledge required to integrate new components and materials.[74] As China grew into a hub of commercialization for the most advanced renewable energy technologies, Chinese firms used innovative manufacturing capabilities to find applications for novel components, materials, and production equipment developed by global firms.[75] Although the duration of such collaborations varied, six out of seven solar PV suppliers interviewed for this project reported working with Chinese solar manufacturers on the commercialization of new

---

[73] For a discussion of noninnovative contract manufacturing in the context of the electronics industry, see Lüthje 2002.
[74] Author interview: CEO of American nanomaterial manufacturer, October 13, 2011.
[75] Neuhoff 2012.

technologies. In the wind sector, suppliers of complex components such as gearboxes and generators similarly described collaborating with Chinese customers to integrate their largest and most advanced technologies.[76]

Innovative Manufacturing in Global Supply Chains

Although some firms expanded into multiple production steps and displayed different degrees of vertical integration, virtually no Chinese manufacturer established the technological competencies to bring an idea to mass production without external input. The capabilities of renewable energy firms remained too narrow to autonomously develop and commercialize new technologies. In all three variants of innovative manufacturing, wind and solar firms relied on collaboration in global supply chains to access talents and resources they did not establish in-house.

Initially, firms in China's renewable energy fields relied on foreign firms to tap into the technologies required for industry entry. In the wind industry, Chinese firms had access to foreign wind turbine technologies through licensing agreements and joint development agreements with foreign manufacturers. Wu Gang, the founder of Goldwind, reasoned that there was no need to replicate existing technologies. When government programs encouraged domestic turbine development, Goldwind licensed a design from Germany's Jacobs Energie and used R&D funds to solve production challenges instead.[77] The vast majority of Chinese wind turbine manufacturers entered similar relationships with foreign partners to access global technologies. Sinovel signed joint development agreements for a 1.5 MW turbine with Fuhrländer of Germany in 2003, followed by agreements with Austria's Windtec for 3 MW and 5 MW turbines in 2007. Dongfang Electric purchased a license for a 1.5 MW turbine from Germany's REpower in 2004 and entered a joint development agreement for a 2.5 MW turbine with the German wind engineering firm Aerodyn in 2005.[78] Nordex entered a joint venture with Ningxia Electric Power Group, and REpower set up a joint venture turbine assembly firm with North Heavy Industrial Group, both in 2006.[79]

China's domestic turbine manufacturers also sourced technology from global suppliers, many of which eventually established production facilities in

[76] Author interviews: engineer, Chinese gearbox supplier, January 4, 2016; plant manager at a German gearbox supplier, May 16, 2011; plant manager at a German generator manufacturer, May 17, 2011.

[77] Osnos 2009.

[78] See Zhang et al. 2009, 559.

[79] Compiled from company websites.

China as foreign turbine manufacturers attempted to meet strict local content requirements. The early foreign suppliers to Chinese turbine manufacturers included the Swiss multinational ABB; the German firms Euros, Bachmann, Jake, and VEM; the Danish blade manufacturer LM; and the Austrian control systems firm Windtec (now part of US-based AMSC).[80] FAG/Schaeffler of Germany, a bearings manufacturer, opened a facility in China in 2006; Bosch Rexroth, a gearbox manufacturer, and SKF, a Swedish bearings multinational, followed in 2008. As foreign turbine manufacturers set up facilities in China, they not only brought suppliers with them but also trained local firms. Gamesa of Spain opened its first facilities in China in 2005; Vestas opened a blade factory in Tianjin in 2006, the same year that GE began the assembly of turbines in Shenyang. Nordex of Germany and Suzlon of India opened plants in Dongying and Tianjin in 2007. Foreign manufacturers began sourcing from local suppliers such as NTC, a generator producer, and Nanjing Highspeed Gear, a gearbox manufacturer, and in turn helped these suppliers meet global technical standards.[81]

Unlike China's wind turbine producers, which entered the industry from a position of technology lag, many of the original solar companies were founded by returning scientists trained at the world's top solar laboratories. The skills and training of these foreign-trained returnees obviated the need for technology licenses and joint development agreements common in the wind industry. But solar firms still tapped into global technology networks, in particular for production equipment. As I discussed in Chapter 4, the first German suppliers of cell and module production lines began selling their products to China's solar firms as early as 2000. Other foreign equipment suppliers quickly followed and set up sales networks in China, particularly as European and US-based solar manufacturers only slowly expanded production facilities.[82]

Many international suppliers of production equipment, particularly those offering turnkey lines, went unchallenged by domestic competitors. As late as 2014, no producers of turnkey production lines existed in China, though a number of Chinese firms began to offer equipment that solar manufacturers could modify and connect to construct their own production lines.[83] For complicated production equipment and supplies—including chemical vapor deposition equipment, screen printers, firing furnaces, and silver pastes—Chinese firms continued to rely on foreign suppliers.[84] Since solar producers from around the world sourced from and cooperated with the same producers of manufacturing equipment to

[80] Wang Q. 2010, 197–203.
[81] Retrieved from China Wind Power Center database (http://www.cwpc.cn), Windpower Monthly, and Li 2011a.
[82] Nussbaumer et al. 2007, 109.
[83] de la Tour, Glachant, and Ménière 2011, 765.
[84] Ball et al. 2017, 137–38.

incorporate new technologies into their production machinery, sourcing equipment from external firms was not just a way to access instruments and machinery that remained unavailable internally. It also offered access to global technological developments and pooled knowledge—resources that solar producers risked losing if they relied on production equipment developed in-house.[85]

Collaboration remained essential to the viability of China's specialization in innovative manufacturing, even as China's wind and solar producers acquired ever more advanced technological capabilities. Challenging the notion that technological upgrading would entail moving beyond manufacturing to higher value-added activities, renewable energy producers continued to rely on external capabilities through relationships with third-party firms; but they invested in skills that could not be accessed in global supply chains. Such collaboration took place in a variety of legal relationships, ranging from joint development agreements to licensing contracts.

In a typical example, a German firm granted a license to a Chinese wind turbine supplier to produce a generator, one of the core turbine components. Because of engineering constraints, the German firm had been unable to incorporate the most cost-effective fan model into its generator design. The Chinese licensee, however, in the process of scaling production of the licensed generator, redesigned the original model to accommodate the cheaper fan. The backward design capabilities of the Chinese firm permitted it to realize a product alternative that the German firm had dismissed as unworkable. Once the alternative was demonstrated to be feasible, the German firm agreed to pay for this proprietary information through reverse licensing.[86] In this case, the Chinese firm contributed production knowledge within a formal contractual relationship. In other cases, however, Chinese firms used their skills to develop cheaper, mid-level products that competed directly with the product archetypes and their originator firms.[87] Particularly in the Chinese domestic market, many established multinationals were unable to engage in such cost-driven design processes and lost market share to cheaper alternatives as a result.[88]

Innovative manufacturing capabilities also appeared in firm partnerships centered on the commercialization of new technologies. In 2009, for instance, a Chinese wind turbine producer acquired a ten-year exclusive license for the

[85] de la Tour, Glachant, and Ménière 2011, 764. Author interviews: CTO of solar PV manufacturer, May 23, 2011; head of research and development, Chinese solar manufacturer, January 7, 2019.

[86] Author interviews: plant manager, German generator manufacturer, May 17, 2011; executive, Chinese generator manufacturer, August 26, 2011.

[87] This phenomenon has occurred in other industrial sectors; see Brandt and Thun 2010; Ge and Fujimoto 2004.

[88] Author interviews: director of China office, German turbine supply firm, March 31, 2017; head of China operations at foreign wind turbine manufacturer, August 30, 2011; executive, foreign wind turbine manufacturer, November 11, 2011; head of China operations, foreign wind turbine manufacturer, August 17, 2011.

manufacture of a groundbreaking, new-to-the-world wind turbine design from a German supplier. The German firm selected the Chinese manufacturer from multiple potential partners, choosing largely on the basis of manufacturing capabilities that would ensure reliability for the product, speed in commercialization, and marketable viability for the project as a whole.

Although the European firm developed this turbine design—a new turbine technology that offered greater reliability and versatility through new and lightweight components—the design for manufacturability occurred during small batch production on the site of the Chinese manufacturer. Engineers employed by the Chinese firm made design changes to simplify tooling and assembly processes and, in cooperation with other local firms, reduced costs by localizing sourcing and by introducing substitute materials. This particular turbine concept proved especially challenging, because its novel product architecture required all the components to be produced in-house.[89] Additional design adjustments were made during the process of scale-up to accommodate requirements for mass production. Reflecting on the partnership, the head of the China office for the German supplier emphasized the importance of the skills brought by their Chinese partner. "The turbine is now completely different from the prototype because of the design changes that occurred in China to make it manufacturable. Nobody else was willing to take that risk, and willing to put in the time and effort to make this new idea work. It took seven years to get it right, but now they are doing very well with the product."[90]

The cooperation between US-based Innovalight and the Chinese solar cell manufacturer JA Solar illustrates the third variety of innovative manufacturing, in which a foreign firm relied on China's manufacturing infrastructure as a platform for product development. A Silicon Valley start-up founded in 2002, Innovalight developed a nanomaterial with potential applications in products ranging from integrated circuits and displays to solar PV. With Department of Energy funding and support from the National Renewable Energy Laboratory (NREL), the firm developed an understanding of how the nanomaterial, a silicon ink, might be applied in the solar PV industry. However, while Innovalight and NREL could determine how the material might improve a single solar cell, neither had the know-how required to apply the material in a cost-effective manner in high-volume solar PV production. The firm was unable to raise the capital needed to build a solar PV production facility.[91]

[89] Author interviews: head of China operations, German wind turbine supplier, April 1, 2017 and January 13, 2011; CEO, German wind turbine supplier, May 20, 2011; CTO, Chinese wind turbine manufacturer, August 29, 2011.

[90] Author interview, head of China operations, German wind turbine supplier, April 1, 2017.

[91] Wang 2011.

In 2009, nearly out of business, Innovalight found a partner in Chinese cell manufacturer JA Solar. Looking to gain an edge over its competitors, JA Solar made the decision to invest in the collaborative development of a component that could substantially improve the efficiency of its main product. After a year of joint R&D, the two firms announced the successful production of high-efficiency solar cells using Innovalight's silicon ink technology. In 2010, the two firms signed a three-year agreement for the supply of silicon ink, as well as a strategic agreement for the joint development of high-efficiency cells.[92] The process of joint development with JA Solar finally verified Innovalight's silicon ink technology as a product capable of contributing value in solar PV. Now established as a legitimate player in the solar industry, Innovalight began licensing its technology to other solar manufacturers.[93]

Contrary to expectations that firms who worked together would become more similar over time, collaboration actually allowed firms to reinforce the distinctiveness of their different industrial practices. Technological cooperation allowed firms to jointly develop successive generations of renewable energy technologies, yet the fundamental division of labor remained durable over time. The US strength in invention, Germany's specialization in complex components and production equipment, and China's focus on technological innovation within commercialization and scale-up were interdependent and mutually reinforcing.

The Manufacturing Economy

China's wind turbine and solar PV producers made use of their nation's national science and technology infrastructure to develop their skills in innovative manufacturing. At the same time, the technological learning underway within these firms relied heavily on the repurposing of institutions within the manufacturing economy. These institutions retained their value precisely because firms no longer had to be one-stop shops: institutions no longer had to support the full range of activities required to invent and commercialize new technologies within national borders.

In contrast to science and technology funding, which often involved top-down administrative structures and directives set by China's central government ministries in Beijing, resources for the manufacturing economy came largely from subnational governments. Often these resources were provided in outright defiance of central government plans, which had encouraged local governments to push firms toward invention.[94] For China's wind and solar firms, local policies

92 JA Solar 2010.
93 Stuart 2012.
94 Cao, Suttmeier, and Simon 2006; Kroll, Conlé, and Schüller 2008, 172–77.

for the manufacturing economy provided an important supplement to the central government's focus on technological independence and its narrow definition of innovation as invention.[95] Firms relied on local government support to construct the physical manufacturing plants they needed to succeed in new forms of mass production, but they also repurposed that local support to establish new engineering capabilities. Just as firms had utilized central government science and technology policies to respond to opportunities for scale-up and commercialization, so entrepreneurial firms used resources for mass production provided at the local level for industrial upgrading in ways not anticipated by the state.

The importance of local government policy for industrial upgrading in the wind and solar sectors corresponds to the central role played by subnational administrations in China's political economy since the onset of economic reforms. In the 1980s, a series of fiscal and administrative reforms had made local governments dependent on local tax revenue while granting them decision-making autonomy in local economic affairs. Fiscal decentralization aimed to promote growth-enhancing economic measures at the local level while carving out space for localities to experiment on economic policy.[96] The central government sought to further encourage experimentation in local policymaking by evaluating local officials on a series of development outcomes, rather than prescribing the specific policies required to achieve those outcomes.[97] In a word, they encouraged creativity. Even though fiscal decentralization underwent a reversal in the 1990s—a move aimed at improving the revenue situation of China's central government—local governments continued to wield discretion in economic governance and enjoyed considerable autonomy in the implementation of central directives, key features of China's post-Mao political economy.[98]

In addition to experimenting with local growth-enhancing policies, subnational governments also implemented and financed many national policies, including programs introduced under China's indigenous innovation strategy. Research and development appropriations of the subnational governments rose in accordance with central government budget increases, growing from RMB 10.6 billion in 1996 to RMB 69.9 billion in 2006.[99] By 2015, R&D appropriations of the subnational governments had increased to RMB 338 billion, far surpassing the RMB 248 billion set aside by central government agencies.[100]

---

[95] Nahm 2017a.

[96] Jin, Qian, and Weingast 2005; Oi 1995.

[97] Although social and environmental factors have been added to the cadre evaluation system over time, economic parameters have been paramount. For an introduction to cadre evaluation in China, see Edin 2003; Landry 2008, chapter 5; Whiting 2004, 106–12.

[98] The process of fiscal recentralization is described in detail in Huang 2008, chapter 3.

[99] Ministry of Science and Technology 2007a.

[100] China Science and Technology Statistical Yearbook 2016.

Although the central government's directives increasingly emphasized a broad reorientation away from the mass production of standardized commodities and toward an innovation-based development strategy, local administrations remained primarily concerned with meeting immediate economic targets and raising local revenue. R&D appropriations at subnational levels were diverted toward programs that yielded more immediate economic results. In practice, this shift entailed supporting the manufacturing activities of local firms, often making financial support conditional on meeting production targets and tax revenue requirements. Even as they implemented central-level directives to support lab-based R&D and product innovation, local officials quietly prioritized measures to enhance growth in their existing industrial base. If we look, for example, at the provincial implementation plans of China's 2009 decision to support seven strategic emerging industries (SEIs), we find striking differences across localities, with local administrations picking between six and ten sectors and selecting local SEIs to match to the existing industrial base. In provinces such as Jiangxi, solar PV industries were included on this list; other localities disregarded renewable energy industries in their interpretation of the original directive.[101] The implementation of central government policies thus provided an opportunity for localities to adjust these policies to match their local needs. It seems important to note, however, that local economic policy did not always produce optimal outcomes. Embracing local development and rapid growth, some local policymakers also produced unintended negative consequences, most notably when localities refused to stop supporting industries already characterized by overcapacity and a lack of scale economies.

Wind and solar firms could access two sets of manufacturing resources at the local level. First, they benefited from investment incentives, such as tax breaks and discounted lands, that offered general support for the manufacturing economy. These financial incentives were offered relatively uniformly across China's economic development zones and industrial parks and aimed to attract foreign—and, increasingly, domestic—investment. Second, firms benefited from the resources, institutions, facilities, and infrastructure provided by localities to support the existing local industrial base. Such institutions were regionally divergent, as they targeted the needs of specific industrial sectors in the local economy.

Although China's HTZs, established under the Torch Program in the late 1980s, provided incubator services for small and medium-sized high-technology enterprises, the economic constraints placed on local governments encouraged a reorientation toward mass manufacturing and export processing in these

---

[101] For details about provincial SEI implementation plans, see US-China Business Council 2013, 16–22.

high-technology zones. According to a 2013 study by Heilmann et al., out of a sample of fifty-three HTZs, thirty-nine deviated from their original purpose to promote domestic R&D activities and instead focused on mass production.[102] For local governments, high-technology zones had become convenient vehicles to increase economic growth and tax revenues within their jurisdiction; production, rather than innovation, appeared to many officials as the most promising use of HTZs.[103] Although the original definition of HTZs excluded production activities, China's high-technology zones became the fastest-growing regions precisely because of the manufacturing facilities that they successfully attracted.[104]

Accordingly, many of the preferential policies available to firms in China's HTZs supported mass production rather than the construction of R&D labs or the creation of new ties to local universities and research institutes. Across most HTZs, firms were exempted from income tax for two years after becoming profitable, after which their rates rose to a mere 7.5 percent for three years and topped out at 15 percent after that, a substantial discount on the 33 percent income tax imposed on businesses outside such zones. Additional tax benefits existed for foreign-invested enterprises and firms producing "advanced technologies," a category that generally included wind turbines, solar panels, and their components. For newly established firms seeking to build manufacturing facilities, including those in wind and solar sectors, HTZs cut building taxes, accelerated planning permits, waived taxes and import tariffs on imported parts and equipment, and allowed rapid depreciation for high-tech equipment.[105]

Localities further competed for investment by offering discounted land rates to firms seeking to establish manufacturing facilities.[106] The development and sale of land for urban construction became one of the most important sources of revenue for subnational governments after fiscal recentralization in the 1990s reassigned a large share of overall tax revenue back to the central government.[107] In development zones, however, local officials were willing to forgo these profits on land because production facilities presented an appealing source of future tax revenue, and productive output remained an important factor in the cadre evaluation system. Because HTZ administrators knew about land (and tax) packages being offered by neighboring municipalities and were willing to match their own deals to compete, land prices became relatively uniform across development zones. Moreover, mandatory compensation levels for rural farmland converted

---

[102] Heilmann, Shih, and Hofem 2013, 903.

[103] Breznitz and Murphree 2011, 78.

[104] Sutherland 2005, 91.

[105] Liu and Martinez-Vazquez 2013, 4; Sutherland 2005, 95.

[106] Kremzner 1998, 628; Kroll, Conlé, and Schüller 2008, 191.

[107] For a discussion of land as a source of revenue for municipal governments, see, for instance, Lin and Yi 2011; Rithmire 2013; Whiting 2011; Zhao 2011.

to industrial use—levels determined by the central government—set a lower price boundary of sorts. A senior official at one of the Torch Program HTZs, Suzhou New District, explained:

> If you represent a manufacturing company and they want to come to Suzhou, you will come to different investor parks. Suzhou New District will hopefully be one of them. But Wuxi and Changzhou will compete with us. Our function is to recommend Suzhou New District and try to persuade them to put their investment here. In Suzhou we have at least five national level investor parks. There are more than ten provincial and city level investor parks. So there are at least 15–20 parks which are all competing. And that's just Suzhou. The benefits that we offer are pretty much the same across industrial parks. We cannot lower the taxes because we are not allowed to subsidize that way. We can speed up approval and help firms with the bureaucracy. We cannot lower the electricity price because that's not determined by us. Same with water. We cannot control the price for that locally. Wuxi and Changzhou give some subsidies to recruit high-level talent employees, which is one way to attract firms. What we can do is to lower the price of land, but not indefinitely. The land is never free. That also is beyond our control. Before we transfer the land to the companies, we have to relocate the farmers on the land. And that requires quite a bit of money, as compensation levels are centrally determined. After they are relocated, we need to tear down everything; and then we need to pay fees to the provincial authorities and the central government. So there is high burden for the local government, and we have to pass on that cost to some extent.[108]

As less and less agricultural land was available for industrial development in China's sprawling HTZs, local officials grew increasingly selective about the kinds of industries targeted and the types of incentives offered to firms. High-tech industrial sectors—independent of central-government guidelines that encouraged the preferential treatment of high-tech firms—were particularly sought after because they promised higher returns on smaller plots than the manufacturing of consumer products that had dominated economic development zones during the 1990s.[109] To ensure that firms would rapidly contribute to the local economy, local administrations made tax breaks and land deals conditional on meeting production targets and revenue requirements. At times, firms were contractually obliged to build facilities with a predetermined manufacturing capacity by a particular date or risk losing government grants, tax reductions, and discounts on land prices. In other cases, local governments informally exerted

---

[108] Author interview, senior official at Suzhou New District HTZ, January 9, 2012.
[109] Author interview, senior official at Suzhou New District HTZ, January 9, 2012.

pressure on firms to rapidly scale production. The CEO of one European wind turbine engineering firm reported that a Chinese collaborator "constructed a 25,000 square meter facility practically overnight, because local officials had provided financial support and wanted to see results."[110] The president of a solar start-up disclosed that steeply discounted land prices required meeting tax revenue targets; otherwise, fines equal to the land discount would be imposed.[111]

Most of China's wind and solar firms were established in the growing number of HTZs created under the Torch Program, building their manufacturing capabilities in an environment that not only offered investment incentives but also encouraged rapid scale-up and mass production. Goldwind built its first manufacturing facilities in a high-tech industrial development zone in Urumqi's Xinshi District, created under the Torch Program in 1994. There, Goldwind participated in a tax refund program for high-tech manufacturing enterprises that returned RMB 15 million in taxes to local firms in 1999 alone.[112] In 1998, the Baoding municipal government supported the creation of Yingli Solar in Baoding's High-Tech Industrial Zone with an RMB 166 million investment. The local administration required the establishment of 3 MW of production capacity, an ambitious goal for a single firm at a time when the United States, then the global leader in PV production, boasted a national production capacity of 54 MW.[113] Trina Solar relocated its operations to a Changzhou HTZ in 2002 to qualify for preferential income taxes, but it moved to a neighboring zone in 2004 after its original tax discount expired.[114] Canadian Solar and GCL Solar opened manufacturing facilities in Suzhou's New District HTZ.[115] Mingyang, China's largest private wind turbine manufacturer, set up headquarters in the National Torch High Technology Industry Development Zone in Zhongshan, Guangdong province, in 2006.[116] Mingyang subsequently opened manufacturing facilities in other parts of China, including in the Jilin High-Tech Industrial Development Zone, a Torch HTZ, and Tianjin Binhai High-Technology Zone, a state-level HTZ that targeted renewable energy manufacturing.[117] In 2010, after the company was listed on the New York Stock Exchange, its annual report disclosed RMB 111.1 million in cash grants by local governments to support R&D, the improvement of manufacturing facilities, and the acquisition of land.[118]

[110] Author interviews: CEO, European wind turbine engineering firm, May 20, 2011; CTO, Chinese wind turbine manufacturer, August 29, 2011; senior official at Suzhou New District HTZ, January 9, 2012; CEO, European wind turbine manufacturer, August 17, 2011.

[111] Author interview, president, solar PV start-up firm, August 24, 2011.

[112] Urumqi Year Book 2000, 116.

[113] Baoding Year Book 1999, 111.

[114] Trina Solar 2008, 36.

[115] Author interview, senior official at Suzhou New District HTZ, January 9, 2012.

[116] Guang Dong Mingyang Wind Power Technology Co. Ltd 2007.

[117] Tianjin Yearbook 2010, 241–42.

[118] China Ming Yang Wind Power Group Limited 2011, 53.

High-tech development zones and local government officials offered a range of additional services that encouraged local firms to rapidly increase production output. For firms setting up production facilities, the HTZ administrations acted as scale-up consultants of sorts, fast-tracking planning permits and navigating the Chinese bureaucracy not just for foreign investors but also for domestic ones.[119] More importantly, however, local governments offered access to financing, channeling bank loans and other funding to firms in development zones. Local S&T offices often demonstrated willingness to invest directly in new energy firms, if only to show their commitment to central government directives on technological innovation. The grants and incentives described earlier are illustrative of this kind of investment.

The special focus on new energy industries in national S&T plans appealed to China's state-owned financial institutions, leaving them willing to lend to wind and solar companies. But local governments were critical brokers in such deals, particularly when the first wind and solar firms were founded. Loans were frequently guaranteed by municipal government entities or by local state-owned firms that partnered with wind and solar firms. The city of Wuxi, for instance, invested USD 6 million in return for a 75 percent equity stake in the solar PV producer Suntech in 2001, after the company's founder, Shi Zhengrong, had compared offers from a number of local high-tech development zones. To fund the rapid expansion of Suntech in the following years—by 2006, Suntech ranked as the world's third-largest producer of solar panels—local officials brokered a series of bank loans for the company.[120] For a production facility launched in 2005, an RMB 200 million investment was financed through such connections.[121] In 2007, Yingli Solar borrowed USD 17 million from the Bank of China, backed by a local state-owned firm.[122] In 2009, Trina Solar secured a five-year credit line of USD 303 million from a syndicate of banks to expand its manufacturing capacity.[123] Not only was local government support critical in securing this loan, but local guarantees also allowed Trina to obtain waivers on loan conditions usually attached to large investments in high-risk, emerging industries.[124]

Access to large-scale financing of course provided no guarantee for upgrading. Localities at times lent indiscriminately and contributed to overcapacity in global renewable energy markets. Between 2009 and 2011, the capacity utilization of existing solar PV manufacturing plants fell from just over 60 percent in

[119] Sutherland 2005, 95–96.
[120] Ahrens 2013, 3–4. See also Kevin Bulls, 2011, "The Chinese Solar Machine," *MIT Technology Review*, December 19.
[121] Wuxi Yearbook 2006, 293.
[122] Yingli Green Energy Holding Company Limited 2008, F-28.
[123] Trina Solar 2010, F-30.
[124] Trina Solar 2013, F-35–36.

2009 to just under 50 percent in 2011.[125] Even though, in the aggregate, only half of China's solar PV plants were running at capacity, solar PV firms continued to receive credit to expand their manufacturing facilities, preventing industry consolidation and protecting firms that were no longer able to compete.

Yet access to local financing also provided the basis for engineering capabilities in innovative manufacturing: these funds guaranteed the infrastructure within which such skills could be applied, and they did so in ways that the limited central-government R&D funding alone could not. Both during the infancy of the wind and solar sectors in the early 2000s and again after the 2009 financial crisis, wind and solar manufacturers in China successfully raised capital, even as funds dried up in the United States and Europe. Media reports suggest that the China Development Bank alone extended USD 29 billion in credit to fifteen solar and wind companies; others have calculated that China's publicly listed wind and solar companies took out some USD 18 billion in loans with loan guarantees from municipal governments.[126] Although little reliable information exists on what interest rates such deals entailed, it is safe to assume that at least some of these loans were provided at submarket rates.[127]

Although firms could not buy their way into the seasoned knowledge and particular engineering skills needed for commercialization, the availability of such funds for production facilities enabled the most capable of China's wind and solar firms to forge ahead and specialize in innovative manufacturing. In interviews, the foreign partners of solar firms frequently praised the R&D conditions in Chinese manufacturing facilities, where access to capital allowed firms to dedicate entire production lines—Golden Lines—to testing and experimenting with new technologies under production conditions.[128] Lacking such facilities themselves, R&D engineers in Europe and the United States struggled to obtain time slots during which they could conduct such tests using regular production lines.[129]

High-tech development zones provided access to the financial capital required to build capabilities in mass production; at the same time, they also attracted the *human* capital necessary for leading expertise in rapid commercialization. Between 1990 and 2006, China's S&T personnel—defined in China as staff who spend at least 10 percent of their time in activities "closely related to the production, development, dissemination, and application of knowledge in natural sciences, agricultural science, medical science, engineering and technological

[125] Zhao, Wan, and Yang 2015, 183.
[126] Bradsher 2012; Sustainable Business News 2012.
[127] Deutch and Steinfeld 2013.
[128] Author interview, chief engineer, State Key Laboratory, March 29, 2015.
[129] Author interviews: CEO, Chinese solar manufacturer, August 20, 2011; CTO and director of R&D, Chinese solar manufacturer, August 26, 2011; CEO, German equipment manufacturer, May 10, 2011; CTO, German equipment manufacturer, May 11, 2011.

science, humanities and social sciences"—nearly doubled, from 23 to 41 million. Scientists and engineers constituted more than two-thirds of S&T personnel. The share of such workers with university degrees increased from 10 million in 2000 to 14.5 million in 2005, with a growing percentage of S&T workers employed by enterprises, rather than by universities and research institutes. By 2006, nearly half of S&T employees worked in large and medium-sized enterprises, up from 36 percent during the early 1990s.[130]

A disproportionate number of this young and educated workforce gravitated to high-technology development zones. In 2000, for instance, when the first wind and solar firms were just beginning to engage in the commercialization of new technologies, enterprises in China's Torch Program HTZs jointly employed a workforce of 7.5 million, a third of whom held university degrees. Although the Ministry of Science and Technology estimated only 30,000 staff with masters' degrees and 4,000 graduates of doctoral programs at work in HTZ enterprises that year, the figures far exceeded average Chinese educational levels at the time.[131] For wind and solar firms, HTZs thus presented a rich environment within which to recruit engineering staff, men and women who not only held above-average levels of educational achievement but also came to the table with experience in mass production from a range of other sectors, including foreign-invested firms that had come to China during the 1990s and settled in high-tech zones.

In addition to such general incentives, local governments provided resources, institutions, facilities, and infrastructure to support the existing local industrial base. Local conditions in high-tech development zones remained relatively uniform in what basic resources they offered to attract investment and in the stipulations (scale-up and mass production) they attached to their support.[132] Once localities had successfully attracted firms, however, a second set of policies and institutions stepped forward, supporting the activities of local firms in a more targeted manner. Such resources, policies, and institutions differed depending on the composition of the local economy. But they held something important in common: these policies supported rapid commercialization and mass production through the creation of new capabilities in the local economy, rather than through financing ever-larger production facilities.

Municipal governments themselves were active agents in reinventing and structuring the local economy. They interpreted central directives to promote strategic industries in ways that supported the existing industrial structure.

[130] Simon and Cao 2009, 67–79.

[131] Ministry of Science and Technology data cited in Sutherland 2005, 96.

[132] A large literature has documented different regional political economies in China, emphasizing differences in institutions, training of local officials, sequencing of economic reforms, and local economic rules. See, for instance, Rithmire 2013; Segal 2003; Thun 2006.

Although many of the early wind and solar firms began in the proximity of their parent companies or near the hometown of their founders, municipalities later attracted supplier firms and companies from related industrial sectors to create cluster effects and synergies. Wuxi, the city where Suntech had its beginnings in 2001, attracted glass manufacturers, producers of production equipment, and firms supplying silicone and other materials required for PV production. Semiconductor firms, which rely on a production method that bears similarities to the process that produces a solar cell, also settled in local HTZs.[133] Baoding, where Yingli had started the domestic solar PV industry in 2001, ultimately branded itself as a "green city," attracting a wide range of renewable energy firms and suppliers with complementary capabilities to its local industrial parks. The local government also targeted foreign equipment manufacturers and component suppliers at international conferences, including at the 2004 Global Wind Power Exhibit held in Beijing, less than 100 miles from the city.[134]

In other cases, particularly among late entrants, domestic wind and solar firms sought out high-tech development zones specifically for their existing industrial base. A history of shipbuilding and the presence of related supplier industries, including bearings manufacturing, persuaded Sinovel to open its first manufacturing facilities in Dalian.[135] Tianjin became a popular destination for domestic wind turbine producers after successfully attracting a wide range of foreign wind turbine manufacturers and their suppliers, including REpower, Sinovel, and Vestas.[136] In Changzhou, where Trina Solar and EGing Solar were producing cells and solar PV modules, the municipal government counted 109 firms that manufactured products and components for power generation equipment, including transformers, inverters, electrical insulation, and switching equipment.[137]

The agglomeration economies born from local government coordination promoted collaboration between foreign and domestic firms. For domestic manufacturers seeking to upgrade their capabilities in manufacturing, however, these local economies also created supplier networks that allowed the purchase of large quantities of raw materials at short notice. They permitted close interaction with suppliers to fine-tune equipment and adjust material composition to match product designs and manufacturing processes. For engineering teams seeking to accelerate product commercialization, regional economies thus offered a wide range of tools and partners focused precisely on the large-scale production of renewable energy technologies. In interviews, firms confirmed the benefits of

---

[133] Wuxi Yearbook 2003, 219; 2006, 292.
[134] Baoding Year Book 2004/2005, 155.
[135] Dalian Yearbook 2007b, 130–39.
[136] Tianjin Yearbook 2010, 241–42.
[137] Changzhou Yearbook 2005, 173.

these local environments. The president of a solar PV manufacturer explained his company's chosen location as the result of a decision to operate in proximity to other solar PV manufacturers who were likely to have used production equipment available: his engineering teams could acquire this equipment to cheaply test the manufacturing of their new product designs.[138] Others emphasized the availability of local suppliers to collaborate on substitute materials or new equipment design, describing how these partnerships enabled them to move rapidly through multiple configurations until the right setup was pinpointed.[139]

Beyond the benefits that firms naturally derived from agglomeration economies, specialization in local industrial composition also permitted local governments to design more targeted institutions to support firms in the process of developing knowledge-intensive capabilities. In contrast to the broad national educational reforms that increased the number of graduates from China's engineering schools over time, local administrations created educational facilities for vocational training and continuing education that matched the needs of their home firms. These local colleges did not aim to graduate engineers with doctoral degrees; rather, they focused on creating a manufacturing workforce capable of understanding manufacturing blueprints while grasping the requirements of mass production. Regardless of whether such programs allowed firms to send existing workers for continuing education or trained high-school graduates for manufacturing jobs, many of these vocational colleges, set up by local governments in China's high-technology institutes, collaborated with local firms. For instance, the municipal government in Changzhou set up a program for technological upgrading in manufacturing firms as early as 1997, around the time that Trina Solar was founded as a solar installation company. The city estimated that about 25 percent of local large- and medium-sized enterprises had employees with Computer Assisted Design training (CAD), with a total of 5,000 CAD-trained workers in the city. To augment this number and promote advanced manufacturing skills in the local workforce, the city set up CAD demonstration platforms, established training programs, and offered loans to local companies seeking to upgrade their manufacturing infrastructure and improve the skill level of their employees.[140]

Other locations with sizable renewable energy industries launched similar programs, including in Changzhou, Baoding, and Urumqi.[141] In Wuxi, the local government founded a vocational college for S&T training in 2003. By 2005, the

[138] Author interview, president, solar PV start-up firm, August 24, 2011.

[139] Author interviews: CTO and director of R&D at Chinese solar manufacturer, August 26, 2011; CTO, Chinese wind turbine manufacturer, August 29, 2011.

[140] Changzhou Yearbook 1998, 288.

[141] Changzhou Yearbook 2004, 249–50; Baoding Year Book 2004/2005, 523; Urumqi Year Book 2007c, 226.

school was offering applied vocational training programs for 6,000 students in collaboration with Suntech, Sony, and thirty-seven other firms with facilities in the region.[142] In some cases, local enterprises themselves took the initiative to set up such programs, collaborating with the local government and other firms for support. Spearheaded by Dalian Daxian Group, a supplier of electronic components, vocational training was offered in Dalian for electromechanical technicians, supplying workers with knowledge of mechanical components and electronic circuitry to local industrial sectors, including wind turbine manufacturing.[143]

At the same time that wind and solar manufacturers were rapidly increasing the average training levels of their educated workforce, they were increasingly automating their production lines to avoid the high turnover rates associated with unskilled labor. Although innovative manufacturing capabilities continued to reside in designated engineering teams and did not extend into the manufacturing workforce in the same way that advanced manufacturing capabilities in Germany did, the training of manufacturing staff permitted Chinese firms to translate design and process changes into manufacturing practice more rapidly. Efforts to increase the skills and training of local members of the existing workforce thus complemented central government innovation policy, which focused on technology development but paid little attention to the types of skills required in commercialization and production.

In addition to promoting workforce training, municipalities supported the technology commercialization efforts of local firms by funding individual commercialization projects and improving the R&D infrastructure available in the local economy. Such R&D infrastructure included China's 800 universities and 5,000 research institutes, 60 percent of which were located in close proximity to one of the high-technology industrial zones.[144] Many of these institutions set up laboratories working on technologies of importance to industrial sectors; municipal chronicles boast an increasing number of patent activities and journal citations for local research laboratories. In Baoding, for example, Hebei University of Technology established a School of Energy and Environmental Engineering in the early 2000s, after the arrival of Yingli and other renewable energy companies prompted the city to promote itself as a green technology cluster.[145] Although almost all renewable energy firms indicate some connections to research institutes, collaborative R&D activities mostly occur with other firms.[146]

[142] Wuxi Yearbook 2006, 305.
[143] Dalian Yearbook 2007b, 140.
[144] Heilmann, Shih, and Hofem 2013; Sutherland 2005, 96.
[145] Author interview, senior official, Baoding Municipal Government, January 7, 2012.
[146] Sutherland 2005, 96.

Local programs focused not on laboratory research but on the commercialization of new technologies and the transition to mass production, thus, proved more central to the success of innovative manufacturing. Almost all localities set up municipal innovation funds, providing grants for innovation-related activities in local firms. Often these grants funded activities to overcome challenges in the commercialization of new technologies, rather than to create such technologies themselves. Although most grants went directly to firms, localities also used the programs to publicly fund facilities such as test centers, thereby providing complementary capabilities for firms in the local economy.

In Dalian, the municipal government supported Sinovel in 2006 with the commercialization of a 1.5 MW turbine technology based on a license from a German firm. In the process, engineers adapted the turbine for deployment under harsh climate conditions with temperatures as low as -40 degrees Celsius. Two local suppliers, Dalian Tianyuan Electrical Machinery and Dalian Wazhou Group, supplied components for the new turbine. The local government helped Dalian Wazhou construct a test platform for industrial-scale precision bearings to aid the commercialization of new bearing designs. Beyond supporting the commercialization of wind turbine components, however, this testing platform enabled the commercialization of bearings for other local industries, such as shipbuilding and railway engines.[147] In collaboration with Suntech, in 2006 the Wuxi government initiated a so-called 530 Program, providing funds to attract Chinese engineering graduates back into local high-tech development zones and offering grants of RMB 1–3 million for the commercialization of promising technologies. By 2012, 876 local firms were participating in the 530 Program, and available funds had grown to RMB 2.5 billion.[148] In Baoding, the provincial government funded the development of two public engineering centers in the local high-tech development zone, a center of virtual engineering and an engineering center of blade development, both of which offered access to advanced computer workstations and test facilities. The government emphasized the importance of industry associations in setting up these facilities to meet the needs of the local industry and boost the competitiveness of local firms.[149]

Local government policies, training institutions, and innovation support programs did not add up to a comprehensive strategy for industrial upgrading. Rather, they presented ad hoc responses to the perceived needs of local industrial sectors, to directives on innovation from the central government, and to the desire of local officials to promote economic growth. For wind and solar firms, these policies created a broad range of resources capable of bolstering

---

[147] Dalian Yearbook 2007b, 130–39.
[148] Wuxi Yearbook 2008, 241.
[149] Baoding Year Book 2004/2005, 155.

engineering capabilities and funding the expansion of manufacturing facilities. But just as central government policies had not deliberately created institutions to support the establishment of capacities in innovative manufacturing, so local governments and high-tech development zones did not strategically choose capabilities in technology commercialization as an overt goal. At the local level, policymaking was instead driven by the much more immediate necessity of growing the economy through the rapid scale-up and mass production of potentially game-changing technologies. China's wind and solar firms utilized this manufacturing infrastructure to respond to new opportunities, laying their engineering expertise in innovative manufacturing on top of a strong foundation of local institutions supportive of mass production. The specialization in innovative manufacturing entailed advanced capabilities in product design, yet it differed from the conception of autonomous technology development at the core of Beijing's indigenous innovation strategy. Chinese wind and solar firms engaged in learning and industrial upgrading, but they did so without developing the full range of industrial capabilities required to invent, commercialize and produce green energy technologies. In spite of government plans to create autonomous local enterprises, China's wind and solar firms developed highly specialized capabilities within collaborative relationships in global supply chains.

Conclusion

Policymakers and industry associations in the West long suspected a centralized government effort behind China's rise in renewable energy sectors. Political economists focused on China frequently raised an opposite set of observations: from the perspective of statist literatures on economic development, which have provided a more nuanced perspective on the role of the state in fostering industrial upgrading, the development of innovative capabilities in China's wind and solar sectors was unexpected because of the fragmentation of the Chinese state. Among other East Asian late developers, centralized and hierarchical planning bureaucracies orchestrated targeted policy interventions to support technological learning and industrial upgrading. China lacked such centralized institutions.[150] Although the central government in Beijing provided various incentives for technology transfer and the establishment of advanced R&D capabilities in Chinese firms, the responsibility for policymaking was distributed across numerous ministries and administrative levels. China lacked

---

[150] On strategic government intervention among the East Asian developers, see Amsden 1989, 2001; Evans 1995; Johnson 1982; Wade 1990.

the institutions to implement the concerted policy effort necessary to prompt upgrading in high-technology industries in a centralized manner.[151]

This fragmentation of industrial policy implementation was particularly visible in policies to promote domestic innovation, where different levels of government demonstrated divergent priorities. Central government plans called for the establishment of autonomous technological capabilities in virtually all segments of the wind turbine and solar supply chains.[152] Literature on China's decentralized development model focused on the ways in which incentives for local governments to create short-term economic growth collided with these long-term central government plans, creating an implementation gap between central goals and local outcomes.[153] Divergent policy goals at subnational levels were here regarded as a threat to the implementation of central government policies, as they offered firms the option of shirking their duty by prioritizing short-term economic gains over long-term policy goals.[154]

In this chapter, I have argued that collaborative advantage allowed Chinese wind and solar firms to use the fragmented industrial policy framework to establish knowledge-intensive capabilities focused on preparing complex technologies for mass production. As in Germany and the United States, firms entered global supply chains with specialized capabilities that relied on collaboration with others. Although these skills fell short of government goals, they nonetheless represented a form of industrial upgrading. Chinese firms repurposed policies and institutions intended for the manufacturing economy to establish new knowledge-intensive capacities within manufacturing itself, incrementally building on China's industrial legacy of mass production. The state enabled such industrial upgrading among China's wind and solar producers not only by providing the resources required for technological learning, but, as I have argued here, by attracting foreign-invested high-technology manufacturers into China's economic development zones. The end result was the establishment of an industrial ecosystem for mass production eminently capable of supporting a new generation of innovative manufacturing.

China's wind and solar firms have achieved sustained growth despite divergent—and often outright conflicting—government policies, which have not followed the hierarchical, centralized, and highly disciplined template of the East Asian developmental states. And China's renewable energy firms have avoided the main hazard associated with participation in such fragmented global production systems, namely the possibility of becoming trapped in low-skill and

---

[151] See, for instance, Huang 2002; Thun 2006, 52–60.
[152] See, for instance, Ministry of Science and Technology 2012; National Energy Administration 2012.
[153] Amsden 1989; Johnson 1982; Kostka and Nahm 2017; Nahm 2017.
[154] For a discussion of policy bundling in China, see Kostka and Hobbs 2012, 768–70.

low-value activities within global supply chains.[155] Instead, Chinese capabilities in scale-up and commercialization have attracted global innovators, allowing Chinese firms to bring wind and solar technologies to market, even if they do not do so alone. At least in renewable energy industries, Chinese firms learned to compete on skills, not on labor cost. In consequence, wind and solar production did not chase labor cost to cheaper manufacturing locations in the Chinese interior or in neighboring economies, even as wage differentials remained large and growing.[156]

At the same time, however, such upgrading-within-manufacturing required Chinese firms and regulators to assume risks. Participation in global processes of technology development required Chinese firms to make large investments in manufacturing capacity, often funded by state-owned banks and local governments. In contrast to German suppliers of components and production equipment, which maintained customers in several industries despite small firm sizes, China's investments were industry-specific. In the wind and solar sectors, where demand continues to rely on demand-side subsidies, the fate of China's innovative manufacturers depends not just on their ability to innovate and further reduce cost, but also on government policy in China and abroad. The global financial crisis, which led many European governments to cut or eliminate subsidies for wind and solar products, created overcapacity in global renewable energy sectors. Antidumping legislation against Chinese solar panels has further threatened export markets, as have widespread calls in the United States for economic decoupling from China.[157] In times of crisis, Chinese firms were thus left with the most capital-intensive part of the global innovation processes.

A number of firms have declared bankruptcy as a result. Suntech, for instance, exported 38 percent of its solar panels to Spain in 2008. By 2009, after the Spanish government had all but shut down its domestic support for renewable energy markets, Spanish demand accounted for less than 3 percent of Suntech's revenue.[158] By 2013, the company, once the largest solar manufacturer in China, had filed for bankruptcy protection.[159]

Ultimately, the sustainability of China's specialization in innovative manufacturing could depend on the ability of China's manufacturers to apply their capabilities in scale-up and commercialization to a wide range of industrial sectors. Breznitz and Murphree, in a study on China's electronics industry, found that manufacturers there also embarked on a manufacturing-centric upgrading

---

155 Steinfeld 2004.
156 In 2009, the wage gap between urban workers in coastal provinces—where most of China's renewable energy manufacturing is located—and urban workers in interior provinces was 55 percent, up from 28 percent two decades earlier. Li et al. 2012, 62.
157 US.International Trade Commission 2012.
158 Ahrens 2013, 4.
159 Bradsher, 2013b.

trajectory.[160] Thun and Brandt similarly found that in the machine tools and automotive sectors, Chinese firms benefited from engineering capabilities in advanced manufacturing.[161] Germany's small and medium-sized wind and solar suppliers, which improved and adapted their core capabilities over decades and applied them to successive industrial sectors, illustrate that diverse strengths in manufacturing can, in principle, be the source of long-term advantage.

The importance of manufacturing institutions for economic development and technological innovation was not lost on central government planners in Beijing, as the renewed push to support upgrading-within-manufacturing through China's Made in China 2025 initiative illustrates. If the experience of China's renewable energy industries is any guide, however, it will be up to entrepreneurial firms, not the state, to identify new applications for advanced skills in manufacturing and use a broad range of institutions to support such strategies.

[160] Breznitz and Murphree 2011.
[161] Brandt and Thun 2010.

6

Wind and Solar Invention in the United States

Driving along Interstate 10 from Los Angeles to Palm Springs gives the viewer a panoramic view onto one of the largest experiments in the commercial generation of renewable energy. As the freeway crosses into the Coachella Valley past an outlet mall and the Cabazon dinosaur museum, the California desert opens up to one of earliest wind farms in the United States. First installed in the 1980s, some 4,000 turbines remain today of the original 6,000 that once dotted the moonlike landscape in the narrow channel between the San Gorgonio and San Jacinto peaks. The remnants of first-generation wind turbines—with their tripod-like towers and two-blade designs—remind the visitor of the technological ambition possessed by US engineers, a drive to create that long buttressed America's reputation as a seedbed for technological innovation. Yet the turbine parts strewn across the California desert also evoke the rapid end of the first wind energy boom—a frustrating closure caused by technical difficulties and a changing political environment in the mid-1980s. Despite American strengths in aerospace design, US-made turbines remained inferior to imported models in efficiency and reliability. Foreign manufacturers reaped most of the benefits from the initial wind farms in California.[1]

Three decades after the first wind turbines were installed on the San Gorgonio pass, the United States once again became one of the largest markets for wind and solar power in the world. In 2015, the United States accounted for 17 percent of global wind turbine installations and 11 percent of installed solar photovoltaic (PV) capacity.[2] Not unlike in the 1980s, US renewable energy industries maintained strengths in the invention of new technologies but established few capabilities in commercialization and production. To a far greater degree than in Germany or China, wind and solar sectors in the United States were populated by high-technology firms that spun off from universities and research institutes. By 2009, out of 100 solar photovoltaic firms in the United States, at least 73 were start-ups, and many of these were racing to commercialize thin-film technologies that broke with the conventional use of silicon as the basic raw material for solar

[1] Gipe 1995, 31–36.
[2] GWEC 2017; IEA 2016.

cell production.[3] In the wind industry, US firms developed turbines that abandoned traditional designs, including gearless drivetrain concepts and small-scale turbines based on jet engine technologies.[4] Small in size and boasting advanced technological capabilities, these firms built up strengths in early-stage research and development, but rarely did they establish capabilities in scale-up and mass manufacturing. US multinational companies, which also entered American renewable energy industries, maintained a similar focus on inventing new technologies in their home operations, while offshoring or outsourcing much of their production to locations abroad. US industrial capabilities in renewable energy industries strongly targeted early-stage R&D, without establishing the full range of skills necessary to bring new products from lab to market.

By 2008, the United States accounted for more than 61,000 renewable energy patents filed in US, European, and Japanese patent offices, roughly double the number of patents filed by German entities.[5] In 2016 alone, US entities filed some 5,000 clean energy patents with the US Patent and Trademark Office (USPTO), compared to 1,800 European patent applications and 300 from China.[6] Still, local content rates for US wind turbines hovered around a modest 40 percent, as high-value components—gearboxes, metal castings, and turbine blades—were imported from abroad. As late as 2017, local content rates for many internal components of the turbine remained as low as 20 percent.[7] A 2011 study by the American Wind Energy Association (AWEA) estimated that European wind turbine manufacturers created three to four times as many jobs per megawatt of installed wind turbine capacity as their US counterparts, as local supply chains in Europe obviated the need for imported components.[8] In the solar sector, where US firms and research institutes developed the foundations for virtually all of the main solar technologies in production today, US firms accounted for less than 5 percent of global manufacturing in 2010. New technologies were brought to market in other parts of the world, and key components for domestic solar PV manufacturing—including wafers, thin film feedstock, and inverters—were imported from abroad.[9]

The emphasis on early-stage research and development (R&D) in US wind and solar industries is particular striking when we compare it to the manufacturing-based capabilities in Germany and China. German and Chinese renewable energy sectors attracted firms with a wide range of production skills, including

---

[3] Knight 2011, 176.
[4] Bullis 2008.
[5] Bierenbaum et al. 2012, 6–7. Bolinger 2013, 18–19.
[6] Helveston and Nahm 2019, 796.
[7] Wiser 2017, 20.
[8] AWEA Manufacturing Working Group 2011; David 2009.
[9] Data compiled by Earth Policy Institute, 2020. The US maintained a positive trade balance in the production of manufacturing equipment and silicon feedstock. See GTM Research 2011.

those specializing in component and equipment manufacturing, scale-up, and mass production. At the most basic level, scholars have evoked theories of comparative advantage to explain American strength in invention and not production.[10] Proponents of this view have frequently cited examples like Apple, a company that used strengths in upstream R&D to generate economic benefits in the United States, even if production activities were mostly located in Asia.[11] Policymakers and industry representatives, meanwhile, claimed that the cost of labor in the United States prevented competitiveness in manufacturing. This argument was often made in conjunction with calls for trade barriers, following accusations that China and other Asian economies lowered their production cost through subsidies and lax environmental regulations.[12] Yet this same argument, when posed against a German backdrop, failed to play out: for all the competition from China and other economies with low factor prices—competition that led to a series of high-profile bankruptcies among German solar PV manufacturers—Germany still retained a supply chain of highly specialized small and medium-sized wind and solar suppliers with manufacturing facilities. And it did so while remaining a high-wage environment, in which hourly compensation for manufacturing workers in 2012 was nearly 50 percent above manufacturing wages in the United States.[13] At the very least, then, the case of Germany suggests that high-wage economies can in principle retain domestic production activities even in emerging high-tech sectors. So why have US wind and solar supply industries built capabilities in early stage R&D without adding complementary skills in scale-up and mass production?

In this chapter, I trace the development of US renewable energy sectors to show that new opportunities for collaboration in global supply chains made the co-location of innovation and production activities in the United States unnecessary for the commercialization of new technologies. New options for industrial specialization in the global economy allowed German and Chinese firms to maintain manufacturing-based industrial specializations; in the United States, they had the opposite effect, helping firms cut ties with the domestic manufacturing economy. US investments in R&D and demand-side subsidies created domestic jobs in the installation and maintenance of wind farms and solar parks, but left a far smaller industrial footprint than the German and Chinese renewable energy sectors.

In the wind and solar sectors, American firms responded to renewable energy policies set at state and federal levels by creating R&D teams as spinoffs from

[10] Kraemer, Linden, and Dedrick 2011; Mankiw and Swagel 2006.
[11] See, for instance, Bonvillian and Weiss 2015, 11–12; Kraemer, Linden, and Dedrick 2011; Sturgeon 2002.
[12] US International Trade Commission 2011.
[13] Levinson 2014, 14.

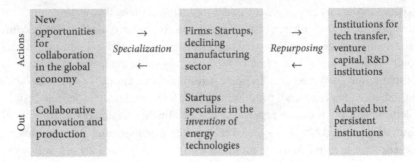

Figure 6.1 Industrial Specialization in the United States

universities and research institutes and focused these teams on the *invention* of new technologies. I show here that firms made use of domestic institutions for technology transfer, including the Bayh-Dole act of 1980 and subsequent legislation that permitted the licensing of federally funded research. They also repurposed funding institutions for R&D activities, often the only sources of income for start-ups that had not yet found a pathway to commercialize their technologies. Firms were able to use such institutions, set up long before the growth of renewable energy industries, because collaborative advantage allowed them to enter the wind and solar sectors without domestic capabilities in mass production. A weak supplier base in adjacent industries reduced the number of firms with capabilities in scale-up and mass production that could enter wind and solar supply chains.[14] The United States' industrial specialization in invention and its ability to collaborate with global partners thus left firms less willing to revitalize domestic institutions within the manufacturing economy (Figure 6.1).

The chapter proceeds with a discussion of structural trends in the US economy that favored the creation of start-ups over the diversification of existing manufacturing businesses into renewable energy industries. It then describes the technological capabilities of these rapidly proliferating start-ups before highlighting the role of collaboration in allowing these firms to use federal R&D institutions to shape the development of US renewable energy sectors. The conclusion returns to the political implications of this particular industrial specialization and argues that their small industrial footprint prevented these wind and solar firms from becoming forceful advocates for stable clean energy legislation.

[14] Pisano and Shih 2012, 8–13.

Innovation without Production

Measured purely in terms of public financial support, the United States spent more than any other advanced economy on wind and solar R&D.[15] Many of the technological advances underlying traditional silicon-based solar cells and thin-film PV applications emerged from federally funded R&D institutes and enterprise laboratories, making possible the spread of solar technologies from their initial application in the space industry of the 1950s to the grid-connected solar PV models widely available today. Even in the wind sector, where European researchers made many of the critical contributions that enabled the gradual increase of turbine capacity, research consortia led by US corporations made efforts to leapfrog to the design of large-scale wind turbines in the wake of oil crises in the 1970s. These costly investments were almost entirely funded through federal government programs.[16]

Government support for R&D activities in universities, research institutes, and the private sector rested on two broad assumptions about the links between innovation and economic outcomes.[17] First, public investments in R&D assumed that market failures justified state intervention. Since technological innovation creates spillovers that firms often have a hard time appropriating, the private sector is assumed to underinvest in innovation in the absence of government intervention.[18] In light of innovation's central role in maintaining technological leadership, economic growth, and national competitiveness, the federal government in the postwar decades faced strong incentives to support technological innovation in the domestic economy.[19]

Second, underlying US public R&D spending in the postwar decades was a notion that a linear relationship existed between innovation and industrial development. The invention of new technologies—from this perspective, largely a function of sufficient investments in basic research—was expected to trickle into the market by way of applied research and commercialization in domestic industries. Although the exact origins of this linear model are difficult to trace, the "belief that scientific advances are converted to practical use by a dynamic flow from science to technology has been a staple of research and development (R&D) managers everywhere."[20] A linear view of the relationship between innovation

[15] International Energy Agency (IEA) 2008, 31. National Science Board 2018, Figure 6–35.

[16] On the contributions of European research, see Heymann 1998. The role of US conglomerates is discussed in Righter 1996, 149–69.

[17] In addition to such economic objectives, the United States of course also pursued environmental concerns unique to the renewable energy industries examined here. Particularly in the postwar decades, much R&D spending pursued military goals that I do not examine here in detail, although early solar PV technologies found military applications in satellites, for instance. On the military origins of Silicon Valley, see, for example, Lécuyer 2007.

[18] Mazzucato 2016, 143.

[19] Boskin and Lau 1992; Romer 1994; Schumpeter 1934; Solow 1956.

[20] Stokes 1997, 10.

and application also applied to the international division of labor. According to the theory of the product cycle, introduced by Vernon in the 1960s, only firms in advanced economies possessed the engineering capabilities required to develop new technologies and to manage challenges in commercialization. Such firms further benefited from sophisticated domestic markets and consumers able to afford price premiums commanded by new technologies. Implicit in this theory was the assumption that close geographic and managerial linkages between invention and production were required in the early stages of product development. Only once products were reliable, manufacturing processes standardized, and price premiums gained from initial technological advantage had been depleted—in other words, once products were fully commodified—only then would manufacturing activities shift to developing economies with lower technical capabilities and less sophisticated market demand.[21]

In the wind and solar industries, public investments in basic research and government support for R&D peaked after the 1970s oil shocks but remained ahead of other nations from the postwar decades to the present. In the early 1980s, supported by bipartisan agreement on the need to diversify the US energy supply, federal investment in renewable energy R&D peaked at USD 1.3 billion.[22] This unprecedented level of R&D funding for renewable energy technologies encouraged research into wind and solar technologies in universities, supported a growing governmental research infrastructure for energy technology (in the form of national research laboratories), and funded research activities in US conglomerates from the aerospace, energy, and defense industries.[23] While the programs failed to yield a single commercially viable turbine—design flaws, manufacturing problems, and structural failures had cut short the operating hours of most of the turbines, and even when turbines did operate reliably, their efficiency remained far below expectations—federal funding for research continued at levels far above those of other countries (Table 6.1).[24]

Although renewable energy budgets decreased during the Reagan presidency in the 1980s, national institutions for energy research that had been created during the oil crises survived the chopping block. SERI, the federal Solar Energy Research Institute, continued to advance renewable energy research throughout the 1980s despite budget cuts. In 1991, its broad mandate beyond solar PV earned it the designation as the National Renewable Energy Laboratory (NREL), one of seven such laboratories set up by the Department of Energy (DOE).[25]

---

[21] Vernon 1966, 1979.
[22] Martinot, Wiser, and Hamrin 2005, 3.
[23] Righter 1996, 158.
[24] Ackermann and Söder 2002.
[25] NREL 2002, 2.

Table 6.1 Select Industrial Policies for US Wind and Solar Sectors

	United States
Technology Push	1973–1988 US Wind Research Program 1991–2000 PVMaT R&D Program Since 1990s NREL R&D Grants 2008 American Recovery & Reinvestment Act: Loans Since 2009 ARPE-E Program
Market Pull	1978 Public Utility Regulatory Policies Act (PURPA) 1992 Production Tax Credits (since then renewed 7 times) Since 1997 Renewable Portfolio Standards (30 states by 2012)

NREL subsequently established a National Wind Technology Center in Boulder, Colorado, in 1993.[26] The national laboratories provided demonstration sites, test centers, and accreditation for manufacturers, who came to rely on their highly specialized staff for technical expertise.[27]

The continuation of federal R&D funding and the maintenance and expansion of the energy national laboratories allowed the United States to maintain a global lead in renewable energy research (see Figure 6.1). Technological advances that originated in the federal R&D programs of the late 1970s, for instance, decreased the cost of solar PV technologies from USD 300 per watt in 1980 to USD 4 per watt in 1992.[28] The price for wind turbine installations dropped from USD 4,040 per kW in the early 1980s to an average of USD 1,340 per kW in the early 2000s, at least partially as a result of technology improvements.[29]

Between 1974 and 2008, the US federal government spent USD 3.3 billion on solar PV research alone, significantly more than Japan (USD 2.1 billion) and Germany (USD 1.9 billion), the largest solar PV market in the world at the time. By 2018, the DOE had spent over USD 28 billion on renewable energy research, or roughly 18 percent of the research spending by the DOE.[30] Such funds were awarded through a number of technology-specific programs. Between 1991 and 2008, for instance, the DOE invested USD 289 million in R&D for new solar technologies as part of the so-called Photovoltaic Manufacturing Technology (PVMaT) program. A separate program targeted research on thin-film technologies.[31] In the wind sector, the DOE invested in research on offshore wind

---

[26] See http://www.nrel.gov/wind/nwtc.html (accessed March 25, 2014).
[27] Harborne and Hendry 2009, 3582.
[28] Loferski 1993, 74.
[29] Wiser and Bolinger 2008, 21; Wiser, Bolinger, and Barbose 2007, 81.
[30] Clark 2018, 3–4. Critics have argued that such funds nonetheless are insufficient to combat the climate crisis. See Sivaram et al. 2020.
[31] O'Connor, Loomis, and Braun 2010, 3–14.

turbine technologies, next-generation turbine technologies, and research to improve turbine reliability and grid integration.[32]

Although public investments in research allowed the United States to remain at the forefront in the invention of new technologies, broad structural changes in the US economy undermined the linear model that underpinned such public spending. Beginning in the 1970s, the decline of manufacturing sectors in the United States drastically reduced the number of domestic firms that possessed technological capabilities with potential application in wind and solar industries. Between 1999 and 2010 alone, the number of manufacturing establishments in the United States declined by 14 percent.[33] The number of manufacturing plants that employed more than 1,000 workers dropped by half between 1977 and 2007.[34] Losses were particularly strong in the aerospace, semiconductor, machine tool, and automotive components sectors—precisely the type of industries from which suppliers had entered wind and solar sectors in Germany.[35] Between 1998 and 2010, nearly 1,200 plants closed in the semiconductor industry, a decline of 37 percent among facilities with more than 500 employees and a loss of 41 percent of medium-sized plants with 100–500 staff.[36] In the machine tool sector, foreign penetration of the US market rose from 30 percent in 1983 to 72 percent in 2008, with subsectors, including metal forming, reaching import rates of 91 percent. Domestic shipments for metal forming machines dropped by more than 50 percent between 1990 and 2009. Over the same period, the US aerospace industry lost 10 percent of mid-sized firms and 28 percent of large firms with more than 500 employees.[37] Although the United States remained one of the world's largest manufacturers—second only to China by dollar value of its output, and ahead of both Germany and Japan—by the time renewable energy sectors became sizable global industries, much US manufacturing activity was concentrated in the hands of a few multinational firms. Growth in technology- or resource-intensive sectors such as pharmaceuticals, medical devices, and petrochemicals masked declines in other industries.[38]

A multitude of factors contributed to these changes in the American manufacturing economy. China's accession to the World Trade Organization (WTO) in 2001 increased import competition.[39] Other factors were homegrown and far preceded the shifts in the global economy caused by China's WTO accession.

---

[32]   Department of Energy 2006, 2017b.
[33]   US Census Data cited in Yudken 2010, 2.
[34]   Holmes 2011, 6.
[35]   Pisano and Shih 2012, 8–13; Whitford 2005, 2012.
[36]   Yudken 2010, 7.
[37]   Pisano and Shih 2012, 11–12; Yudken 2010, 6–12.
[38]   Ramaswarmy et al. 2018, 21.
[39]   For a discussion of the impact of changing US–China trade relations on American manufacturing sectors, see Autor, Dorn, and Hanson 2012; Berger 2013b, 41–44; Pierce and Schott 2014.

Over the course of the 1970s, financial markets in the United States had rewarded large firms for outsourcing non-core production activities; and falling tariffs and trade barriers subsequently permitted US multinationals to look to low-cost economies to find suppliers.[40] The declining number of suppliers in the US economy had its basis, at least in part, in the difficulties small and medium-sized firms faced when they tried to adapt to the reorganization of production in the global economy and the lack of state institutions that could facilitate such adjustment. For instance, after decades during which metalworking manufacturers in the American Midwest essentially served as production buffers for larger firms, many were ill-equipped to meet the new requirements in design and customization imposed by their customers in the 1990s. Although in principle, small and medium-sized firms were capable of making investments in new technological capabilities and design skills, they shied away from doing so in the face of economic uncertainty, an absence of guaranteed markets, and little public institutional support for technological upgrading in manufacturing.[41]

The accounting standards required to claim R&D tax credits, for instance, had traditionally favored technological innovation developed in traditional R&D departments over the type of incremental manufacturing innovation that would be involved in retooling a production facility for application in new sectors. Claiming federal R&D credits was an onerous reporting process, and many small and medium-sized firms lacked designated R&D departments. For all the R&D funding available for early-stage R&D, little public funding existed to upgrade existing technological capabilities.[42] Few banks wanted to fund manufacturing investments in the absence of order guarantees, a reluctance that compelled suppliers who were willing to enter new sectors to rely on retained earnings for financing.[43] Many struggled to do so. Firms willing to invest in emerging renewable energy industries also struggled to find qualified staff trained to handle increasingly complex machinery. In a survey on skills and training in manufacturing establishments, smaller firms with high-skill demands reported significantly more difficulty filling vacancies, suggesting that those firms willing to move into new emerging high-tech sectors were not served well by existing skills, training institutions, and local community colleges.[44]

Among those that weathered the decline in the number of manufacturing establishments in the semiconductor, machine tool, and automotive supply industries, few were able to make the investments required to enter renewable

[40] Davis 2009, 87–96, 195–200.
[41] Whitford 2005, 95–120; 2012, 259.
[42] Author interviews: CEO of metal-forming manufacturer, October 24, 2012; CEO of aerospace supplier, April 27, 2012.
[43] Berger 2013b, 115–16; Cetorelli and Strahan 2006, 459.
[44] Osterman and Weaver 2013, 33–35.

energy industries. One steel manufacturer seeking to diversify into the wind industry stated that a contract to supply parts for a local offshore wind park would necessitate a USD 20 million investment in a new manufacturing facility, a risky investment in the absence of any guarantees that a contract would ultimately be awarded to the firm. Even with such guarantees, bank loans would be difficult to obtain, and the manufacturer's only hope of finding external financing involved federal loan guarantees. At the time of my interview with this steel manufacturer, legal challenges and debates over subsidies had left the offshore project in limbo, yet this small manufacturer with fifty employees had already spent USD 1 million of retained earnings to prepare a bid.[45] By the time construction commenced on the offshore wind park a few years later, a different supplier had been chosen, leaving the metal fabrication firm without a viable path to pay for its manufacturing facility.[46]

By comparison, a German manufacturer of similar components, whom the steel firm relied on for technical advice, received a USD 45 million grant for a USD 90 million facility from the German government and was able to secure three years of guaranteed orders from German turbine manufacturers prior to making the investment. Asked if any competitors were also trying to enter the wind industry, the steel manufacturer recounted how all twelve of his local competitors had gone bankrupt over the past two decades, as their core markets eroded and they failed to diversify into growing industries.

As I chronicled in Chapter 4, German suppliers from legacy industries entered the wind and solar sectors by applying core capabilities to new applications in renewable energy—the production of components, materials, and manufacturing equipment required to bring new technologies to scale. In the United States, the declining number of manufacturing establishments had left fewer firms that could potentially do the same, particularly in sectors where firms had industrial strengths applicable to wind and solar. Among those who remained, slim margins often prevented investments in new skills. Weak institutional support for repurposing and reinventing existing industrial capabilities—these included the absence of local banks, training institutions, and collaborative research funds that had enabled suppliers in Germany to enter the renewable energy industries—further prevented firms from entering new economic sectors.

Because broad structural change in the US economy had reduced the number of supply firms with industrial capabilities applicable to the wind and solar sectors, US wind and solar supply chains remained considerably less diverse than those in Germany and China. US strength in early-stage research and development manifested in large numbers of high-technology start-ups, yet the failure

---

[45]   Author interview, CEO of steel manufacturing firm, October 24, 2012.
[46]   Cardwell 2014.

of small and medium-sized manufacturing firms to mobilize and enter the renewable energy supply chains left large gaps in the types of industrial capacities that could be accessed domestically. Ultimately, top-down investments in technological innovation in universities and research institutes led to vibrant start-up activity but were not matched by an equally forceful mobilization of skills in commercialization and production.

Inventing Wind and Solar

The primary benefactors of public investments in research and development were start-up firms with technological capabilities in the invention of new technologies. Even before legislation created the first domestic markets for wind turbines or solar panels, firms built on the strength of US research and development activities by spinning off from universities and government research institutes in an attempt to commercialize recent discoveries. In contrast to the aerospace and defense conglomerates that had begun working on large-scale wind turbines with the help of federal programs beginning in the 1970s, these new firms were small and specialized, growing directly out of publicly funded research. In 1974, entrepreneurs Stanley Charren and Russell Wolfe founded US Windpower as a spinoff from MIT's Lincoln Lab. The MIT laboratory provided the core technology and the company's chief engineer. US Windpower, later named Kenetech, began building a demonstration wind farm on Crotched Mountain in New Hampshire, long before the first large wind markets were created in the United States.[47] Six years later, ESI, another turbine manufacturer, was established by two government engineers working at a wind turbine testing site set up as part of the national wind energy program in Rocky Flats, Colorado. The engineers left to launch their own company and licensed the technology from the federal government.[48] In the 1980s, Zond began building variable-speed wind turbines based on a technology developed at and in collaboration with NREL. The firm was one of the few who had survived the rapid end of California's wind energy boom in the 1980s; Enron eventually purchased it in 1997.[49]

In the solar sector, small firms produced solar PV cells for niche applications and benefited from state funding for utility-scale demonstration projects.[50] Former employees of Spectrolab, a firm that had supplied solar modules for

---

[47] Jeff Ackerman, 1981, "Putting the Wind to Work; Breeze Power Is Serious Business for Founder of Farm in N.H.," *Boston Globe*, May 3. See also: MIT Lincoln Lab, "Spin-Off Companies," http://www.ll.mit.edu/about/TechTransfer/spinoffs.html (accessed March 27, 2014).

[48] Gipe 1995, 71.

[49] Department of Energy 2003.

[50] West 2014, 7.

space applications since the 1950s, founded Solec International in 1976. It was located in proximity to Caltech and NASA's Jet Propulsion Lab in Pasadena, and it collaborated with both institutions on the improvement of terrestrial solar technologies throughout the 1980s.[51] Solar Technology International, also founded by former Spectrolab employees, similarly participated in joint research with Caltech and the Jet Propulsion Lab to improve its solar PV technologies.[52]

With the exception of a brief period in the early 1980s, during which a combination of federal and state-level subsidies created short-lived demand for wind power installations in California, renewable energy firms struggled with a lack of market demand. Even though California's wind energy boom was not replaced by new domestic markets for renewable energy technologies until the early 2000s, new wind and solar firms continued to be founded on technologies originating in federally funded research. The first generation of terrestrial solar PV firms specialized in traditional silicon PV modules derived from earlier products for space applications. Beginning in the 1990s, a second generation of solar firms launched research on new solar PV technologies designated for grid-connected, civilian applications.

In the early 2000s, both California and Texas passed renewable portfolio standards that required utilities to meet ambitious renewable energy targets, leading to large local markets for wind turbine installations.[53] Fueled by regional investments in renewable energy, in addition to federal production tax credits, the United States ballooned to become the largest market for wind turbines in 2005.[54] A federal solar investment tax credit of 30 percent was passed as part of the 2005 Energy Policy Act and renewed in 2006 and 2008; together with state-level policies such as the 2007 California Solar Initiative, this tax credit led to a surge in US domestic demand for solar PV after decades of stagnation.[55] By then, the introduction of generous subsidies for solar PV installations had created the world's first large solar market in Germany. Other nations, most notably Spain and Italy, bolstered domestic solar demand in the years that followed.[56]

The expansion of global markets prompted a new wave of industry entry. In the solar sector, many of the new firms revolved around the attempt to commercialize thin-film solar cells. Although thin-film cells promised to replace costly silicon as the basic raw material in solar cell production, complex manufacturing processes had kept thin-film technologies prohibitively expensive. Firms such as Nanosolar and Nanosys, both founded in California in 2001, were testing

[51] Colatat, Vidican, and Lester 2009, 5.
[52] Solar Technology International was purchased by the oil firm ARCO in the late 1970s and changed its name to ARCO Solar. Colatat, Vidican, and Lester 2009, 5; West 2013, 6.
[53] Bird et al. 2005, 1401–2.
[54] Wiser et al. 2008, 4.
[55] Colatat, Vidican, and Lester 2009, 7; Solar Energy Industries Association 2014.
[56] Campoccia et al. 2009, 290–91.

alternate deposition technologies that could potentially reduce the cost of thin-film manufacturing. Heliovolt, established in Austin, Texas, in 2001, and Day Star, founded in Halfmoon, New York, in 2006, sought to solve the same problem. Konarka was founded in Massachusetts in 2001 as a spinoff from the University of Massachusetts, Lowell, to fabricate solar cells from flexible plastics.[57] Scientists from NREL founded Solyndra in 2005, a company that used a deposition technology developed by NREL to build cylindrical, higher efficiency cells.[58] In 2007, Emanuel Sachs spun off a new company, 1366 Technologies, to introduce new production processes for solar wafers.[59] By 2009, at least forty-six solar PV start-ups were operating in California alone.[60]

The wind sector also attracted a growing number of start-ups. In 2001, former employees of the legacy wind turbine manufacturer Zond founded a new turbine manufacturer, Clipper Windpower, in California. Clipper proposed replacing a single turbine generator with several smaller generators to increase efficiency and reliability.[61] In Florida, a manufacturer of superconducting magnets, diversified into the wind energy business in 2002 and began developing gearless wind turbines.[62] Ogin, a spin-off from the aerospace sector, began designing new wind turbine technology in 2008, borrowing principles from jet engines to increase turbine efficiency.[63] In 2009, NREL employees founded Boulder Wind Power to commercialize an alternative gearless wind turbine technology.[64]

Although American strengths in science and technology remained the envy of policymakers around the world, American capabilities in large domestic manufacturing sectors did not. Start-ups were far more specialized than the vertically integrated firms that had formed the main engines of technology commercialization in previous decades. They shared with those older firms similar abilities in the invention of new technologies, yet few possessed skills in the commercialization and production of wind turbines and solar panels.[65] In the postwar decades, public investments in R&D had, at the very least, led to domestic manufacturing facilities for early product generations of new technologies. But these domestic links, which fueled the assumption that a linear connection existed between the invention, commercialization, and production stages, were finally

[57] Morton 2006, 21.
[58] David R. Baker and Carolyn Said, 2011, "Solyndra: Energy Superstar's Rapid Rise and Fall," *San Francisco Chronicle*, September 18.
[59] Kevin Bullis, 2010, "Making More Solar Cells from Silicon," *Technology Review*, March 4.
[60] Colatat, Vidican, and Lester 2009, 6.
[61] Goudarzi and Zhu 2013, 199.
[62] Angela Lazazzera, 2009, "New Innovations in 19th Century Technology," *Spacecoast Business Magazine*, May.
[63] Gertner, 2013.
[64] See www.boulderwindpower.com (accessed March 29, 2014).
[65] SunPower and First Solar were an exception to this rule and invested in sizable manufacturing facilities in the solar sector.

undermined—as firms that specialized in the invention of new technologies were not accompanied by firms with equally strong capabilities in scale-up and mass production.

In contrast to Germany and China, where large numbers of domestic manufacturers entered renewable energy industries in response to growing global markets, few domestic suppliers with diverse industrial capacities populated the US wind and solar sector markets; and despite a number of notable exceptions, few large domestic manufacturers did, either. In part, uncertainty over domestic markets generated this reluctance within existing manufacturing firms. The patchwork of federal and state-level regulations and the volatility of the US demand-side policies deterred these firms from entering wind and solar industries. Faced with a costly retooling of their existing plants, the need to acquire new skills to customize products for renewable energy industries, and supplier qualification processes lasting twelve months more, many small and medium-sized manufacturers decided that investing in renewable energy sectors was a bet they'd rather not place.[66] A study by the Lawrence Berkeley Laboratory on the effects of policy volatility in wind power found that uncertainty "in the future scale of the U.S. wind power market has limited the interest of both U.S. and foreign firms in investing in wind turbine and component manufacturing infrastructure in the U.S." Short-term extensions to policy support "may lower the willingness of private industry to engage and invest in long-term wind technology R&D that is unlikely to pay off within a one-to-two year [cycle]," the report concluded.[67] Renewable energy firms showed particular reluctance to invest in states that had previously shown policy volatility in energy market regulation, a problem exacerbated by uncertainty over federal policy support.[68] Wind turbine manufacturers, which sought to localize component production to reduce transportation costs and currency risks, conceded that they were unable to guarantee long-term order volumes necessary to attract local suppliers.[69]

The existence of global sectors with highly specialized skills—including the German renewable energy suppliers focused on complex componentry and China's firms with skills in commercialization and mass production—absolved firms from having to co-locate activities that used to be located within the four walls of the firm. Many firms that successfully entered US wind and solar supply chains were multinational corporations, less reliant on any particular market and able to draw on global supply chains for parts and manufacturing expertise. Such firms included the multinational equipment manufacturer Applied Materials, the silicon producer Hemlock, and the global bearings manufacturer Timken.

[66] Rogowsky and Laney-Cummings 2009, 13–14.
[67] Wiser, Bolinger, and Barbose 2007, 81.
[68] Fabrizio 2012.
[69] Baker 2010; Spada 2010.

Their core competitors, however, resided outside the United States. Independent US suppliers operated only three out of ten blade manufacturing facilities located in the United States in 2009, with the majority of blade plants run by European wind turbine manufacturers who serviced the growing US market.[70] Although more than 10,000 metal casting firms existed in the United States in 2010, not a single firm had retooled its manufacturing facilities to supply metal castings for wind turbines—a gap that required turbine manufacturers to source castings for turbine hubs in Europe and Asia.[71] Only two American firms were manufacturing wind turbine generators.[72] Likewise, in the solar sector, the majority of suppliers were multinational corporations that had diversified into renewable energy industries. In addition to Applied Materials, which entered the solar sector through a series of acquisitions beginning in 2006, one firm, GT Solar, offered domestically manufactured turnkey production equipment.[73] More suppliers existed in glass manufacturing, wire production, laser technology, and other areas in which products required little or no customization for the solar PV sector.

In the face of difficulties faced by small manufacturers, many firms that successfully entered US wind and solar supply chains from existing industries were multinational corporations, less reliant on any particular market and able to invest in new facilities without the need for external financing. Multinational corporations frequently entered the renewable energy sector through acquisitions of start-up firms with promising technologies for select wind and solar components and production equipment. GE, perhaps the most visible example, entered the wind sector in 2003 by purchasing Enron's wind turbine division in the aftermath of Enron's accounting scandal and bankruptcy in 2003.[74] Applied Materials, a multinational firm with forty years of experience in producing manufacturing equipment and software for the semiconductor industry, decided to enter the solar PV industry in 2006. The firm had already modified some of its semiconductor equipment for manufacturers of conventional silicon-based solar cells. Anticipating growing markets for thin-film solar technologies, it embarked on a series of acquisitions to establish a solar PV division that could serve both traditional silicon and thin-film solar manufacturers. In 2006, Applied Materials invested USD 464 million to purchase Applied Films Corp, a producer of thin-film deposition equipment.[75] In 2007, it acquired two

---

[70] Rogowsky and Laney-Cummings 2009, 11.
[71] Spada 2010. See also Brian Rogal, 2012, "Foundries Twisting in Breeze over Wind Tax Credit," *Midwest Energy News*, March 27.
[72] Baker 2010; Rogowsky and Laney-Cummings 2009, 9–10.
[73] Platzer 2012a, 7.
[74] Lewis 2013, 95; Windpower Monthly 1997.
[75] Mark LaPedus, 2006, "Applied Materials Enters Solar Gear Markets," *EE Times*, May 4. http://www.eetimes.com/document.asp?doc_id=1161175 (accessed November 14, 2020).

European manufacturers of solar PV production equipment.[76] In 2009, the US start-up Advent Solar joined the Applied Materials portfolio.[77] In addition to these acquisitions, the firm's in-house venture capital fund, Applied Ventures, invested smaller sums in start-up companies whose technologies were not yet mature.[78]

Other multinationals followed Applied Materials' diversification into renewable energy sectors. In 2011, Dupont Chemical bought the Silicon Valley start-up Innovalight to expand its materials portfolio for the solar industry. As I mentioned earlier, Innovalight had previously received funding from NERL and the DOE to develop a silicon ink and first commercialized the technology through a joint development agreement with the Chinese firm JA Solar. Dupont's acquisition thus occurred after the technology was fully commercialized, thereby allowing Dupont to benefit from a decade of R&D activities without incurring technology risk.[79] Dow Chemical, which had participated in federally funded research consortia to develop building-integrated solar PV technologies and had received USD 20 million from the DOE for research into new types of solar arrays, struggled with delays in the commercialization of its technologies. In 2013, Dow Chemical acquired NuvoSun, a California start-up producing solar shingles for rooftop applications. NuvoSun's technology was ripe for commercialization, but the firm had struggled to fund the expansion of its manufacturing facilities to achieve scale economies.[80]

In the wind industry, growing domestic markets encouraged foreign wind and solar manufacturers to set up production facilities in the United States. Some of these manufacturers persuaded their European suppliers to join them. The Spanish wind turbine producers Acciona and Gamesa were among the first foreign wind firms to open manufacturing plants in the United States.[81] Siemens,

[76] Katie Fehrenbacher, 2007, "Applied Materials to Buy Italian Solar Equipment Maker for $330M," *Gigaom*, November 19. http://gigaom.com/2007/11/19/applied-materials-to-buy-italian-solar-equipment-maker-for-330m/ (accessed April 14, 2014).

[77] Josie Garthwate, 2009, "Applied Materials Buying Advent Solar Assets, Cheap," *Gigaom*, November 6. http://gigaom.com/2009/11/06/applied-materials-buying-advent-solar-assets-cheap/ (accessed April 14, 2014).

[78] Applied Ventures Brochure, 2014. See http://www.appliedmaterials.com/sites/default/files/AV_Handout_0812.pdf (accessed March 27, 2014). In its solar business, Applied Materials bet almost entirely on the future success of thin film solar technologies, which ultimately were unable to compete on price with the rapidly falling cost of traditional silicon-based PV technologies. See Nemet 2019, 126.

[79] Nahm and Steinfeld 2014, 297. See also Kevin Bullis, 2011, "DuPont Inks a Deal to Improve Solar Cells," *MIT Technology Review*, August 1.

[80] Department of Energy, 2008, "DOE Selects 13 Solar Energy Projects for up to $168 Million in Funding," http://energy.gov/articles/doe-selects-13-solar-energy-projects-168-million-funding (accessed March 27, 2014.) Ucilia Wang, 2013, "Dow Chemical Buys NuvoSun for Making Solar Shingles," *Forbes*, March 7. Emma Hughes, 2009, "New Product: Dow Chemical Introduces Solar Shingle BIPV," *PV-Tech*, October 09. www.pv-tech.org/product_reviews/new_product_dow_chemical_introduces_solar_shingle_bipv.

[81] Rogowsky and Laney-Cummings 2009, 4.

which had opened a manufacturing site for turbine blades in Iowa in 2007, established a full assembly plant in Kansas in 2010, one year after the American Recovery and Reinvestment Act had extended federal support for wind turbine deployment. Nordex of Germany started local production in the same year.[82] A number of European suppliers of turbine components established US manufacturing plants in the years that followed. These multinational suppliers included the blade producer LM, the gearbox manufacturers Winergy, Hansen, and Moventas, and the Portuguese tower firm Martifer. Local manufacturers that diversified from other industries—such as machine tool firm K&M, transmission firm Brad Foote, and blade manufacturer TPI Composites—remained the exception.[83]

Global Partners

US wind and solar firms made inventing new technologies a priority despite the absence of large domestic supply chains that could provide matching technological capabilities, components, and production experience. Where clusters of renewable energy firms emerged in the United States, they were frequently made up of start-ups pursuing similar strategies, not functionally diverse groups of firms with complementary skills. In Northern California, for instance, the density of venture capital funds and research universities created advantageous conditions for start-ups; but the area did not attract a network of vertically differentiated suppliers.[84] Instead, collaborative advantage—and the ability to specialize because of new opportunities for collaboration—allowed wind and solar firms in the United States to work with global partners on technology commercialization and the scale-up to mass production. In the best case, America's research and development infrastructure brought its fruits to market through such collaborative relationships, benefiting not just US firms and institutions but a range of global actors, each of which contributed skills and bore associated risks. In the worst case, start-up firms failed to find complementary capabilities in global supply chains, abruptly ending the trajectory from lab to market even for promising technologies.

In the hunt for global partners, large multinational firms—many of which had acquired start-ups to enter renewable energy—enjoyed an advantageous position. Many already benefited from global supply networks and possessed resources to manage their global links. Large firms could also internalize tasks

---

[82] Platzer 2012b, 32.

[83] Platzer 2012b, 32; Rogowsky and Laney-Cummings 2009, 9–10.

[84] Böttcher 2010, 16–24; Colatat, Vidican, and Lester 2009, 5–7.

that they could not find in global supply chains or that local institutions did not support. GE, for instance, the only large US wind turbine manufacturer, entered the wind energy sector through the purchase of Enron's wind turbine division during Enron's bankruptcy in 2003.

This acquisition gave GE immediate access to the turbine technologies under Enron's portfolio, including those of Zond, US Windpower, and the German manufacturer Tacke.[85] Zond's variable speed wind turbines, which had originally been developed at the University of Massachusetts, Lowell, and matured through collaboration with DOE and the national wind power program at NREL, provided the foundation for GE's turbine business. Enron's foreign assets, including the German manufacturer Tacke, further contributed patents, technologies, and supplier networks.[86] In addition to taking on 1,600 employees and production facilities in Germany and Spain, where large wind energy markets already existed, GE's purchase of Enron's wind energy division included turbine technologies that had been developed over decades of federal R&D support: GE was able to build on three decades of federally funded wind turbine R&D without incurring any of the initial technological risks itself.[87]

Despite having ceased the in-house development of utility-scale wind turbines when federal research support dried up during the 1980s, the purchase of Enron's wind assets allowed GE to quickly become one of the largest wind turbine manufacturers in the world. By 2005, GE held 61 percent of the US market for wind turbines.[88] To further improve its wind turbine technology, GE conducted both in-house R&D and acquired start-ups with specialized technologies. In 2011, for instance, GE purchased the tower manufacturer Wind Tower Systems LLC, to access its proprietary technology for the construction of low-cost wind turbine towers of more than 300 feet.[89]

GE retained the relationships with German gearbox suppliers such as Eickhoff, Winergy, and Bosch Rexroth, which had previously supplied Tacke. GE continued to source generators from VEM Sachsenwerke and maintained an R&D facility in Munich, Germany, to coordinate the development of new components with its European suppliers. Its membership in the German Engineering Federation's (VDMA) wind chapter allowed GE to participate in collaborative research activities conducted among German suppliers.[90] At the same time, GE began expanding its global supplier network, sourcing blades from Brazil and

[85] Mazzucato 2013, 148.

[86] Lewis 2013, 95; Windpower Monthly 1997.

[87] Mazzucato 2013, 148–49.

[88] Gleitz 2006, 1.

[89] Ehren Goossens, 2011, "GE Acquires Wind Tower Systems to Build Taller Wind Turbine Towers," *Bloomberg*, February 11.

[90] VDMA website, http://wind.vdma.org/en/article/-/articleview/599526 (accessed March 15, 2013). Author interview, German Engineering Federation, May 25, 2012.

metal castings and gearboxes from China, where it also maintained an R&D facility.[91] Strong institutional and financial capabilities allowed GE not only to systematically identify potential suppliers and collaborators, but also made possible the assignment of engineering staff to the production facilities of its partners. A Chinese manufacturer that developed gearboxes in collaboration with GE reported a permanent presence of GE design and manufacturing engineers on site to improve product designs and supervise manufacturing processes.[92] Even as it advertised itself as the "American" wind turbine manufacturer, GE's local content rates were among the lowest in the industry.

The resources to manage a global supply chain allowed GE to focus on assembly and research in the United States while sourcing the majority of components internationally. Local content rates for GE turbines assembled in the United States remained lower than those of its foreign competitors, many of which had established local component production.[93] As a consequence, approaches to reduce gearbox wear through novel lubricants, which GE's predecessor, Zond, had developed in collaboration with NREL, were introduced and carried out in Chinese gearbox manufacturing plants.[94] GE continued to participate in federally funded research—collaborating, for instance, with NREL and Virginia Tech on developing new blade designs through a project funded by ARPA-E—yet it was less dependent than other manufacturers on finding local partners for implementation of the results.[95]

Large suppliers such as Applied Materials maintained similarly global relationships to commercialize their products. In 2009, Applied Materials opened a solar technology R&D center in China, not primarily to source components, but to improve solar PV production technologies in collaboration with China's growing number of solar manufacturers.[96] With US start-ups working on disruptive technologies not yet in mass production, Applied Materials looked to China's 120 solar manufacturers to partner on the incremental improvement of silicon and thin-film solar PV technologies. In 2011, Applied Materials announced a new selective emitter product developed in its

[91] Author interview, head engineer of Chinese gearbox manufacturer, August 26, 2011. "Tecsis Signs US$1bn Wind Turbine Blade Deal with GE," *Business News Americas*, December 4, 2006, http://www.bnamericas.com/news/electricpower/Tecsis_signs_US*1bn_wind_turbine_blade_deal_with_GE (accessed April 14, 2014).

[92] Author interview, head engineer of Chinese gearbox manufacturer, August 26, 2011; December 5, 2016.

[93] Rogowsky and Laney-Cummings 2009, 9, 20.

[94] NREL, 2010, "Wind Turbine Design Innovations Drive Industry Transformation," http://www.nrel.gov/docs/fy10osti/47565.pdf (accessed March 27, 2014).

[95] NREL, 2013, "Fabric-Covered Blades Could Make Wind Turbines Cheaper and More Efficient," http://www.nrel.gov/wind/news/2013/2066.html (accessed March 27, 2014).

[96] Katherine Bourzac, 2009, "Applied Materials Moves Solar Expertise to China," *MIT Technology Review*, December 22.

R&D facility in China. The Italian firm Baccini, acquired by Applied Materials in 2007, contributed the underlying production technology, but this technology was subsequently tested and fine-tuned in the manufacturing plants of Chinese PV producers, who used components and materials developed by Honeywell in the United States.[97]

Applied Materials found less success developing manufacturing technologies for thin-film lines. A plan to build turnkey production lines for thin-film cells—based on the core technologies of several US start-up firms it had acquired—failed when falling silicon prices bolstered the competitiveness of conventional silicon cells.[98] The firm's 2010 exit from the thin-film business effectively ended research and development on a technology that had received USD 300 million in federal research funding.[99] Because its thin-film division was based on global relationships, the consequences of Applied Material's exit reverberated far beyond the United States. With few prospects for further technology improvements, early adopters of Applied Materials' thin-film production lines, such as the Chinese firm Suntech, closed their thin-film divisions as Applied Materials shuttered its thin-film division in China.[100]

Yet smaller wind and solar start-ups *also* benefited from global supply chains to find complementary capabilities, even if their limited institutional and financial resources precluded the type of global supply chain management common to multinational corporations. Since venture capital funds were rarely willing to fund investments in capital-intensive manufacturing facilities, and since start-up firms frequently lacked production experience, these start-ups frequently sought knowledge in scale-up and mass production, not access to technology, from global partners. Innovalight had received funding from the DOE and had collaborated with the NREL to apply its technology to the solar sector. Neither the federal research infrastructure nor the American solar industry could supply the type of production skills required to apply the silicon ink to large-scale manufacturing. Before SolarWorld, a German solar manufacturer, constructed a manufacturing plant for silicon-based solar PV technologies in 2008, almost all US solar plants were producing thin-film solar PV technologies, which were incompatible with Innovalight's product. A plan to build its own production facility faltered when venture capital funders refused to invest the sums required for a manufacturing plant.

---

[97] "Advisory: Applied Materials Reports Innovations in Solar Cell Manufacturing at SCNEC," *Reuters*, February 21, 2011.

[98] Jennifer Kho, 2010, "Applied Materials and the $1.5 Billion Sunfab Flameout," *Fast Company Magazine*, December.

[99] Gallaher, Link, and O'Connor 2012, 31–34.

[100] Michael Kanellos, 2010, "Suntech Abandons Thin Film, Wafer Experiments," *Greentech Media*, August 6, http://www.greentechmedia.com/articles/read/suntech-abandons-thin-film-experiments-revenue-up-for-2q (accessed April 14, 2014).

Ultimately, Innovalight, like many of its peers, looked to China for a partner to commercialize its technology.[101] It joined forces with JA Solar, which had a production line designated to manufacturing research and the production capabilities necessary to integrate Innovalight's silicon ink. With few engineers and depleted finances, it is unlikely that Innovalight was able to conduct a systematic search for potential partners. Rather, JA Solar's close connections to Silicon Valley facilitated the match. JA Solar's CEO at the time, Peng Fang, had completed his PhD at the University of Minnesota, conducted research as a postdoctoral student at the University of California, Berkeley, and had worked for Applied Materials and the semiconductor firm AMD in Silicon Valley before returning to China.[102] Innovalight's CEO, Conrad Burke, was also a Silicon Valley veteran, suggesting that the two firms were able to broker a collaboration through the networks of Northern California's start-up clusters.[103] The partnership between the two firms resulted in the successful commercialization of Innovalight's silicon ink technology, eventually leading to Innovalight's acquisition by Dupont.

Other start-ups followed a similar strategy, building personal ties to China in search of complementary skills—albeit in componentry. Ogin, the Massachusetts wind turbine company that developed the jet-engine turbine design, hired Lars Anderson in 2010; Anderson had previously managed the China business of Denmark's multinational turbine manufacturer Vestas.[104] Unable to find customized components for the novel turbine design in the US wind power supply chain, Ogin hoped its new CEO's familiarity with the Chinese supply chain would help identify suitable suppliers.[105] Ogin subsequently opened an R&D and component sourcing facility in Beijing to facilitate collaboration with Chinese partners.[106]

The CEO of a Silicon Valley solar start-up that had opened a production facility within China with local partners explained that Northern California gave the firm access to trained engineers, test facilities, and the technological expertise of universities and research laboratories. In China, however, the firm found manufacturing engineers with experience in the rapid scaling of new technologies. The density of solar manufacturers in China had also created a local market for used manufacturing equipment, which the firm could buy cheaply and subsequently repurpose to test and produce its thin-film technology. An abundance of local suppliers permitted the solar start-up's production engineers to easily try new materials and work with partners to improve the manufacturing process.

---

[101] Nahm and Steinfeld 2014, 297.
[102] "Peng Fang: Executive Profile," 2014b.
[103] "Conrad Burke: Executive Profile," 2014a.
[104] Gertner 2013.
[105] Author interview, Ogin engineer, November 30, 2010.
[106] US–China Energy Cooperation Program 2014.

Although the CEO insisted that basic research should stay in Silicon Valley for the time being, he expected more and more research staff to move to the Chinese facilities, as cost reductions through improvements to the manufacturing process were becoming more important over time.[107]

Although start-ups were able to find partners in global supply chains, managing R&D activities through such relationships posed considerable difficulties for smaller firms. Evergreen, an MIT spinoff that began the development of string-ribbon manufacturing technologies for solar wafers in the early 1990s, was unable to find US partners willing to adjust their production practices to Evergreen's nonstandard wafer size. Evergreen's string-ribbon technology lacked the maturity to produce wafers in the standard formats expected by cell manufacturers, a disadvantage that prevented Evergreen from becoming a regular wafer supplier on the global component markets. In 2005, the firm partnered with Norwegian silicon producer REC and German cell manufacturer Q-Cells to set up a manufacturing facility in Germany, where large solar markets existed at the time.[108] For the R&D engineers at the small Massachusetts-based start-up, however, such collaboration required countless trips to Germany, as incremental improvements to the technology had to be tested and implemented in its manufacturing facility. Any changes to wafer production and size necessitated subsequent adjustments of the entire production line, including cell and module manufacturing. R&D engineers involved in the commercialization of the string ribbon technology maintained that the geographical distance between the partners proved challenging for a small firm like Evergreen, slowing technological progress and preventing rapid—albeit incremental— improvements.[109]

Despite more than USD 43 million in grants from the state of Massachusetts, Evergreen's attempts a few years later to localize production in the United States failed, due to the continued high cost of the firm's technology. Evergreen gradually moved its facilities to China in 2009, where it conducted R&D and production in close proximity to a local partner, a manufacturer of cells and modules. Local suppliers of production equipment contributed to cost reductions for Evergreen's proprietary production lines; a greater number of local firms offered opportunities for more rapid incremental improvements for the firm's technology. Even with this change and a wide range of partners, however, Evergreen was unable to stay in business. In 2011, a Chinese investor bought Evergreen for USD 6 million in cash and 7.6 million in stock, a mere fraction of the state R&D funds and production subsidies that the firm had received in the United States.[110]

---

[107] Author interview, CEO of Silicon Valley solar start-up, August 24, 2011; January 6, 2015.
[108] QCells 2005.
[109] Author interviews: former Evergreen engineers, May 16 and October 13, 2011.
[110] Bradsher 2011.

Many start-up firms depended on global partners to commercialize their technologies, yet global relationships were not the only reason US-funded technologies were brought to market abroad. For the wind and solar industries, where the skills and expertise required to bring new technologies from lab to market often resided across multiple firms in far-flung locations, attempts to single-handedly manage the commercialization process could also result in failure. MiaSole, a Silicon Valley manufacturer of high-efficiency thin-film solar modules, had long struggled to scale the manufacturing of its technology. The start-up had received more than USD 500 million in venture financing since its founding in 2004 but was unable to increase its production from 50 MW to 150 MW annually. In 2011, it hired manufacturing experts from INTEL to improve its manufacturing operations. Falling silicon prices, overcapacity in global markets, and difficulties raising further funds to expand its facilities compounded its production problems. In 2012, the Chinese industrial manufacturer Hanergy bought MiaSole for USD 30 million, a fraction of the original VC investment. Although its facilities in California have remained in place for the time being, Hanergy has since begun to scale MiaSole's technology in larger manufacturing plants in China.[111]

As is the case with most disruptive technologies, not all innovations were destined for success, whether firms managed to find global partners or not. Ultimately, changes in the global market environment, technology failures, lack of sufficient financing at critical development junctures, and high production costs prevented many innovations born of US research institutions from finding a home in consumer markets. Start-up firms incurred risks in developing new technologies and bringing them to large-scale production and deployment; many struggled to manufacture their products at a competitive price, even with the help of global suppliers. Prices for conventional wind and solar technologies were falling rapidly, as multinational firms with large manufacturing facilities entered the US market, raising longer-term questions about problems of technology lock-in and the ability of next-generation energy technologies to compete against the products now mass-produced in China.[112] The global financial crisis led many European governments to cut their renewable energy subsidies, causing renewable energy markets to decline in other parts of the world. The discovery of large natural gas reserves in the United States lowered the price of fossil fuels there, increasing the price gap between renewable energy and conventional sources of electricity and offsetting the cost reductions in renewable energy technologies from previous decades.[113] As a result, a wave of bankruptcies shut US

---

[111] Bradsher 2013a.
[112] Bourzac 2009; Hart 2020.
[113] Koch 2014.

high-technology solar firms, and wind turbine producers struggled to stay afloat. Evergreen Solar ceased operations.[114] Solyndra, which had benefited not only from R&D subsidies but also from a sizable loan guarantee to build a large manufacturing facility, declared bankruptcy after the decline in global silicon prices eroded the competitiveness of its products and its venture capital investors withdrew their support.[115] SunPower and First Solar closed manufacturing facilities in the United States and abroad.[116] Out of the 200 solar start-ups that had received venture capital funding by 2008, less than half were still operating as independent businesses by 2013.[117] Where technologies did succeed in traveling the full trajectory from lab to market, they relied on federal support for R&D as much as on the contributions of firms in global supply chains. Gaps in domestic supply chains forced innovators to look outside the United States for engineering capabilities in scale-up and mass production.

Institutions for Invention

The United States has long been the single largest funder of energy research in the world. In 2017 alone, the federal government committed USD 7 billion to energy technology research, development, and demonstration.[118] As I have chronicled in this chapter, such public investments in research did not yield the same domestic industrial development that innovation yielded in the postwar decades. Collaborative advantage allowed firms to focus on capabilities on invention, as they repurposed existing public institutions for research and development to enter renewable energy supply chains. These institutions were originally established to funnel federal R&D funds into the development of new technologies that were assumed to attract complementary capabilities in commercialization and mass production into the US economy. Changes in the organization of the global economy severed those ties and allowed firms to enter renewable energy sectors without building the full range of skills required to take new technologies from lab to market. Institutions that were really intended to support much broader sets of industrial activities—those that promoted the visits of worldwide government groups to Silicon Valley referenced in the introduction to this book—were instead used by firms to support specialization in invention without these the development of such complementary skills.

---

[114] Turner 2011.
[115] Mazzucato 2013, 129–32.
[116] Leone 2012.
[117] Wesoff 2013.
[118] IEA 2019, 108.

The federal R&D infrastructure influenced the development of American renewable energy sectors in two central ways. First, American wind and solar firms—start-ups as well as the multinational companies that in many cases acquired the smaller tech firms—utilized the federal innovation infrastructure to access core technologies by deploying institutions for technology transfer dating back to the 1980s. As part of a series of legislative changes that eased the flow of technologies from universities to the private sector, the Bayh-Dole Act of 1980 permitted universities and research institutes to patent discoveries that resulted from federally funded research and to offer exclusive licenses to third parties. The Bayh-Dole Act was just one of series of legislative changes that spurred increased university patenting and licensing over following decade.[119] In 1965, fewer than 200 patents were granted to American universities; by 1988, more than 1,000 patents were granted to universities annually, as universities enjoyed permission to commercially exploit the results of their research through patents and licensing. By 1993, many US universities and research institutes had established designated technology transfer and licensing offices and jointly held more than 4,000 active license agreements with firms, together generating USD 375 million in royalties.[120]

In Germany, a network of publicly funded applied research centers, the Fraunhofer Institutes, offered consulting services to private sector firms. The content of research collaborations was determined by the consulting clients, whose fees covered part of the cost. In renewable energy industries, such clients were manufacturers of equipment and components.[121] In the United States, by contrast, the legislative framework to encourage technology transfer allowed wind and solar firms to access technologies created with the help of vast federal investments in renewable energy research. It also provided incentives for researchers to follow innovative technologies to private sector firms. The private sector did not set research priorities, however—universities and federal research programs held that authority. Consequently, much research targeted the invention of new technologies, including the next-generation solar PV technologies and novel turbine designs discussed at the beginning of this chapter.

These firms retained close links to research institutes and universities and were often physically located near the institutions that had hosted the original research. First Solar (then named Solar Cells Inc.) was founded in 1990 in Toledo, Ohio, as the first commercial manufacturer of thin-film solar cells, a technology that reduced the use of silicon by depositing a thin layer of PV

---

[119] Patents could be licensed, but private sector firms could not purchase the patents. Mowery et al. 2001, 102. For a discussion of the extensive legislative changes that transformed university–private sector knowledge transfer during the early 1980s, see Mowery et al. 2004.

[120] Henderson, Jaffe, and Trajtenberg 1998, 120–21.

[121] Fraunhofer ISE 2017, 24.

material on alternate substrates. Its initial facilities were located on the campus of the University of Toledo, where collaboration between First Solar and university laboratories was funded by federal and state-level research grants.[122] Similarly, SunPower was founded in 1991 by a Stanford University engineering professor named Richard Swanson. SunPower's core technology offered a new approach to creating high-efficiency solar cells that used all-back contacts to increase energy output. The research for the all-back contacts at Stanford had been funded by DOE and NREL. SunPower financed its first facility with grants from DOE, the Electric Power Research Institute, and venture capital financing.[123] In 1994, MIT professor Emanuel Sachs spun off Evergreen Solar to commercialize a new manufacturing technology for solar wafers. Evergreen employed a so-called string-ribbon technology to manufacture thin solar wafers without cutting them from large silicon blocks, thereby preventing material loss from wire-sawing prevalent in traditional wafer manufacturing.[124]

In addition to providing core technologies, the US research and development infrastructure offered a financial lifeline for start-ups that had already spun off from universities and research institutes but struggled to access funding. Throughout the 1990s, the absence of subsidies for the large-scale deployment of renewable energy technologies in the United States made it difficult for start-up firms to generate revenue from their products. Financial institutions, in particular venture capital funds, resisted funding long-term R&D without a clear prospect of market demand—without government subsidies, even advanced wind and solar technologies were not cost-competitive with fossil fuels.[125] To stay afloat, the majority of start-up firms continued to rely on government research grants for funding and, as a consequence, few were able to invest in capital-intensive mass production facilities as a result of their limited budgets. In the 1990s, SunPower collaborated with NASA to develop a solar-powered airplane.[126] Others, such as the wind turbine manufacturer Zond, worked with utilities to build small demonstration facilities.[127] US research and development programs thereby became a lifeline for firms whose research had advanced beyond initial-stage R&D but was not yet ready for mass production. Between 1991 and 2008, the DOE invested USD 289 million in manufacturing R&D for new solar technologies as part of the PVMaT program. The program supported several solar PV start-ups, including Evergreen, throughout the 1990s when

[122] American Energy & Manufacturing Partnership 2013, 12.
[123] Swanson 2011, 537–38.
[124] For an explanation of how Evergreen's string-ribbon technology differs from conventional solar cell manufacturing practices, see Wallace et al. 1997.
[125] Moore and Wüstenhagen 2004, 243.
[126] Swanson 2011, 539–45.
[127] Department of Energy 2003.

commercial markets were small.[128] A separate program existed for thin-film cell technologies. In the wind sector, too, federal funds remained critical to keeping firms afloat.[129] For instance, Zond, one of two wind turbine manufacturers that had survived the end of California's wind power subsidies in the mid-1980s, received DOE funding for research on large wind turbines in 1995.[130]

Unlike German family-owned businesses, US start-ups did not have long-standing relationships with local banks. The United States also lacked the public infrastructure and policy banks that funded manufacturing expansion in China. Few US financial institutions were willing to invest in emerging, high-risk renewable energy sectors. This changed in the early 2000s, when prospects for global renewable energy markets rose—the result of government policies in the United States and elsewhere. This rosier outlook, in turn, encouraged venture capital funders to support renewable energy start-ups, especially in the solar sector. The percentage of government R&D funding as a share of overall investment in solar energy technologies dropped from 90 percent in 2001 to less than 10 percent in 2007 as private investment increased exponentially.[131] Global venture capital investment in clean energy technologies multiplied from USD 200 million in 2000 to USD 2.5 billion by 2007; US-based venture capital funds investing in US start-ups accounted for 82 percent of overall VC investment in renewable energy. Some 150 renewable energy start-ups received venture capital funding in Silicon Valley alone.[132] By 2011, US venture capital firms invested USD 11 billion in American clean technology businesses, compared to USD 9 billion globally.[133] The combination of global markets and domestic capital prompted a new wave of industry entry, particularly in the solar sector, where cumulative federal R&D funding had continually surpassed investments in wind turbine research and new technologies were ready for commercialization.[134] New entrants clustered close to major research institutions and venture capital firms, with California and Massachusetts emerging as two centers of start-up activity.

But venture capital funding for the renewable energy industry remained insufficient to meet capital needs. After peaking in 2008, venture capital investment decreased, dropping to USD 2 billion by 2013. The number of renewable energy start-ups that successfully vied for funding dropped from 75 in 2007 to 24 in 2013. Increasingly, venture capital funds focused on later-stage technologies and avoided early-stage projects with long development horizons and uncertain

[128] O'Connor, Loomis, and Braun 2010, 3–11.
[129] O'Connor, Loomis, and Braun 2010, 3–14.
[130] Department of Energy 2003.
[131] Jennings, Margolis, and Bartlett 2008, 8.
[132] Gaddy, Sivaram, and O'Sullivan 2016, 2; Jennings, Margolis, and Bartlett 2008, 9.
[133] Mazzucato 2013, 127.
[134] Jennings, Margolis, and Bartlett 2008, 8.

future payoffs.[135] Against a backdrop of waning enthusiasm—coupled with widespread doubt about the ability of energy start-ups to produce the returns common in the software industry—wind and solar start-ups continued to experiment with federal R&D programs and other federal subsidies to stay afloat. ARPA-E, a federal program to support the commercialization of high-risk energy technologies, provided USD 130 million to 66 start-up firms and university labs in its first round of funding, including the MIT spinoff 1366 Technologies and the wind turbine manufacturers Ogin.[136] Other firms received grants and technical assistance from NREL and the DOE, which supported, for instance, Clipper's work to develop a turbine for low wind speeds between 2002 and 2006, covering half of the USD 19 million in R&D expenses to develop a prototype.[137] Similarly, DOE's Thin-Film Partnership program, first established in the 1990s, funded the pilot production of thin-film modules through 2008.[138] The American Recovery and Reinvestment Act provided USD 1.3 billion in loan guarantees to four solar start-ups—Solyndra, 1366 Technologies, Abound Solar, and SoloPower—to help fund investments in production facilities.[139]

Although venture capital funds played a critical role by allowing start-up firms to test and improve their early-stage products after they had left their home universities and research institutes, the basic technologies of most start-up firms sprang from federally funded research. Not only did federal R&D support encourage the development of new renewable energy technologies but federal research grants provided an important source of revenue for start-ups that had not yet found markets for their technologies. For further testing and improvements to their technologies, firms relied on resources and technical expertise provided through national laboratories. Investments in the riskiest technologies—very early research in fields with no clear market application—were thus made by the state. Venture capital funders wanted little part of this action. They shied away from investing in the highest-risk early-stage R&D, as well as the capital-intensive manufacturing facilities required for scale-up and mass production. Instead, they supported technologies that had achieved sufficient maturity to leave the university and that had an established path toward commercialization.[140] Ultimately, the large number of start-ups in the US wind and solar sectors responded to renewable energy policies by using legacy research institutions of the federal government.

[135] Gaddy, Sivaram, and O'Sullivan 2016, 2–3.
[136] ARPA-E 2009; Wald 2011.
[137] Hamilton 2011, NREL 2012.
[138] O'Connor, Loomis, and Braun 2010, 3–17.
[139] Brown 2011, 4.
[140] Mazzucato 2013, 127–29.

US strengths in innovation without capabilities in scale-up and mass production did not result from global competitive pressures and the disadvantages of a high wage environment. Strong research and development institutions did not by themselves result in broader industrial outcomes because federal policies were not complemented by policy support for the type of bottom-up industrial change that brought production capabilities to China's and Germany's renewable energy supply chains. Absent an industrial base of firms with skills applicable to the commercialization and production of wind and solar technologies and lacking the types of institutional support—including skills and training institutions, financing, and collaborative research opportunities—that could help smaller firms apply their capabilities to new industrial sectors, the US start-ups relied on collaboration in the global economy to reproduce historical strength in the invention of new technologies.

Conclusion

Just as the wind and solar sectors in Germany and China reproduced the industrial capabilities of the broader economy by employing collaborative advantage, so US R&D capabilities also benefited from policy support beyond the domain of renewable energy policy. US renewable energy firms used broad institutional support for high-technology research, including a legal framework that facilitated spinoffs (and licensing of the results of federally funded research) and a large venture capital community willing to invest in high-risk technology projects. These resources allowed for large numbers of high-technology start-ups, the majority of which focused on the development of disruptive renewable energy technologies that had originated in federally funded research programs.

Federal and state-level policies jointly created large markets for wind turbines and solar PV technologies, yet US start-up firms were not accompanied by comprehensive domestic supply chains focused on scale-up and manufacturing. A weak supplier base in adjacent industries reduced the number of firms that could enter wind and solar supply chains. Absent a vibrant industrial base and lacking the types of institutional support—including skills and training institutions, financing, and collaborative research opportunities—that could help smaller firms apply their capabilities to new industrial sectors, the United States reproduced its historical strength in the invention of new technologies without creating the vertically integrated industries that had originally motivated public spending on R&D.

The presence of collaborative advantage allowed firms to look for partners with complementary skills outside the United States. Firms in Germany and China possessed precisely the types of skills required to bring new energy technologies to market, and many American firms relied on global partners to commercialize their technologies. In practice, however, such global linkages proved easier to maintain for large, multinational corporations than for the high-tech start-ups that spun off universities and research institutes. Firms like GE and Applied Materials, which could quickly enter new industrial sectors through the acquisition of start-up firms, systematically matched their own capabilities with complementary skills in global supply chains. For smaller start-up firms, finding such partners required considerably more effort. With limited financial and human resources, such global collaborations were equally hard to maintain over time.

Governments around the world have attempted to replicate American strength in technological innovation. Despite outsized public investments in renewable energy research and development, however, the US specialization in invention has not generated vertically integrated domestic industries. In 2016, some 777,0000 Americans were employed in renewable energy sectors, making wind and solar some of the fastest growing sources of employment in the country. But less than a quarter of employment in the wind industry and a fraction of jobs in the solar sector were related to manufacturing.[141] The vast majority of jobs resided in the construction, operation, and maintenance of wind turbines and solar panels—products that in most cases contained technologies originally invented in the United States, but commercialized and produced in other parts of the world. New options for industrial specialization in the global economy allowed German and Chinese firms to maintain manufacturing-based industrial specializations. In the United States, by contrast, integration into global networks of innovators enabled firms to cut ties from the domestic manufacturing economy.

The fragmentation of domestic wind and solar sectors into firms with varying business interests and different domestic ties prevented US renewable energy industries from mounting a concerted lobbying effort in support of favorable policies against the opposition from vested interests.[142] Start-ups without capabilities in commercialization, multinational firms reliant on global markets and international suppliers, and international manufacturers without roots in the United States pursued individual political strategies. A key consequence of the American prioritization of invention over commercialization was the notably small size of the US manufacturing lobby in renewable energy sectors. In the wind industry, local content rates for US-manufactured wind turbines— even though they gradually increased over time—remained below 50 percent, even as the United States became the largest wind power market in the world.

---

[141] IRENA 2017, 14.
[142] Stokes 2020.

Local content rates improved after 2012, as larger turbine sizes over time made transportation more costly and motivated manufacturers to produce closer to end market. Yet they remained well below the rates of 80 or more achieved in Germany and China, and in some cases they dipped as low as 20 percent for individual turbine components.[143]

In the solar sector, where US firms and research institutes developed the foundations for virtually all of the main solar technologies in production today, US firms accounted for less than 5 percent of global manufacturing in 2010. New technologies were brought to market in other parts of the world, and key components for domestic solar PV manufacturing—including wafers, thin-film feedstock, and inverters—were imported from abroad. Although employment in renewable energy sectors has soared over the past decades, only a small share of this workforce today is employed in the development, commercialization, and production of wind and solar technologies. The DOE estimated that, in 2016, 373,807 Americans worked at least part-time in the solar industry, yet only 18.5 percent of employment was in manufacturing. The majority of solar jobs revolved around the installation of solar PV facilities, trade, and services for the solar industry.[144]

The fragmentation of industry interests appeared, among other ways, in the failure to mount an effective campaign supporting public subsidies for domestic renewable energy installations. Production tax credits for the wind industry and investment tax credits for the solar industry—the key federal incentive programs to create market demand for renewable energy technologies—had been notoriously volatile for decades. Even as the domestic markets for wind turbines and solar panels grew, they did not fully stabilize. After years of expirations and renewals, the Obama administration renewed the Production Tax Credit for three years in 2009. Again, it was not made permanent; and its renewal was as contested in 2012 as in previous years. The PTC was renewed for one year the day after it expired in 2012, yet wind turbine installations slowed dramatically in 2013.[145] The tax credit lapsed for 11 months in 2014, before a five-year extension and gradual phase-out of the wind tax credit was passed with bipartisan support in 2015.[146] But the damage was done: the uncertainty of previous years had already caused a number of turbine manufacturers, including the start-up firm Clipper, to close facilities and lay off staff.[147] In the solar sector, a 30 percent investment tax credit had been extended for eight years (starting in 2008) after

[143] AWEA Manufacturing Working Group 2011; David 2009; Nahm and Steinfeld 2014, 292.
[144] Department of Energy 2017a, 37–39.
[145] Barradale 2010, 7699; Schwabe, Cory, and Newcomb 2009, 8. Christopher Martin, 2013, "U.S. Wind Power Slumps in 2014 after Tax Credit Drives 2012 Boom," *Bloomberg*, October 31.
[146] Department of Energy 2015, 38; Mai et al. 2016.
[147] Diane Cardwell, 2012, "Tax Credit in Doubt, Wind Power Industry Is Withering," *New York Times*, September 30.

several one-year-renewals.[148] In 2015, the solar investment tax credit was extended by five years. The extension stipulated a gradual phase-out in line with the policies for the wind industry.[149]

Divergent interests among start-ups seeking to find ways to commercialize their technologies, established manufacturers, and developers who relied on cheap imported products also affected trade policy. In the wind sector, a coalition of US manufacturers filed a trade complaint against wind turbine tower companies from China in 2011, leading the International Trade Commission to approve antidumping tariffs in 2013. While the move was applauded by firms with tower manufacturing capacity in the United States, developers of wind farms warned that tariffs wouldn't solve the broader problem of insufficient domestic manufacturing capacity.[150] In 2010, a coalition of solar manufacturers initially succeeded in calling for trade barriers against Chinese solar panels—making their voices heard against the opposition of solar developers and consumer advocates. A "Coalition for Affordable Solar Energy" was not able to prevent the tariffs, which were implemented in 2012. As Chinese manufacturers shifted their manufacturing locations to Malaysia and Taiwan to avoid the tariffs, US solar manufacturers appealed. In 2014, the US Department of Commerce and the International Trade Commission expanded the geographical scope and increased the tariffs in response to the request.[151] While the national industry association for the solar sector, the Solar Energy Industries Association (SEIA), had remained neutral in the initial trade cases, it now began to side with installers in opposition to domestic manufacturers. It did so, for instance, in the case of Suniva, a Georgia-based solar start-up that in April 2017 filed a petition with the US International Trade Commission to seek protection from import competition. SEIA subsequently issued a statement warning that further tariffs would threaten 88,000 jobs in the US solar industry due to price hikes for imported panels.[152]

Historically, strong links between public investments in R&D and the domestic production of at least the early versions of a new product ensured some commonality of interests among firms in a particular industry. Globalization—and the distribution of different types of innovation and manufacturing capabilities across global supply chains—severed the link between public investments in the invention of new technologies and the growth of domestic manufacturing sectors and fragmented the political strategies of domestic firms. The absence of a manufacturing coalition in support of renewable energy policy in the

---

[148] Solar Energy Industries Association 2014.
[149] Mai et al. 2016.
[150] Cardwell 2012; International Trade Administration 2013.
[151] Lewis 2014, 16–17.
[152] Solar Energy Industries Association 2017.

United States is of course not inevitable. In the long-run, the creation of supportive manufacturing institutions in the United States may well change the division of labor in future green industrial sectors, and indeed there is no shortage of proposals for such institutions. In the short-run, however, meeting climate policy goals in the United States will require reliance on technologies that may originate domestically but are at least in part manufactured abroad, which makes ambitious climate policy both harder to pass politically and more difficult to sustain against the opposition from vested interest.

7

Conclusion

For all the urgency surrounding climate change and its potentially catastrophic effects, governments have supported clean energy transitions not just for environmental reasons, perhaps not even primarily so. The tendency to link climate actions with economic goals has not fundamentally changed over the past two decades. In China, the Made in China 2025 Initiative has continued to promote the development of export industries for clean energy technologies. Like China, Germany has begun to pass policies to electrify its transportation sector, not just out of environmental concerns but also to maintain competitiveness of the domestic auto industry. In the United States, debates around the possibility of a Green New Deal have explicitly linked climate policy to broad economic development strategies. In Chapter 2, I showed that political support for public investments required to initiate technological change in the energy sector have long depended on the promise of broader economic benefits, in particular through the creation of domestic renewable energy industries. Against the backdrop of such common political goals, why have nations maintained divergent patterns of industrial specialization and distinct constellations of firms? In the cases examined in this book, governments did not employ fundamentally different industrial policy strategies to support domestic industries, nor did they shield the domestic economy from the forces of globalization to differing degrees.

This book argues instead that the key to explaining the persistent and consequential divergence of national patterns of industrial specialization is an understanding of globalization as primarily a process of collaboration. Globalization allowed for two types of experimental action that enable firms to reap benefits from participating in the global economy: the ability of firms to specialize, thanks to new opportunities for collaboration, and their ability to repurpose existing institutions of the domestic economy. Rather than having to maintain inhouse the skills required to develop, commercialize, and produce wind turbines and solar panels, collaboration allows firms to focus on distinct and narrow sets of capabilities. Under these conditions, even when governments aim to create comprehensive national industries, firms respond with narrow competitive strategies that build on existing skills and prior experience in other industries. As I have shown in the empirical chapters, specialization also allows firms to appropriate and repurpose existing institutions in the domestic economy as part of their effort to compete in new industrial sectors, even when these institutions were originally established to support other sectors of the economy. The impact of collaborative advantage is therefore refracted through distinct institutional legacies, yielding distinct national profiles in the global economy. The concept of collaborative advantage at the heart of this argument reverses the conventional wisdom that has portrayed distinct national political economies as threatened by competition in the global economy. By providing new opportunities for collaboration, globalization allows for persistent and consequential divergence of both domestic institutions and national industrial specializations over time.

Findings

Political economists have often portrayed globalization as a phenomenon of increasing international competition, one with major consequences for the ability of nations to organize distinct domestic political economies. In my third chapter, I developed a theoretical approach to understanding globalization that positions collaboration firmly at the center of firms' engagement with the global economy. I argued that the forces that have prompted concern about heightened competition also put within reach of domestic firms a far greater range of collaborators with diverse skills and capabilities. German equipment producers were able to partner with Chinese wind and solar manufacturers on R&D projects that required production skills not available domestically. Chinese manufacturers were able to work with US start-ups to access core technologies and focus their R&D efforts instead on scaling the production of such technologies, often on German-made production equipment. The distinct strategies of renewable energy firms in different parts of the world became possible precisely because the firms found ways to work together.

Central to this book is *collaborative advantage*, a concept I use to capture the connection between changes in the global economy and the endurance of distinct national industrial specializations. The presence of collaborative advantage in renewable energy sectors allowed renewable energy to find partners for the development and commercialization of new technologies. On the whole, advances in transportation and information technologies made it easier to forge these partnerships, though establishing such connections was certainly more straightforward for some firms than others. China's manufacturers could lure global partners with the promise of a large and rapidly growing domestic economy. American start-ups often lacked international links and relied on far more informal networks to find counterparts for collaboration. Nonetheless, the very existence of other specialized firms in renewable energy sectors allowed wind and solar firms to access capabilities necessary for the development of new technologies in global supply chains. Collaboration thereby relieved firms in these postglobalization industries of the need to establish the full range of skills to bring their products to market and freed up new opportunities for specialization.

Those opportunities, in turn, empowered new strategies for entering renewable energy industries, including the decision to repurpose existing domestic institutions and public resources. In choosing strategies to enter the rapidly growing renewable energy sectors in the late 1990s and early 2000s, firms picked technical skills that made use of existing industrial capabilities, could not easily be bought or licensed in global networks, and enjoyed robust support from existing institutions in the domestic economy. German firms seized the opportunity to develop designated production equipment and off-the-shelf components, Chinese manufacturers identified a need for skills in scale-up and mass production, and US firms recognized the invention of new technologies as their leading edge. Of course, not all firms in each economy followed these patterns exactly: multinational firms at times established a broader range of capabilities, primarily through acquisitions of smaller firms. Some specialized renewable energy firms broke with national blueprints, including some manufacturers in the United States, start-ups in Germany, and makers of production equipment in China. Nonetheless, the majority of wind and solar firms focused on innovative manufacturing in China, customization in Germany, and the invention of new technologies in the United States.

Firms relied on the appropriation and repurposing of familiar public resources at the domestic level—many of which were originally established for legacy industries well before the emergence of renewable energy as a viable industrial sector. These institutions retained value in wind and solar industries precisely because they no longer had to support the full range of activities required to invent and commercialize new technologies within national borders. This was perhaps most obvious in the case of China. Chinese manufacturers learned to use the resources of the production economy to capture a sizable share of global markets through manufacturing innovation, even though domestic institutions did not support the invention of new technologies to the same degree. German equipment producers, collaborating with Chinese partners, boldly built on a set of legacy institutions that many saw as threatened by the competitive forces of globalization, including vocational training institutions, a financial sector centered around local banks, and research and development (R&D) support for the traditional Mittelstand of small and medium-sized businesses.

The impact of collaborative advantage is best studied at the level of the shop floor, from the perspective of the firm. In Chapters 4–6 I examined the emergence of a global division of labor, tracking how firms responded to state industrial policies and which public resources became most important to them in this process. By placing the firm as the center of inquiry, I found that they relied on a far broader range of state-provided resources than is commonly associated with industrial policies for renewable energy sectors. Traditional tools of industrial policy—subsidies, R&D funding, and regulation—allowed the state to mobilize interests behind emerging industries and to encourage firms to enter new sectors. Under conditions of collaborative advantage, however, such sectoral intervention did not fully determine firms' technological specializations. Nor, for that matter, did sectoral industrial policies provide sufficient support to allow them to do so. Rather, firms carved out space for experimentation in their responses to state industrial policies, imagining new ways to specialize and collaborate with others—while at the same time repurposing existing institutions and public resources for application in new industries.

In Germany, where federal policies created large domestic markets for wind turbines beginning in the early 1990s and for solar PV modules beginning in the early 2000s, small and medium-sized suppliers from the machine tools, automotive, and equipment manufacturing sectors entered renewable energy industries in large numbers. Government support for renewable energy markets provided incentives for entry, while collaboration with Chinese manufacturers made it possible for these firms to prioritize narrow, competitive specializations in customization. Skills, training, and labor market institutions, local banks, and an infrastructure for collaborative industrial research supported these firms as they applied their capabilities to new industrial sectors. These supportive institutions had not been established for the purpose of encouraging firms to enter renewable energy industries, of course. But they found new life when they enabled firms from Germany's legacy industries to respond to novel opportunities created by federal energy policies, thereby building new constituents in support of legacy institutions.

Central government policies in China encouraged the emulation of advanced R&D capabilities of foreign companies through R&D funding and by fostering technology transfers from foreign-invested firms. Although domestic wind and solar producers participated in central government science and technology programs, they used government support to establish engineering capabilities in manufacturing. Firms found a helping hand in their endeavors from China's infrastructure for mass manufacturing, which subnational governments often maintained in disregard of central government preferences for advanced R&D. The ability to access components and technologies in global supply chains permitted China's firms to repurpose domestic support for R&D and local policies for manufacturing. The end result was the creation of powerful engineering capabilities in scale-up and commercialization, neither of which had been mastered in other parts of the world.

While wind and solar firms in Germany and China established innovative capabilities very closely linked to production activities, renewable energy firms in the United States focused on the invention of new technologies, often without locating scale-up and commercialization domestically. Regulatory and tax policies supported the creation of domestic markets, yet industrial policy for renewable energy industries primarily took the form of R&D funding for universities and national laboratories for energy research. Also in the United States, specialization allowed firms to take advantage of legacy institutions. Start-ups made use of institutions for the licensing and commercial spin-off of technologies born of federally funded research—institutions created through series of legislative reforms dating back to the 1980s. But these firms were often unable to access skills in scale-up and mass manufacturing in their home country, requiring them to hunt for global partners in order to bring their technologies to market.

Comparative literatures on innovation often share the notion that innovation occurs in distinct national industrial ecosystems. Such research assumes that firms are relying on the institutional arrangements of the domestic economy to establish different types of innovative capabilities, but it is within the domestic economy firm that resources, capabilities, and market opportunities are combined and coordinated. Such coordination takes the form of tight organizational links between R&D and manufacturing in early stages of product development and relies on the resources of the broader economy to create knowledge within the firm.[1] Although existing scholars part ways over which elements of industrial ecosystems stand as most important for innovation outcomes, most still agree that the capabilities required for innovation are established, combined, and coordinated by firms embedded in the domestic industrial base.

Renewable energy industries have not followed these core assumptions in the literature. In both industries, firms collaborated to develop new products with distant partners, leapfrogging, obviating, or reversing the traditional sequence of innovation activities. In doing so, wind and solar firms circumvented the traditional division of labor between industrialized and developing economies and transcended the national economies expected to anchor and support them. Perhaps counterintuitively, globalization allowed firms to craft such distinct and specialized paths for participation in wind and solar industries. In the United States, start-ups maintained capabilities in the *invention* of new technologies, but rarely developed skills in commercialization and mass production.[2] In Germany, wind and solar firms clustered in the development of production equipment and customized components, offering expertise in *customization*.[3] In China, large wind and solar manufacturers focused on *innovative manufacturing*

[1] Hall and Soskice 2001; Nelson 1993; Vernon 1966.
[2] Knight 2011, 176.
[3] Arbeitsgemeinschaft Windenergie-Zulieferindustrie 2012; Germany Trade & Invest 2010, 2011b.

capabilities required for commercialization and scale-up.[4] National diversity in the structures of production and in firms' industrial strengths did not result from the state's ability to successfully protect the domestic economy from the competitive pressures of globalization or sticky institutions constraining firm behavior. The persistent and consequential divergence of national patterns of industrial specialization emerged from aggregate firm decisions to compete through the augmentation of existing industrial strengths, actively renewing and repurposing domestic legacy institutions and public resources in the process.

Collaborative Advantage in Comparative Perspective

Three structural conditions enabled collaborate advantage in renewable energy. As I laid out in Chapter 3, these sectors benefited from the presence of potential partners for collaboration in global supply chains, from firms' ability to engage in collaboration owing to flat hierarchies in global supply chains and a lack of incumbent firms that could prevent access for newcomers, and from governments that tolerated firms' divergence from stated industrial policy goals.

As I have argued, these structural conditions are more likely to be present in sectors that developed after the reorganization of the global economy in the 1990s—my central reason for selecting renewable energy industries for this study. The near-simultaneous development of wind and solar industries in China, Germany, and the United States allowed for the emergence of global supply chains that were necessary for specialization. Over time, such specialization became self-reinforcing, as vertically integrated firms would have had to compete with highly specialized firms across the full range of activities to invent, commercialize, and produce new wind and solar technologies. The lack of incumbent firms in renewable energy sectors allowed new entrants to take full advantage of new opportunities for collaboration. As I noted in Chapter 3, incumbents in other sectors often responded to globalization by defending legacy production structures, raising barriers to new competitors, and controlling access to global supply chains. Wind and solar sectors instead found ways to experiment. As a result, large discrepancies often existed between industrial policy targets and the responses of firms, but governments tolerated firms' divergence from their goals.

The structural conditions for collaborative advantage are, of course, not unique to wind and solar. A growing body of research suggests, for instance, that Chinese firms have been able to acquire knowledge-intensive manufacturing capabilities in the auto and electronics sectors, forging similar patterns of global collaboration even in cases where incumbent firms seek to protect

[4] See Nahm and Steinfeld 2014, 294–98.

preglobalization arrangements. In the automobile industry, among others, the engineering capabilities of Chinese firms have allowed them to create products particularly suited for China's "middle market" (based on cost and function-ality).[5] Although China's automakers are not outcompeting global incumbents for high-end products, the changes to product designs to reduce cost and optimize functionality are not entirely different from the findings presented here, even if their improvements in design and manufacturing process target mid-tier markets. The ability of Chinese automotive suppliers to build such capabilities marks an unintended consequence of the sequencing of China's economic reforms, which first focused on nurturing domestic manufacturing capabilities before allowing foreign direct investment and trade liberalization.[6] At the same time, Western incumbents, established long before the opening of China's economy to foreign firms in the 1980s, prevented Chinese firms from moving into desirable parts of the supply chain.[7] The impact of collaborative advantage in China's auto sector was therefore limited by the presence of incumbent firms and nonhierarchical forms of industrial organization.

In today's automotive sector, incumbent firms appear to be losing—however gradually—their ability to control global supply chains.[8] Technological change, including the growing importance of electronics in engine control and safety equipment, has made auto manufacturers dependent on collaboration with suppliers who offer expertise that automakers historically did not possess (nor did they need to). These changes have only accelerated in the transition to electric vehicles, which introduced new components, including batteries and electric drivetrains. The division of labor in the electric vehicle sector now bears some resemblance to what I have outlined in the renewable energy sectors, as Chinese firms have applied their capabilities in innovative manufacturing to focus on scale-up and mass production. Relying on the same domestic resources that buoyed aspiring wind and solar manufacturers, Chinese firms now control more than two-thirds of the global production capacity for lithium-ion batteries while rapidly reducing the associated costs.[9]

State goals of building comprehensive industries wholly within national borders—particularly in industries deemed critical to national competitiveness—continue to resemble claims about a "clean energy race" that we heard from governments in the mid-2000s. China's share of global production capacity for electric vehicle batteries is similar in scale to China's role in solar PV, but it presents a far different threat to the legacy industries that form

---

[5] Brandt and Thun 2010.
[6] Brandt and Thun 2010, 1571.
[7] Brandt and Thun 2016, 88–90.
[8] Sabel and Herrigel 2018, 236.
[9] Helveston and Nahm 2019, 794.

the backbone of advanced industrialized economies elsewhere. In an interview with *The Financial Times*, Bruno LeMaire, France's finance minister, has argued that "the auto industry is vital to Europe's industrial base. But if it has to import batteries, which account for about 40 percent of the cost of an electric vehicle, Europe risks losing the value-added part of the production chain and the technological knowhow that stems from it. . . . Mobility is a matter of sovereignty."[10] As China reemphasizes its goals of technological independence in the Fourteenth Five-Year Plan, the European Union has forged ahead with initiatives to establish a domestic battery industry to reduce reliance on China.[11] If the development of wind and solar technologies is any guide, however, such industrial policy goals are likely to clash with the economic reality on the ground.

While the politics surrounding the global division of labor in the auto industry clearly differed from early renewable energy sectors—advanced industrial economies were fighting for the survival of existing vertically integrated industries rather than competing for future ones—governments faced a similar divergence between state goals and industrial outcomes. Germany has thus far failed to attract significant battery manufacturing despite government goals to reduce dependence on Chinese imports, yet German suppliers are again specializing in production equipment and complex components. A 2019 trip to a solar supplier I first visited in 2011 revealed that the firm had since used its experience in the development of complex production equipment to develop test equipment for electric vehicle engines. As demand for new production equipment in the solar industry had flattened over time, the firm had shifted much of its production to the electric vehicle sector, where it was building equipment for new assembly plants around the world.[12] In the United States, which lost much of its battery manufacturing industry, start-ups have nonetheless developed new battery chemistries that promise to surpass current lithium-ion technologies in performance.[13] This suggests that globalization created new opportunities for collaboration in the automotive sector, yet these changes were more easily perceived as an economic loss when compared to the vertically integrated domestic supply chains of the past. It remains to be seen whether governments will allow for firm experimentation in response to state industrial policies, the third structural condition of collaborative advantage.

The electronics industry has a shorter history than the automotive sector and has witnessed a more wholesale shift of global manufacturing capacity to East Asia.[14] Research on electronics and semiconductor firms in China suggests that

---

[10] Hall and Milne 2019.
[11] Nahm 2020; Tang 2020.
[12] Author interview, managing partner, Solar PV Supplier. October 15, 2019.
[13] Zaleski 2019.
[14] Pisano and Shih 2009, 2012.

engineering capabilities in manufacturing allowed local firms to improve and reengineer existing products.[15] Similar to the dynamic I describe in the wind and solar industries, electronics and semiconductor manufacturers were able to build such capabilities with the help of local governments, which, due to limited resources, favored investments in the improvement of existing technologies over high-risk technology ventures. Research shows that Chinese firms in these sectors mixed established technologies to come up with new solutions, a tactic that might have to do with the existence of global incumbents in the electronics and semiconductor industries that predated Chinese entrants. Collaborative advantage would predict that such innovation should also be grounded in the ability to access technology in global supply chains and build on the continued support of local governments for mass production. Over time, innovation by Chinese firms in these industries may well turn out to be an integral step along the trajectory from lab to market innovation, as Chinese firms build unique strengths in commercialization and mass production to outcompete manufacturing capabilities in other parts of the world.

This book explains the persistent and consequential divergence of national patterns of industrial specializations by examining China together with two advanced industrialized economies. Comparing the contributions of German and American firms allowed me to identify the role of China's renewable energy manufacturers in collaborative processes of innovation, a role that, in turn, permitted German and Chinese firms to enter the wind and solar industries with highly specialized skills. How do Chinese capabilities in innovative manufacturing stack up against those of other developing economies? Collaborative advantage would predict that firms in other economies should also use collaboration to incrementally build on existing industrial legacies. It is possible that China—with its large domestic market, its extensive support for manufacturing, and its ability to bring partners for collaboration within arm's reach of local firms by attracting foreign direct investment—is uniquely equipped to establish engineering capabilities in manufacturing. But can such upgrading through the repurposing of industrial legacies be replicated in other contexts?

One possibility might be that variations in the existing manufacturing activities of domestic firms affect the specialization of producers. Chapter 4 described how wind and solar suppliers carried Germany's industrial legacy of customization and small-batch production into new economic sectors. Differences in local industrial capabilities, public resources, and institutional support should affect upgrading trajectories in developing economies, as well. In Malaysia, the combination of flexible labor policy and state investments in training institutions attracted semiconductor firms that specialized in making rapid changes to

---

[15] Breznitz and Murphree 2011; Murphree and Breznitz 2020.

production volumes. Semiconductor firms in Penang took advantage of opportunities for collaboration by building on existing strengths in managing such volatility among local producers.[16] The Malaysian state encouraged local firms to develop skills in chip design and early-stage R&D, yet firms built on existing strengths to respond to niche markets instead. For instance, producers of technology-intensive test equipment for flexible production processes utilized local expertise in rapid scale-up and scale-down of production. Although semiconductor manufacturers who specialized in managing volatility were the early collaborators and customers of such equipment producers, their products were eventually sold into global markets.[17]

Another scenario, and one that possibly applies to a larger number of economies, could be that few industrial capabilities exist locally, or that such capabilities remain concentrated in a few sectors shielded from the broader economy. The central argument of this book implies that in such cases, the establishment of innovative manufacturing skills should be significantly more difficult: even at its best, industrial policy can only mobilize firms to incrementally improve on existing strengths. The framework presented in this study correspondingly suggests that firms in this situation are not without recourse, however: they can access manufacturing capabilities through collaboration and still find pathways into global industries. In Vietnam, for instance, the state spent much of its resources on the state-owned sector, which targeted extractive industries, provided little revenue or skill upgrading, and remained shielded from the broader economy. In spite of these state preferences, a growing number of private sector firms in software and services such as e-commerce moved into global supply chains through higher-value activities, without possessing capabilities in physical manufacturing.[18] These firms creatively redeployed resources and policies aimed at the state-owned sector, relied on investment from overseas Vietnamese, and worked with global partners to move into new industries.

India's strength in software and services without accompanying proficiencies in mass production might represent another case of innovation without production. With half of the population employed in agriculture and a small manufacturing sector that historically struggled to compete despite low labor costs, Indian firms built on their strengths in elite education to enter global supply chains. Sixty percent of India's GDP stemmed from firms in services and software.[19] Possibly as a consequence of weak domestic manufacturing capabilities, Suzlon, a global wind turbine manufacturer headquartered in Pune, entered the wind industry not through capabilities in production, but through aggressive

---

[16] Samel 2013.
[17] Samel 2013, 71.
[18] Chirot, Anh, and Steinfeld 2012; Chirot 2016.
[19] Iyer and Vietor 2014, 8–13.

foreign acquisitions funded by its founder, a local textile magnate. Established in 1995, Suzlon purchased R&D subsidiaries in Germany and the Netherlands as well as European gearbox, generator, and blade manufacturers by 2007.[20] Recent research on India's solar industry—a key target of Modi's attempts to spur the development of a domestic manufacturing sector—confirm the difficulty of establishing mass production capabilities in this context. Although the absence of domestic legacies in India's mass production likely precluded the possibility of upgrading trajectories akin to China's, collaborative advantage nonetheless opened opportunities for the nation to participate in innovation—through collaboration for firms unable to draw on local manufacturing strengths.[21]

Prospects for Collaboration

Arguments about national diversity in the global economy are not new to scholars of political economy. Globalization—the increasing interdependence and integration of national economies in global markets—has led many to ask whether competitive pressures, emulation, and the diffusion of best practices in the global economy will ultimately lead to the convergence of national production structures, regulatory institutions, and economic policies. In the 1980s, the weakness of the American economy and the strong performance of firms from Japan and Germany—economies organized around very different relationships between the state, society, and business—raised questions about whether such national differences were here to stay, or whether distinct national practices would eventually give way to global convergence.[22]

Scholars have since pointed to a range of factors that could shield national economies from such pressures. Some have suggested that the importance of domestic markets leaves significant room for continued differences in the organization of production.[23] Others have argued that mutually reinforcing institutional arrangements lead to divergent but stable national political economies, each suitable to different types of production activities.[24] Yet differences in domestic politics and institutions have continued to allow even small, developing economies to craft divergent paths toward the establishment of domestic high-tech firms in global economic sectors.[25]

[20] Lewis 2007.
[21] Behuria 2020, 2.
[22] For an overview of the debates about national diversity in the global economy, see Berger 1996.
[23] Wade 1996.
[24] Hall and Soskice 2001.
[25] Breznitz 2007.

Such scholarship on the diversity of national capitalisms has concerned it-self with options for the state to protect domestic industrial practices from the pressures of the global economy. Central to this book is an argument that, in ef-fect, turns this older position on its head. The global economy is less a threat than an opportunity for collaboration that allows firms to survive, and in many cases to flourish, by maintaining distinct industrial capabilities. In the case of wind and solar industries, this remained true even as governments sought to locate new activities domestically, effectively encouraging some degree of convergence in domestic industrial activity. Such goals took the most obvious form in China, where central government policy very deliberately encouraged the development of R&D capabilities similar to those of firms in the West. Yet China's wind and solar firms, defying these instructions, chose to improve their proficiencies in scale-up and mass production.

In Germany and the United States, governments also hoped that demand-side subsidies, R&D support, and tax credits for manufacturing in renewable en-ergy industries would lead to the development of industrial capacities along the full trajectory from early-stage R&D to mass production. But in practice, this hope played out differently. In Germany, small and medium-sized suppliers of components and manufacturing equipment found far more success by applying their strengths in customization and small-batch production to wind and solar industries than German manufacturers of solar panels, which competed with China's innovative manufacturing skills head-on. In the United States, beset with a weak supplier base, federal R&D support allowed for the renewal of histor-ical strength in early-stage R&D but did not lead to a broad revival for domestic manufacturing. Distinct national strengths in different industrial activities remained, even in new economic sectors where the absence of global incumbents offered firms myriad options for specialization.

Empowered by collaborative advantage in the wind and solar industries, in-ternational economic integration and distinct domestic political economies found themselves in a strong position. They were not locked into a zero-sum game in which states had to actively push back on global competitive pressures to maintain national differences. Entering new industries through collabora-tion allowed firms to choose industrial specializations that were reinforced by existing economic institutions, most established for other purposes before the dawn of renewable energy sectors. By showing how firms picked competitive strategies in the global economy that built on and were buttressed by existing domestic institutions, I have made the case for a firm-based mechanism for insti-tutional endurance: institutions survived because globalization lent them utility in a diverse array of industrial contexts.

The flip side of this equation, however, may be that different economies are not equally suitable to all types of industrial activities. If the specializations that firms choose have roots in past practices, and if sectoral intervention can only incrementally change how firms take advantage of opportunities in new industries, then governments cannot easily encourage firms to match the skills of foreign competitors. Tensions between state goals and economic outcomes became apparent in each of the three cases examined here. The gap between the promise of vertically integrated industries and the reality of economic specialization had political consequences.

In the fall of 2012, the bankrupt California solar start-up Solyndra filed a lawsuit against the three large Chinese solar manufacturers. The suit alleged that Trina, Yingli, and Suntech had conspired to drive Solyndra out of business by selling their panels below cost in the US market. The defendants, the suit claimed, "employed a complex scheme, in collaboration with each other and raw material suppliers and certain lenders, to flood the United States solar market with solar panels at below-cost prices." Coordination among trade associations, government, and the Chinese solar manufacturers had prompted the decision to "export more than 95 percent of their production and dump their products in the United States to achieve market domination."[26] The 2011 Solyndra collapse had followed a string of bankruptcies in the US solar sector. Because it had received USD 500 million in loan guarantees from the US federal government—that is, taxpayer money—Solyndra's failure attracted particular attention. Republicans quickly accused the Obama administration of granting loan guarantees for political reasons. An evaluation conducted by the Department of Energy later found that Solyndra had misrepresented the true state of its financial affairs to the government on several occasions. Concerned about the politics of a US jury trial, China's solar manufacturers eventually settled the case for a fraction of the damages cited in initial court filings without admission of guilt.[27]

Regardless of the accuracy of the allegations, the lawsuit captured broad sentiments about globalization, China's role in renewable energy industries, and the prospects for US competitiveness. The suit claimed that Chinese government support was behind the dominant role of Chinese renewable energy manufacturers in global markets, reflecting arguments also made in other trade cases against China at the time. The suit affirmed notions about China as a highly coordinated industrial policy regime, capable of strategically mobilizing its various administrative branches in pursuit of aggressive state goals to dominate emerging industries. Finally, the suit made the case that the cost advantages of Chinese firms were devastating to US innovation—and that such cost advantages had their basis in nothing but generous state subsidies and differences in factor prices.

[26] Winston & Strawn LLP 2012.
[27] Friedman 2015; Publicover 2016.

Around the same time, manufacturers of solar panels in Germany and the United States started to call for trade barriers to prevent import competition from China.[28] The theory of collaborative advantage suggests that such measures are unlikely to lead to the establishment of innovative manufacturing capabilities in the West. Collaborative advantage requires a combination of global collaboration, local ecosystems for mass production, and central government science and technology policy for success to be realized. Trade barriers work against this type of activity and could effectively ban Chinese solar panels and wind turbine components from entering Germany and the United States. Such barriers might even encourage the relocation of some manufacturing activities. Absent similar industrial ecosystems and institutional legacies, renewable energy producers in the West, "supported" by these trade barriers, will probably not be able to replicate the engineering specializations of their Chinese competitors in the short term.[29]

Even worse effects could be felt in the collaborative processes of technology development that currently span geographical and organizational boundaries. If opportunities for global collaboration, as I have argued, enable firms to focus on existing strengths while relying on partners for complementary capabilities, then trade barriers undermine the very basis on which firms participate in wind and solar sectors. The protests of Germany's component suppliers and manufacturers of production equipment, who vehemently opposed European Union plans to enact antidumping measures against China's solar producers, stemmed from their recognition that their contributions to solar technology development relied on collaboration with these Chinese partners.[30] Although US news outlets in 2013 somewhat gleefully reported the bankruptcy of one of China's largest solar manufacturers, Suntech, the troubles besetting the Chinese solar industry had consequences for technology development in the United States, as well.[31] Applied Materials, the US-based manufacturer of production equipment that had invested large sums in thin-film solar research, all but shut its solar PV division after its Chinese partners ran into trouble, ending lines of research originally funded by US government grants.[32]

Today, each trajectory of industrial specialization lives or dies based on a firm's ability to access complementary capabilities in other parts of the world. Tensions between those who successfully find a niche in global industries and those who suffer from competition in global markets are unlikely to dissipate anytime soon. Differences among these specializations are visible, for instance, in job creation

[28] Bullis 2012.
[29] Helveston and Nahm 2019.
[30] Meckling and Hughes 2017; Wessendorf 2013.
[31] Plumer 2013; Bradsher 2013b.
[32] Tibken 2012.

numbers and the relative ease or difficulty that firms face when trying to enter global networks. US start-ups created far fewer domestic jobs than their Chinese partners or German suppliers. Even if renewable energy sectors yielded employment in installation and maintenance, the lack of a sizable domestic solar manufacturing sector in the United States sparked political discontent. Insertion into global firm networks was also easier for highly networked German firms and Chinese manufacturers, whose large domestic market naturally attracted foreign partners, than it was for small US start-ups without such support.

Although new opportunities for collaboration broadened the range of firms capable of engaging a global division of labor, they did not eradicate concerns about national competitiveness, the global distribution of growth and employment, and the economic returns from domestic industrial specializations. While policymakers may not be able to change the fundamental risks and rewards of each of these specializations, there is a role for the state in helping firms participate in global networks. The challenge might not be to preserve distinct national structures of production against the pressures of globalization or to prevent competition through trade barriers and import tariffs, but rather to make certain that sufficient numbers of domestic firms can apply their capabilities to new opportunities in global industries. Governments should be advised to craft policies that allow for the creative repurposing and firm experimentation that I described in my empirical chapters, without shuttering access to global partners in the misguided hope that new activities will spring up domestically.

Globalization and Climate Change

There is currently little evidence that governments will heed such advice. In China, the controversial "Made in China 2025" policy has dropped from public discourse, but the underlying ambition—technological independence and global dominance in strategic industrial sectors—has continued to guide policymaking in Beijing. China's Fourteenth Five-Year Plan has renewed ambitions to reduce dependence on foreign technologies, called for China to overtake the United States economy by 2035, and laid out goals to become a global leader in innovation for key industrial sectors.[33] In Europe, antiglobalization platforms helped populist parties gain ground in parliaments across the continent. While collaboration with China on energy and climate formed the top of the political agenda during the Obama administration, the 2016 presidential election in the United States gave rise to a neomercantilist mindset in Washington that saw engagement with the global economy as a zero-sum game. Already during

[33] Tang 2020.

the Obama administration, voices across the political spectrum in Washington began making the case for economic decoupling from China, arguing that economic integration had not in fact led China to align with Western political norms and economic practices. The COVID-19 pandemic has significantly accelerated such tendencies, highlighting not only the vulnerability of the world's economic supply chains to external shocks, but also strengthening mercantilist calls for national self-sufficiency in China, the United States, and elsewhere. There is little indication that a Biden administration is planning a drastic course reversal on these issues.[34]

Few industries have more at stake in these battles than those producing clean energy technologies, including the wind turbines and solar panels discussed in this book, but also electric vehicles and lithium-ion batteries that are increasingly needed for electric cars and on-grid storage. As a result of its specialization in innovative manufacturing, China has increased its share of global solar PV production from less than one percent in 2001 to over 60 percent of the world's solar panels today. China now makes more than one-third of global wind turbines, it is the world's largest producer of electric cars, and it commands more than two-thirds of global production capacity for lithium ion batteries.[35] In large part because of China's unprecedented investment in manufacturing in these sectors, the cost of clean energy technologies has fallen sharply. Since 2009, prices for wind turbines and solar panels have decreased by 69 percent and 88 percent, respectively, making these technologies increasingly competitive with conventional sources of energy. This is particularly the case when they are deployed in conjunction with battery storage, where China's massive investments in new manufacturing capacity have also led to rapid cost declines.[36]

As a global problem of unparalleled dimensions, climate change requires a global response, including in the invention, commercialization, and production of technologies that can forge deep decarbonization. In the United States and Europe, policymakers frequently attribute China's rapid rise in clean energy industries to illegal industrial policies, including forced technology transfer, unfair subsidies, and intellectual property theft. Such accusations have led to a series of problematic policy responses, including the ongoing tariff battles with China, both in the United States and in the European Union. Missing from such conversations is an understanding of Chinese manufacturers' critical contributions of knowledge and innovation to the development and commercialization of clean energy technologies that I have outlined in this book.

[34] Farrell and Newman 2020.
[35] Helveston and Nahm 2019.
[36] Lazard 2018.

We already have many of the technologies needed to begin making rapid progress toward reducing carbon emissions, and recent cost reductions of solar and wind—at least in part attributable to Chinese firms—mean that meeting climate goals is becoming ever more affordable. The geography of wind and solar supply chains—some of the first industries to emerge after globalization led to a wholesale reorganization of the global economy in the 1990s—makes collaboration with China fundamental in any effort to avoid the worst consequences of climate change—and, indeed, beneficial to the United States. Meeting the goals of the Paris Agreement will require net-zero emissions by 2050 and substantial reductions before then. Given the limited remaining carbon budget, emissions must have peaked and begun declining by 2030 at the latest. Transportation and power sectors should be decarbonized by 2035 to meet global climate goals.[37] It is unrealistic to expect that any other economy will be able to replicate or surpass China's capabilities in innovative manufacturing and build comprehensive domestic clean energy industries within that dramatically short time frame. This is especially the case in light of the unique institutional framework and industrial legacies that have supported the development of these skills in China over the past thirty years.

As I have shown in this book, collaboration made possible the development of the contemporary renewable energy sectors, including partnerships among American innovators, German equipment manufacturers, and Chinese producers with their skills in rapid scale-up and cost reduction. Trade battles and widespread talk of decoupling have begun to undermine these relationships, even as we need them now more than ever—to bring new technologies to market quickly and efficiently and to deploy them at the scale required to meet our shared climate challenge. If it proves successful, the current pushback against the global division of labor that has undermined the development of clean energy sectors would also thwart human progress on decarbonization, making it highly unlikely that global warming will be contained to levels that allow us to continue life as we currently know it.

Zero-sum approaches to engaging the global economy also obfuscate what countries stand to gain from such relationships beyond the core benefits of collaborative advantage. This is certainly true for US renewable energy industries, which have suffered losses as a result of trade barriers to Chinese technologies first put in place under the Obama administration and then extended under the Trump and Biden administrations. Such trade barriers have not brought manufacturing "back" to the United States. The removal of these barriers and the restoration of open trade relationships is imperative to meeting global climate

[37] IPCC 2018.

goals. And addressing these grand challenges will continue to require advances in science and technology. For the United States, this means building on strengths in invention through investments in R&D. Yet the new technologies that result from such efforts must eventually be commercialized and brought to mass production. Working with German equipment producers and Chinese manufacturers is, for now, the fastest way to bring these technologies from lab to market.

The global division of labor in the industries at the core of this book is not, of course, fixed or inevitable. Collaboration with China means working with and learning from Chinese partners, but in the long run, it can also take the form of new US efforts to improve domestic competitiveness, including in segments of the clean energy supply chains that are currently not well-supported in the US (and German) economies. American competitiveness in these sectors could improve with the help of new resources for domestic firms. These could include, for example, new domestic infrastructure banks to finance manufacturing projects, renewed investments in US vocational training and technical colleges, and stable regulatory frameworks to support domestic markets for clean energy technologies. Resources like these take on even more importance when we note that China, too, continues to engage in technonationalism and to pursue national self-sufficiency in key technology areas.

Yet only long-term investments in clean energy industries will allow the world to change its relationship with China in these industries without jeopardizing global climate goals. Even then, it is unlikely that entire value chains for complex energy technologies would ever lie entirely within national borders. As trade conflicts between China and the United States threaten efforts to strengthen global ties in clean energy industries, we risk losing sight of the climate challenge confronting our world—and risk missing the narrow remaining window we still have to sufficiently reduce global carbon emissions. Collaboration and a global division of labor in these industries is currently the most promising path toward rapid global decarbonization, but it does not preclude investments to shift the balance in these relationships over time. For now, we cannot solve the climate crisis without collaboration with China, and the politics surrounding the COVID-19 pandemic have made such collaboration even more difficult.

Over the past forty years, scholarship on globalization has examined possibilities for the state to protect distinct national practices from the competitive pressures of the international economy. If recent developments are any guide, globalization itself may stand in need of protection in a world where collaboration is both misunderstood and undervalued. Tensions among political promises, economic opportunities, and domestic outcomes are inherent to the globalization process, but today they threaten to undermine international economic integration even where it has led to widespread benefits. The abrupt end to the world's first economic globalization in the early twentieth century should remind policymakers that progress is reversible. Nowhere would the end of collaboration be more consequential than in the clean energy industries we urgently need to solve our global climate crisis.

References

Abernathy, William J., and James M. Utterback. 1978. "Patterns of Industrial Innovation." *Technology Review* 80:40–7.

Abernathy, William J., and Kim B. Clark. 1985. "Innovation: Mapping the Winds of Creative Destruction." *Research Policy* 14 (1):3–22.

Ackermann, Thomas, and Lennart Söder. 2002. "An Overview of Wind Energy—Status 2002." *Renewable and Sustainable Energy Reviews* 6 (1–2):67–127. doi: http://dx.doi.org/10.1016/S1364-0321(02)00008-4.

Advocate General Jacobs. 2000. "Opinion of Advocate General Jacobs." *PreussenElektra v Schleswag AG* European Court of Justice (Case C-379–98).

Ahrens, Nathaniel. 2013. *China's Competitiveness: Myth, Reality, and Lessons for the United States and Japan. Case Study: Suntech*. Washington, DC: Center for Strategic and International Studies.

Aklin, Michaël, and Johannes Urpelainen. 2018. *Renewables: The Politics of a Global Energy Transition*. Cambridge, MA: MIT Press.

Alexander, Cathy. 2013. "Carbon Cutters." http://www.crikey.com.au/thepowerindex/carbon-cutters/.

American Energy and Manufacturing Partnership. 2013. *Driving Regional Transformation*. Washington, DC: Council on Competitiveness.

American Wind Energy Association. 2015. "Anatomy of Wind Turbine." http://www.awea.org/Resources/Content.aspx?ItemNumber=5083.

Amsden, Alice H. 1989. *Asia's Next Giant: South Korea and Late Industrialization*. Oxford: Oxford University Press.

Amsden, Alice H. 2001. *The Rise of "the Rest": Challenges to the West from Late-Industrializing Countries*. Oxford: Oxford University Press.

Antràs, Pol. 2003. "Incomplete Contracts and the Product Cycle." National Bureau of Economic Research Working Paper No. 9945.

Arbeitsgemeinschaft Windenergie-Zulieferindustrie. 2012. *Komponenten, Systeme Und Fertigungstechnik Für Die Windindustrie*. Frankfurt: VDMA.

Arbeitsgemeinschaft Windenergie. 2019. *Branchenführer Windindustrie 2019*. Frankfurt: VDMA.

ARPA-E. 2009. "ARPA-E Project Selections." http://www.energy.gov/sites/prod/files/edg/news/document/ARPA-E_Project_Selections.pdf.

Aulich, Hubert, and Peter Frey. 2009. "Solarvalley Mitteldeutschland—Strom aus der Sonne." http://www.solarvalley.org/media/Imagebroschuere.pdf.

Autor, David H., David Dorn, and Gordon H. Hanson. 2012. "The China Syndrome: Local Labor Market Effects of Import Competition in the United States." National Bureau of Economic Research Working Paper No. 18054.

AWEA Manufacturing Working Group. 2011. *Demand-Side Policies Will Fuel Growth in Wind Power Manufacturing Sector*. Washington, DC: AWEA.

Bahnsen, Uwe. 2013. "Ölkrise 1973—Leere Tanks Und Leere Straßen." *Die Welt*. https://www.welt.de/regionales/hamburg/article122171969/Oelkrise-1973-Leere-Tanks-und-leere-Strassen.html.

Bailey, Sheila G., Ryne Raffaelle, and Keith Emery. 2002. "Space and Terrestrial Photovoltaics: Synergy and Diversity." *Progress in Photovoltaics: Research and Applications* 10 (6):399–406. doi: 10.1002/pip.446.

Baker, Joseph. 2010. "Spurring Development and Building a U.S. Wind Power Supply Chain Industry." Wind Power Manufacturing and Supply Chain Summit, Chicago, IL.

Baldwin, Carliss, and Kim Clark. 2000. *Design Rules: The Power of Modularity*. Cambridge, MA: MIT Press.

Baldwin, Richard. 2016. *The Great Convergence*. Cambridge, MA: Harvard University Press.

Ball, Jeffrey, Dan Reicher, Xiaojing Sun, and Caitlin Pollock. 2017. *The New Solar System: China's Evolving Solar Industry and Its Implications for Competitive Solar Power in the United States and the World*. Stanford, CA: Stanford University Steyer-Taylor Center for Energy Policy and Finance.

Baoding Year Book [保定年检]. 2004/2005. Beijing: Gazetteer Press [方志出版社].

Baoding Year Book [保定年检]. 1999. Beijing: People's Press [人民出版社].

Barradale, Merrill Jones. 2010. "Impact of Public Policy Uncertainty on Renewable Energy Investment: Wind Power and the Production Tax Credit." *Energy Policy* 38 (12):7698–709. doi: http://dx.doi.org/10.1016/j.enpol.2010.08.021.

Bartlett, John E., Robert M. Margolis, and Charles E. Jennings. 2009. *The Effects of the Financial Crisis on Photovoltaics: An Analysis of Changes in Market Forecasts from 2008 to 2009*. Golden, CO: National Renewable Energy Laboratory.

Bebon, Joseph. 2013. "Top Wind Turbine Supplier in 2012: Vestas or GE." *North American Wind Power*, March 26.

Bechberger, Mischa. 2000. "Das Erneuerbare-Energien-Gesetz (Eeg): Eine Analyse des Politikformulierungsprozesses." *FFU-report 00–06*. Berlin: Forschungsstelle für Umweltpolitik, Freie Universität Berlin.

Becker, Ralf M., and Thomas F. Hellmann. 2003. "The Genesis of Venture Capital—Lessons from the German Experience." CESifo Working Paper No. 883.

Behuria, Pritish. 2020. "The Politics of Late Late Development in Renewable Energy Sectors: Dependency and Contradictory Tensions in India's National Solar Mission." *World Development* 126:104726. doi: https://doi.org/10.1016/j.worlddev.2019.104726.

Belitz, Heike, Alexander Eickelpasch, and Anna Lejpras. 2012. *Volkswirtschaftliche Bedeutung Der Technologie- Und Innovationsförderung im Mittelstand*. Berlin: Deutsches Institut für Wirtschaftsforschung.

Berchem, Andreas. 2006. "Das Unterschätzte Gesetz." *Die Zeit*, September 22.

Bereny, Justin A. 1977. *Survey of the Emerging Solar Energy Industry*. San Mateo, CA: Solar Energy Information Services.

Berger, Suzanne. 1996. "Introduction." In *National Diversity and Global Capitalism*, edited by Suzanne Berger and Ronald Dore, 1–28. Ithaca, NY: Cornell University Press.

Berger, Suzanne. 2000. "Globalization and Politics." *Annual Review of Political Science* 3:43–62.

Berger, Suzanne. 2005a. *How We Compete*. New York: Doubleday.

Berger, Suzanne. 2005b. *How We Compete: What Companies around the World Are Doing to Make It in Today's Global Economy*. New York, NY: Doubleday.

Berger, Suzanne. 2013a. *Making in America*. Cambridge, MA: MIT Press.

Berger, Suzanne. 2013b. *Making in America: From Innovation to Market*. Cambridge, MA: MIT Press.

Berghoff, Hartmut. 2006. "The End of Family Business? The Mittelstand and German Capitalism in Transition, 1949–2000." *Business History Review* 80 (2):263–95. doi: doi:10.1017/S0007680500035492.

Bettencourt, Luis M. A., Jessika E. Trancik, and Jasleen Kaur. 2013. "Determinants of the Pace of Global Innovation in Energy Technologies." *Plos ONE* 8 (10):1–6.

Bierenbaum, Dan, Mary Margaret Frank, Michael Lenox, and Rachna Maheshwari. 2012. *Winning the Green Innovation Economy: An Analysis of Worldwide Patenting*. Charlottesville: Batten Institute at the University of Virginia.

Binz, Christian, and Bernhard Truffer. 2017. "Global Innovation Systems—A Conceptual Framework for Innovation Dynamics in Transnational Contexts." *Research Policy* 46 (7):1284–98.

Bird, Lori, Mark Bolinger, Troy Gagliano, Ryan Wiser, Matthew Brown, and Brian Parsons. 2005. "Policies and Market Factors Driving Wind Power Development in the United States." *Energy Policy* 33 (11):1397–407. doi: 10.1016/j.enpol.2003.12.018.

Bolinger, Mark, Ryan Wiser, Lew Milford, Michael Stoddard, and Kevin Porter. 2001. "States Emerge as Clean Energy Investors: A Review of State Support for Renewable Energy." *Electricity Journal* 14 (9):82–95. doi: http://dx.doi.org/10.1016/S1040-6190(01)00246-9.

Bolinger, Mark. 2013. *Understanding Wind Turbine Price Trends in the U.S. over the Past Decade*. Berkeley, CA: Lawrence Berkeley National Laboratory.

Bonvillian, William B., and Charles Weiss. 2015. *Technological Innovation in Legacy Sectors*. New York, NY: Oxford University Press.

Bosch, Gerhard. 2011. "The German Labour Market after the Financial Crisis: Miracle or Just a Good Policy Mix?" In *Work Inequalities in the Crisis: Evidence from Europe*, edited by Daniel Vaughan-Whitehead, 243–77. Cheltenham: Edward Elgar Publishing.

Boskin, Michael J., and Lawrence J. Lau. 1992. "Capital, Technology, and Economic Growth." In *Technology and the Wealth of Nations*, edited by Nathan Rosenberg, Ralph Landau and David C. Mowery, 17–56. Stanford, CA: Stanford University Press.

Böttcher, Matthias. 2010. *Global and Local Networks in the Solar Energy Industry: The Case of the San Francisco Bay Area*. Neurus Paper. Irvine: University of California, Irvine.

Boudreau, John. 2012. "China Strives to Create Its Own Silicon Valley." *San Jose Mercury News*, June 6.

Boulder Wind Power. 1999. "Boulder Wind Power." www.boulderwindpower.com.

Bouncken, Ricarda B. 2004. "Kooperationen Von Kmu in Jungen Branchen: Empirische Ergebnisse Im Bereich Regenerativer Energien." In *Kooperationen von Kleinen und Mittleren Unternehmen in Europa*, edited by Jörn-Axel Meyer, 206–51. Lohmar: EUL Verlag.

Bourzac, Katherine. 2009. "U.S. Solar Startups Struggling to Compete with Chinese Firms." *Technology Review*, November 4.

Bradsher, Keith. 2011. "Solar Panel Maker Moves Work to China." *New York Times*, January 14.

Bradsher, Keith. 2012. "Glut of Solar Panels Poses a New Threat to China." *New York Times*. http://www.nytimes.com/2012/10/05/business/global/glut-of-solar-panels-is-a-new-test-for-china.html?_r=0.

Bradsher, Keith. 2013a. "Chinese Firm Buys U.S. Solar Start-Up." *New York Times*, January 9.

Bradsher, Keith. 2013b. "Chinese Solar Panel Giant Is Tainted by Bankruptcy." *New York Times*, March 20.

Brandt, Loren, and Eric Thun. 2010. "The Fight for the Middle: Upgrading, Competition, and Industrial Development in China." *World Development* 38 (11):1555–74.

Brandt, Loren, and Eric Thun. 2016. "Constructing a Ladder for Growth: Policy, Markets, and Industrial Upgrading in China." *World Development* 80:78–95. doi: https://doi.org/10.1016/j.worlddev.2015.11.001.

Braun, Boris. 2001. "Regionale Innovationsnetzwerke in der Mittelständischen Maschinenbauindustrie Japans und Deutschlands." In *Regionale Innovationsnetzwerke Im Internationalen Vergleich*, edited by Reinhold Grotz and Ludwig Schätzl, 166–84. Münster: LIT Verlag.

Breetz, Hanna, Matto Mildenberger, and Leah Stokes. 2018. "The Political Logics of Clean Energy Transitions." *Business and Politics* 20 (4):492–522.

Breznitz, Dan, and Michael Murphree. 2011. *Run of the Red Queen: Government, Innovation, Globalization and Economic Growth in China*. New Haven, CT: Yale University Press.

Breznitz, Dan. 2007. *Innovation and the State: Political Choice and Strategies for Growth in Israel, Taiwan, and Ireland*. New Haven, CT: Yale University Press.

Brown, Phillip. 2011. *Solar Projects: DOE Section 1705 Loan Guarantees*. Washington DC: Congressional Research Service.

Bruns, Elke, Dörte Ohlhorst, Bernd Wenzel, and Johann Köppel. 2011. *Renewable Energies in Germany's Electricity Market: A Biography of the Innovation Process*. Heidelberg: Springer.

Bullis, Kevin. 2008. "A Design for Cheaper Wind Power." *MIT Technology Review*, December 1.

Bullis, Kevin. 2012. "The Chinese Solar Machine." *MIT Technology Review*, Jan/Feb.

Bundesministerium für Bildung und Forschung. 2017. "Die Spitzencluster—Solarvalley Mitteldeutschland." http://www.spitzencluster.de/de/solarvalley-mitteldeutschland-1716.html.

Bundesministerium für Umwelt, Naturschutz und Reaktorsicherheit. 2008. *Ökologische Industriepolitik—Wachstumspolitik für Eine Nachhaltige Zukunft*. Berlin: BMU.

Bundesministerium für Wirtschaft und Arbeit. 2005. *Innovation und Neue Energietechnologien—Das 5*. Berlin: Energieforschungsprogramm der Bundesregierung.

Bundesministerium für Wirtschaft und Technologie. 2011. *Forschung für Eine Umweltschonende, Zuverlässige und Bezahlbare Energieversorgung—Das 6*. Berlin: Energieforschungsprogramm Der Bundesregierung.

Bundesregierung. 2005. *Wegweiser Nachhaltigkeit 2005—Bilanz und Perspektiven: Kabinettsbeschluss Vom 10. August 2005*. Berlin: Presse- und Informationsamt der Bundesregierung.

Bürkle. 2013. "Unternehmen." http://www.buerkle-gmbh.de/index.php?id=1132.

Butler, Lucy, and Karsten Neuhoff. 2008. "Comparison of Feed-in Tariff, Quota and Auction Mechanisms to Support Wind Power Development." *Renewable Energy* 33 (8):1854–67. doi: http://dx.doi.org/10.1016/j.renene.2007.10.008.

Campbell, Richard J. 2011. *China and the United States: A Comparison of Green Energy Programs and Policies*. Washington DC: Congressional Research Service.

Campoccia, A., L. Dusonchet, E. Telaretti, and G. Zizzo. 2009. "Comparative Analysis of Different Supporting Measures for the Production of Electrical Energy by Solar PV and Wind Systems: Four Representative European Cases." *Solar Energy* 83 (3):287–97. doi: http://dx.doi.org/10.1016/j.solener.2008.08.001.

Camuffo, Arnaldo. 2004. "'Turning Out a World Car': Globalization, Outsourcing, and Modularity in the Auto Industry." *Korean Journal of Political Economy* 2:183–224.

Cao, Cong. 2004. "Zhongguancun and China's High-Tech Parks in Transition: 'Growing Pains' or 'Premature Senility'?" *Asian Survey* 44 (5):647–68. doi: 10.1525/as.2004.44.5.647.

Cao, Cong, Richard P. Suttmeier, and Denis Fred Simon. 2006. "China's 15-Year Science and Technology Plan." *Physics Today* 59 (12):38–43.

Cao, Jing, and Felix Groba. 2013. *Chinese Renewable Energy Technology Exports: The Role of Policy, Innovation and Markets*. Berlin: Deutsches Institut für Wirtschaftsforschung.

Cardwell, Diane. 2012. "U.S. Raises Tariffs on Chinese Wind-Turbine Makers." *New York Times*, July 27.

Cardwell, Diane. 2014. "U.S. Offshore Wind Farm, Made in Europe." *New York Times*, January 22.

Centrotherm. 2016. "History," http://www.centrotherm.de/en/unternehmen/geschichte/.

Cetorelli, Nicola, and Philip E. Strahan. 2006. "Finance as a Barrier to Entry: Bank Competition and Industry Structure in Local U.S. Markets." *Journal of Finance* 61 (1):437–61. doi: 10.2307/3699346.

Chandler, Alfred D., and Takashi Hikino. 1997. "The Large Industrial Enterprise and the Dynamics of Modern Growth." In *Big Business and the Wealth of Nations*, edited by Alfred D Chandler, Franco Amatori, and Takashi Hikino, 24–62. Cambridge: Cambridge University Press.

Chandler, Alfred D. 1977. *The Visible Hand: The Managerial Revolution in American Business*. Cambridge, MA: Harvard Belknap.

*Changzhou Yearbook [*常州年检*]*. 1998. Changzhou: Changzhou Gazetteer Editorial Committee [常州市地方志编纂委员会].

*Changzhou Yearbook [*常州年检*]*. 2004. Changzhou: Changzhou Gazetteer Editorial Committee [常州市地方志编纂委员会].

*Changzhou Yearbook [*常州年检*]*. 2005. Changzhou: Changzhou Gazetteer Editorial Committee [常州市地方志编纂委员会].

China Daily. 2002. "Wenzhou Lighter Makers Await EU Decision." *China Daily*, April 26.

China Ming Yang Wind Power Group Limited. 2011. Annual Report 2010, Form 20-F.

China Science and Technology Statistical Yearbook. 2016. Beijing: China Statistical Press.

China Statistical Yearbook. 2007. Beijing: China Statistics Press.

Chirot, Laura H. 2016. "The Politics of New Industrial Policy: Sectoral Governance Reform in Vietnam's Agro-Export Industries." Cambridge: Massachusetts Institute of Technology.

Chirot, Laura, Vu Thanh Tu Anh, and Edward S. Steinfeld. 2012. *Private Sector Development: An Alternative Target for Industrial Policy in Vietnam*. Cambridge: Massachusetts Institute of Technology.

Clark, Corrie. 2018. *Renewable Energy R&D Funding History: A Comparison with Funding for Nuclear Energy, Fossil Energy, and Energy Efficiency R&D*. Washington, DC: Congressional Research Service.

Colatat, Phech, Georgeta Vidican, and Richard K. Lester. 2009. "Innovation Systems in the Solar Photovoltaic Industry: The Role of Public Research Institutions." IPC Working Paper Series, Cambridge, MA.

"Conrad Burke: Executive Profile." 2014a. *Bloomberg Businessweek*. http://investing. businessweek.com/research/stocks/people/person.asp?personId=27714739&ticker=J ASO.

Couture, Toby, and Yves Gagnon. 2010. "An Analysis of Feed-in Tariff Remuneration Models: Implications for Renewable Energy Investment." *Energy Policy* 38 (2):955–65. doi: http://dx.doi.org/10.1016/j.enpol.2009.10.047.

Crane, R. A., P. J. Verlinden, and R. M. Swanson. 1996. "Building a Cost-Effective, Fabrication Facility for Silicon Solar Cell R&D and Production." 25th PVSC, Washington DC, May 13–17.

CRESP. 2005. *Zhongguo Fendian Chanyehua Fazhan Guojia Xingdong Fangan [National Action Plan for China's Wind Power Industry Development]*. Beijing: Zhongguo Kezaisheng Nengyuan Guimohua Fazhan.

Culpepper, Pepper D. 1999. "Still a Model for the Industrialized Countries?" In *The German Skills Machine: Sustaining Comparative Advantage in a Global Economy*, edited by Pepper D. Culpepper and David Finegold, 1–36. New York: Berghahn.

Culpepper, Pepper D. 2001. "Employers, Public Policy, and the Politics of Decentralized Cooperation in Germany and France." In *Varieties of Capitalism: The Institutional Foundations of Comparative Advantage*, edited by Peter A. Hall and David Soskice, 275–306. Oxford: Oxford University Press.

Dagger, Steffen B. 2009. *Energiepolitik & Lobbying: Die Novelle Des Erneuerbare-Energien Gesetzes*. Stuttgart: ibidem-Verlag.

Dalian Yearbook [大连年检]. 2007. Dalian: Dalian Yearbook Publishing Office [大连年 鉴编辑部].

David, Andrew S. 2009. *Wind Turbines: Industry and Trade Summary*. Washington, DC: United States International Trade Commission.

Davis, Gerald F. 2009. *Managed by the Markets: How Finance Reshaped America*. Oxford: Oxford University Press.

de la Tour, Arnaud, Matthieu Glachant, and Yann Ménière. 2011. "Innovation and International Technology Transfer: The Case of the Chinese Photovoltaic Industry." *Energy Policy* 39 (2):761–70. doi: http://dx.doi.org/10.1016/j.enpol.2010.10.050.

Department of Energy. 2003. "Wind Power Pioneer Interview: Jim Dehlsen, Clipper Windpower." https://web.archive.org/web/20131015213123/http://windpoweringamerica. gov/filter_detail.asp?itemid=683.

Department of Energy. 2006. "Wind Energy Program Portfolio." http://www.nrel.gov/ docs/fy06osti/37937.pdf.

Department of Energy. 2015. *Wind Vision: A New Era for Wind Power in the United States*. Washington, DC: Department of Energy.

Department of Energy. 2017a. *U.S. Energy and Employment Report*. Washington, DC: Department of Energy.

Department of Energy. 2017b. "Wind Research and Development." Office of Energy Efficiency and Renewable Energy. https://energy.gov/eere/wind/wind-research-and-development.

Deudney, Daniel, and Christopher Flavin. 1983. *Renewable Energy: The Power to Choose*. New York, NY: W.W. Norton & Company.

Deutch, John, and Edward S. Steinfeld. 2013. "A Duel in the Sun: The Solar Photovoltaics: Technology Conflict between China and the United States." Report for the MIT Future of Solar Energy Study, Cambridge, MA.

Deutscher Bundestag. 1990. "Entwurf Eines Gesetzes über die Einspeisung von Strom aus Erneuerbaren Energien in das Öffentliche Netz." 11. Wahlperiode (Drucksache 11/7971, September 25).

Deutscher Bundestag. 2000. "Gesetz Zum Vorrang Erneuerbarer Energien—Erneuerbare-Energien-Gesetz." *Bundesgesetzblatt* 1:305–09.

Deutscher Industrie- und Handelskammertag. 2012. *Ausbildung 2012: Ergebnisse Einer Dihk-Online-Unternehmensbefragung.* DIHK: Berlin.

de Vries, Eize. 2011. "Bard Turbine Know-How Boosts Project Potential." *Windpower Monthly*, July.

de Vries, Eize. 2013. "Close Up—Own Foundries Give Strategic Edge." *Windpower Monthly*, March.

Distelhorst, Greg, and Richard M. Locke. 2018. "Does Compliance Pay? Social Standards and Firm-Level Trade." *American Journal of Political Science* 62 (3):695–711. doi:10.1111/ajps.12372.

Dobbin, Frank. 1994. *Forging Industrial Policy: The United States, Britain, and France in the Railway Age.* Cambridge: Cambridge University Press.

Doner, Richard, Gregory W. Noble, and John Ravenhill. 2006. "Industrial Competitiveness of the Auto Parts Industries in Four Large Asian Countries: The Role of Government Policy in a Challenging International Environment." World Bank Policy Research Working Paper (4106).

Earth Policy Institute. 2020. "Climate, Energy, and Transportation Data." http://www.earth-policy.org/data_center/C23.

Ebner, Christian, Lukas Graf, and Rita Nikolai. 2013. "New Institutional Linkages between Dual Vocational Training and Higher Education: A Comparative Analysis of Germany, Austria and Switzerland." In *Integration and Inequality in Educational Institutions*, edited by Michael Windzio, 281–98. Dordrecht: Springer Netherlands.

Eckl, Verena, and Dirk Engel. 2009. "Benefiting from Publicly Funded Pre-Competitive Research: Differences between Insiders and Outsiders." *Ruhr Economic Paper No. 129.* Essen: Rheinisch-Westfälisches Institut für Wirtschaftsforschung.

Economist, The. 2012. "The End of Cheap China." *The Economist*, March 12.

Edin, Maria. 2003. "State Capacity and Local Agent Control in China: CCP Cadre Management from a Township Perspective." *China Quarterly* 173:35–52. doi: doi:10.1017/S0009443903000044.

EEW. 2013. "About EEW." http://www.eew.de/about-eew.

Eichhorst, Werner, and Paul Marx. 2009. "Kurzarbeit—Sinnvoller Konjunkturpuffer Oder Verlängertes Arbeitslosengeld?" *Wirtschaftsdienst* 89 (5):322–28. doi: 10.1007/s10273-009-0931-x.

Ernst, Dieter. 2011. *Indigenous Innovation and Globalization: The Challenge for China's Standardization Strategy.* Honolulu, HI: East-West Center.

Ernst, Dieter, and Linsu Kim. 2002. "Global Production Networks, Knowledge Diffusion, and Local Capability Formation." *Research Policy* 31 (8–9):1417–29. doi: http://dx.doi.org/10.1016/S0048-7333(02)00072-0.

Ernst, Dieter, and Barry Naughton. 2008. "China's Emerging Industrial Economy: Insights from the IT Industry." In *China's Emergent Political Economy*, edited by Christopher A. McNally, 39–59. New York, NY: Routledge.

Estevez-Abe, Margarita, Torben Iversen, and David Soskice. 2001. "Social Protection and the Formation of Skills: A Reinterpretation of the Welfare State." In *Varieties of*

Capitalism: The Institutional Foundations of Comparative Advantage, edited by Peter A. Hall and David Soskice, 145–83. Oxford: Oxford University Press.

Evans, Peter. 1995. *Embedded Autonomy: States and Industrial Transformation*. Princeton, NJ: Princeton University Press.

Ezell, Stephen J., and Robert D. Atkinson. 2011a. *The Case for a National Manufacturing Strategy*. Washington, DC: The Information Technology & Innovation Foundation (ITIF).

Ezell, Stephen J., and Robert D. Atkinson. 2011b. *International Benchmarking of Countries' Policies and Programs Supporting SME Manufacturers*. Washington, DC: Information Technology & Innovation Foundation.

Fabrizio, Kira R. 2012. "The Effect of Regulatory Uncertainty on Investment: Evidence from Renewable Energy Generation." *Journal of Law, Economics, and Organization* 29 (4) (August 2013):765–98. doi: 10.1093/jleo/ews007.

Fagerberg, Jan, and Koson Sapprasert. 2011. "National Innovation Systems: The Emergence of a New Approach." *Science and Public Policy* 38 (9):669–79. doi: 10.3152/030234211x13070021633369.

Farrell, Henry, and Abraham Newman. 2020. "Will the Coronavirus End Globalization as We Know It?" *Foreign Affairs*, May/June.

Fialka, John. 2016. "Why China Is Dominating the Solar Industry." https://www.scientificamerican.com/article/why-china-is-dominating-the-solar-industry/.

Fischedick, Manfred, and Mischa Bechberger. 2009. "Die Ökologische Industriepolitik Deutschlands am Beispiel der Solar- und Windindustrie. Musterschüler Oder Problemkind?" *Moderne Industriepolitik*. Berlin: Friedrich-Ebert-Stiftung.

Fishman, Ted C. 2005. *China Inc*. New York, NY: Scribner.

Flex, Hansa. 2013. "Unternehmensgeschichte." http://www.hansa-flex.com/en/unternehmen/geschichte.html.

Forschungszentrum Jülich. 1993. *Programm Energieforschung Und Energietechnologien— Statusreport 1993 Photovoltaik*. Bonn: Bundesministerium für Forschung und Technologie.

Fraunhofer ISE. 2017. *Jahresbericht 2016/17*. Freiburg: Fraunhofer-Institut für Solare Energiesysteme ISE.

Frieden, Jeffry A., and Ronald Rogowski. 1996. "The Impact of the International Economy on National Policies: An Analytical Overview." In *Internationalization and Domestic Politics*, edited by Helen V. Milner and Robert O. Keohane, 25–47. Cambridge: Cambridge University Press.

Friedman, Gregory H. 2015. *Special Report: The Department of Energy's Loan Guarantee to Solyndra Inc*. Washington, DC: US Department of Energy, Office of Inspector General.

Gaddy, Benjamin, Varun Sivaram, and Francis O'Sullivan. 2016. *Venture Capital and Cleantech: The Wrong Model for Clean Energy Innovation*. Cambridge, MA: MIT Energy Initiative.

Galey, John. 1979. "Industrialist in the Wilderness: Henry Ford's Amazon Venture." *Journal of Interamerican Studies and World Affairs* 21 (2):261–89. doi: 10.2307/165528.

Gallaher, Michael P., Albert N. Link, and Alan O'Connor. 2012. *Public Investments in Energy Technology*. Cheltenham: Edward Elgar Publishing.

Gawel, Erik, and Christian Klassert. 2013. "Wie Weiter mit der Besonderen Ausgleichregelung im Eeg?" *UFZ Discussion Papers* (9):1–14.

Ge, Dongsheng, and Takahiro Fujimoto. 2004. "Quasi-Open Product Architecture and Technological Lock-In: An Exploratory Study on the Chinese Motorcycle Industry." *Annals of Business Administrative Science* 3 (2):15–24.

Gereffi, Gary. 1994. "The Organization of Buyer-Driven Commodity Chain: How U.S. Retailers Shape Overseas Production Networks." In *Commodity Chains and Global Capitalism*, edited by Gary Gereffi and Miguel Korzeniewicz, 95–112. Westport, CT: Praeger.

Gereffi, Gary. 2009. "Development Models and Industrial Upgrading in China and Mexico." *European Sociological Review* 25 (1):37–51. doi: 10.1093/esr/jcn034.

Gereffi, Gary. 2018. *Global Value Chains and Development: Redefining the Contours of 21st Century Capitalism*. Cambridge: Cambridge University Press.

Gereffi, Gary, John Humphrey, and Timothy Sturgeon. 2005. "The Governance of Global Value Chains." *Review of International Political Economy* 12 (1):78–104.

Germany Trade & Invest. 2010. *Wind Energy Industry in Germany*. Berlin.

Germany Trade & Invest. 2011a. *Leading PV Manufacturers Produce in Germany*. Berlin.

Germany Trade & Invest. 2011b. *Photovoltaic Equipment*. Berlin.

Germany Trade & Invest. 2011c. *Photovoltaics—Made in Germany*. Berlin.

Germany Trade & Invest. 2013. *Facts and Figures 2013—Cash Incentives*. Berlin.

Germany Trade & Invest. 2014. *Leading PV Manufacturers in Germany*. Berlin.

Gertner, Jon. 2013. "Flodesign's Jet-Engine Turbine Will Change the Way You Think about Wind Power." *Fast Company Magazine*, September.

Giesecke, Susanne. 2000. "The Contrasting Roles of Government in the Development of Biotechnology Industry in the U.S. and Germany." *Research Policy* 29 (2):205–23. doi: http://dx.doi.org/10.1016/S0048-7333(99)00061-X.

Gipe, Paul. 1995. *Wind Energy Comes of Age*. New York, NY: John Wiley & Sons.

Gleitz, Robert. 2006. *The Case for Wind: GE Energy's Perspective*. GE Energy.

Goodrich, Alan C., Douglas M. Powell, Ted L. James, Michael Woodhouse, and Tonio Buonassisi. 2013. "Assessing the Drivers of Regional Trends in Solar Photovoltaic Manufacturing." *Energy and Environmental Science* 6 (10):2811–21. doi: 10.1039/C3EE40701B.

Goudarzi, N., and W. D. Zhu. 2013. "A Review on the Development of Wind Turbine Generators across the World." *International Journal of Dynamics and Control* 1 (2):192–202. doi: 10-1007/s40435-013-0016-y.

Graf, Lukas. 2013. "Duale Studiengänge als 'Unerwartete' form der Institutionellen Durchlässigkeit Zwischen Berufs- und Hochschulbildung in Deutschland." In *Vergleiche Innerhalb von Gruppen und Institutionelle Gelingensbedingungen. Vielversprechende Perspektiven für die Ungleichheitsforschung*, Heike Solga, Christian Brzinsky-Fay, Lukas Graf, Cornelia Gresch, and Paula Protsch, 41–42. Berlin: WZB.

Green, Martin A. 2001. "Crystalline Silicon Solar Cells." In *Clean Electricity from Photovoltaics*, edited by M. D. Archer and R. Hill, 149–97. London: Imperial College Press.

Grewe, Hartmut. 2009. "Die Branche Der Erneuerbaren Energien Und Ihre Lobby." *Konrad Adenauer Stiftung—Analysen & Argumente* (December).

Grossman, Gene M., and Elhanan Helpman. 1991. "Endogenous Product Cycles." *Economic Journal* 101 (408) (September 1):1214–29.

Grune, Susann, and Sebastian Heilmann. 2012. "Deutsch-Chinesische Technologiekooperation." *China Analysis* 99 (December):1–14.

Grünhagen, Marc, and Holger Berg. 2011. "Modelling the Antecedents of Innovation-Based Growth Intentions in Entrepreneurial Ventures: The Role of Perceived Regulatory Conditions in the German Renewable Energies and Disease Management Industries." *International Journal of Technology, Policy and Management* 11 (3/4): 220–49.

GTM Research. 2011. U.S. Solar Energy Trade Assessment 2011. Washington, DC: Solar Energy Industries Association.

Guan, Dabo, Glen P. Peters, Christopher L. Weber, and Klaus Hubacek. 2009. "Journey to World Top Emitter: An Analysis of the Driving Forces of China's Recent CO_2 Emissions Surge." *Geophysical Research Letters* 36 (4):L04709. doi: 10.1029/2008GL036540.

Guang Dong Mingyang Wind Power Technology Co. Ltd. 2007. *1.5 Mw Wind Turbine: Germany Technology + China Manufacturing Capacity*. Mingyang: Zhongshan.

Günterberg, Brigitte, and Gunter Kayser. 2004. *SME's in Germany—Facts and Figures 2004*. Bonn: Institut für Mittelstandsforschung.

GWEC. 2017. *Global Wind Report Annual Market Update 2016*. Brussels: Global Wind Energy Council.

Hager, Carol J. 1995. *Technological Democracy: Bureaucracy and Citizenry in the German Energy Debate*. Ann Arbor: University of Michigan Press.

Hager, Carol, and Christoph H. Stefes. 2016. *Germany's Energy Transition: A Comparative Perspective*. New York, NY: Palgrave Macmillan.

Hall, Ben, and Richard Milne. 2019. "Europe First: How Brussels Is Retooling Industrial Policy." *Financial Times*. https://www.ft.com/content/140e560e-0ba0-11ea-bb52-34c8d9dc6d84?shareType=nongift.

Hall, Peter A., and David Soskice. 2001. "An Introduction to Varieties of Capitalism." In *Varieties of Capitalism: The Institutional Foundations of Comparative Advantage*, edited by Peter A. Hall and David Soskice, 1–70. Oxford: Oxford University Press.

Hamilton, Tyler. 2011. "Building Bigger, Better Wind Turbines." *MIT Technology Review*, July 6.

Harborne, Paul, and Chris Hendry. 2009. "Pathways to Commercial Wind Power in the US, Europe and Japan: The Role of Demonstration Projects and Field Trials in the Innovation Process." *Energy Policy* 37 (9):3580–95. doi: http://dx.doi.org/10.1016/j.enpol.2009.04.027.

Hart, David M. 2020. *The Impact of China's Production Surge on Innovation in the Global Solar Photovoltaics Industry*. Washington, DC: Information Technology & Innovation Foundation.

Harvey, Fiona. 2009. "Asia Set to Overtake Us in Green Technology." *Financial Times*, November 18. http://www.ft.com/intl/cms/s/2/68cfa9dc-d45a-11de-a935-00144feabdc0.html#axzz48NiLK2hX.

Hassel, Anke. 2014. "The Paradox of Liberalization—Understanding Dualism and the Recovery of the German Political Economy." *British Journal of Industrial Relations* 52 (1):57–81. doi: 10.1111/j.1467-8543.2012.00913.x.

Hedrich Group. 2013. "Designing Innovations for Wind Power." https://www.hedrich.com/en/products/innovations/innovation-timelinewww.hedrich.com/en.

Heilmann, Sebastian, Lea Shih, and Andreas Hofem. 2013. "National Planning and Local Technology Zones: Experimental Governance in China's Torch Programme." *China Quarterly* 216:896–919. doi:10.1017/S0305741013001057.

Helper, Susan, Timothy Krueger, and Howard Wial. 2012. "Why Does Manufacturing Matter? Which Manufacturing Matters? A Policy Framework." *Metropolitan Policy Program*. Brookings: Washington, DC.

Helveston, John, and Jonas Nahm. 2019. "China's Key Role in Scaling Low-Carbon Energy Technologies." *Science* 366 (6467):794. doi: 10.1126/science.aaz1014.

Henderson, Jeffrey, Peter Dicken, Martin Hess, Neil Coe, and Henry Wai-Chung Yeung. 2002. "Global Production Networks and the Analysis of Economic Development." *Review of International Political Economy* 9 (3):436–64.

Henderson, Rebecca M., and Kim B. Clark. 1990. "Architectural Innovation: The Reconfiguration of Existing Product Technologies and the Failure of Established Firms." *Administrative Science Quarterly* 35 (1):9–30.

Henderson, Rebecca, Adam B. Jaffe, and Manuel Trajtenberg. 1998. "Universities as a Source of Commercial Technology: A Detailed Analysis of University Patenting, 1965–1988." *Review of Economics and Statistics* 80 (1):119–127. doi: 10.1162/003465398557221.

Herrigel, Gary. 2010. *Manufacturing Possibilities: Creative Action and Industrial Recomposition in the United States, Germany, and Japan*. Oxford: Oxford University Press.

Heymann, Matthias. 1995. *Die Geschichte der Windenergienutzung 1890–1990*. Frankfurt: Campus.

Heymann, Matthias. 1998. "Signs of Hubris: The Shaping of Wind Technology Styles in Germany, Denmark, and the United States, 1940–1990." *Technology and Culture* 39 (4):641–70. doi: 10.2307/1215843.

Hiscox, Michael J. 2002. *International Trade and Political Conflict: Commerce, Coalitions, and Mobility*. Princeton, NJ: Princeton University Press.

Hochstetler, Kathryn. 2020. *Political Economies of Energy Transition: Wind and Solar Power in Brazil and South Africa*. Cambridge: Cambridge University Press.

Hoffmann, Kevin. 2012. "Endstation Thalheim—Solarfirma Q-Cells Kämpft Ums Überleben." *Der Tagesspiegel*, January 25.

Holmes, Thomas J. 2011. *The Case of the Disappearing Large-Employer Manufacturing Plants: Not Much of a Mystery after All*. Minneapolis, MN: Federal Reserve Bank of Minneapolis.

Höpner, Martin, and Lothar Krempel. 2004. "The Politics of the German Company Network." *Competition and Change* 8 (4):339–56.

Hsueh, Roselyn. 2012. "China and India in the Age of Globalization: Sectoral Variation in Postliberalization Reregulation." *Comparative Political Studies* 45 (1):32–61.

Hu, Albert G. Z., Gary H. Jefferson, and Qian Jinchang. 2005. "R&D and Technology Transfer: Firm-Level Evidence from Chinese Industry." *Review of Economics and Statistics* 87 (4):780–86. doi: 10.1162/003465305775098143.

Huang, Yasheng. 2002. "Between Two Coordination Failures: Automotive Industrial Policy in China with a Comparison to Korea." *Review of International Political Economy* 9 (3):538–73.

Huang, Yasheng. 2003. *Selling China—Foreign Direct Investment during the Reform Era*. Cambridge: Cambridge University Press.

Huang, Yasheng. 2008. *Capitalism with Chinese Characteristics: Entrepreneurship and the State*. Cambridge: Cambridge University Press.

HYDAC. 2013. "Wir Über Uns." http://www.hydac.com/de-en/company.html.

IHS Solar. 2013. *Integrated PV Market Tracker—Q1 2013*. Englewood CO: IHS.

Inskeep, Benjamin, Ethan Case, Kate Daniel, Brian Lips, Autumn Proudlove, David Sarkisian, Achyut Shrestha, Kathryn Wright, Ryan Cook, Chad Laurend, Eskedar Gessesse, and Will Hanley. 2016. *The 50 States of Solar*. Raleigh, NC: North Carolina Clean Energy Technology Center.

International Energy Agency (IEA). 2008. *Energy Policies of IEA Countries: The United States*. Paris: OECD.

International Energy Agency (IEA). 2016. *Photovoltaic Power Systems Technology Collaboration Programme—Annual Report 2016*. Paris: International Energy Agency.

International Energy Agency (IEA). 2019. *Energy Policies of IEA Countries: The United States*. Paris: OECD.

International Energy Agency (IEA). 2020. *Energy Technology R&D Statistics*. IEA: Paris.

International Trade Administration. 2013. "Utility Scale Wind Towers from the People's Republic of China: Antidumping Duty Order." *Federal Register* 78 (32):11146–148.

IPCC. 2018. *Global Warming of 1.5°C*. Geneva: Intergovernmental Panel on Climate Change.

IRENA. 2017. *Renewable Energy and Jobs—Annual Review 2017*. Paris: International Renewable Energy Agency.

IRENA. 2018. *Renewable Energy and Jobs—Annual Review 2018*. Paris: International Renewable Energy Agency.

Ismar, Georg. 2012. "Kürzung Bei Solarförderung Massiv Entschärft." *Die Welt*, June 26.

Iyer, Lakshmi, and Richard H. Vietor. 2014. *The Challenges of Governance*. Boston, MA: Harvard Business School.

JA Solar. 2010. "JA Solar Signs Strategic Agreements with Innovalight for Joint Development of High Efficiency Solar Cells." JA Solar. http://investors.jasolar.com/ phoenix.zhtml?c=208005&p=irol-newsArticle&ID=1446259&highlight=.

JA Solar Holdings. 2007. *Annual Report 2006, Form 20-F*.

Jacobsson, Staffan, and Volkmar Lauber. 2005. "Germany: From a Modest Feed-in Law to a Framework for Transition." In *Switching to Renewable Power—A Framework for the 21st Century*, edited by Volkmar Lauber, 122–58. London: Earthscan.

Jennings, Charles E., Robert M. Margolis, and John E. Bartlett. 2008. *A Historical Analysis of Investments in Solar Energy Technologies (2000–2007)*. Golden, CO: National Renewable Energy Laboratory.

Jin, Hehui, Yingyi Qian, and Barry Weingast. 2005. "Regional Decentralization and Fiscal Incentives: Federalism, Chinese Style." *Journal of Public Economics* 89:1719–42.

Johnson, Chalmers A. 1982. *Miti and the Japanese Miracle: The Growth of Industrial Policy, 1925–1975*. Stanford, CA: Stanford University Press.

Johnson, Keith. 2009. "Flying Tigers: More Reasons to Worry about Asia's Clean-Tech Push." *Wall Street Journal*, November 18. http://blogs.wsj.com/environmentalcapital/ 2009/11/18/flying-tigers-more-reasons-to-worry-about-asias-clean-tech-push/.

Kang, Junjie, Jiahai Yuan, Zhaoguang Hu, and Yan Xu. 2012. "Review on Wind Power Development and Relevant Policies in China During the 11th Five-Year-Plan Period." *Renewable and Sustainable Energy Reviews* 16 (4):1907–15. doi: http://dx.doi.org/ 10.1016/j.rser.2012.01.031.

Kaplinsky, Raphael. 2013. *Globalization, Poverty and Inequality: Between a Rock and a Hard Place*. Cambridge: Polity.

Karapin, Roger. 2016. *Political Opportunities for Climate Policy: California, New York, and the Federal Government*. Cambridge: Cambridge University Press.

Karmann-Proppert, Yvonne. 2017. "Csr Im Forschungsaktiven Mittelstand—Verantwortung Hat Tradition." In *Csr Und Nachhaltige Innovation: Zukunftsfähigkeit Durch Soziale, Ökonomische Und Ökologische Innovationen*, edited by Gesa Gordon and Astrid Nelke, 123–32. Berlin, Heidelberg: Springer.

Karplus, Valerie J. 2007. *Innovation in China's Energy Sector*. Stanford, CA: Stanford University Center for Environmental Science and Policy.

Kennedy, Andrew B. 2013. "China's Search for Renewable Energy: Pragmatic Techno-Nationalism." *Asian Survey* 53 (5):909–30. doi: 10.1525/as.2013.53.5.909.

Keuper, Armin, Jens Peter Molly, and Christiane Stückemann. 1992. "Windenergienutzung in Der Bundesrepublik Deutschland." *DEWI Magazin* 1:5–25.

Kim, Linsu. 1997. *Imitation to Innovation: The Dynamics of Korea's Technological Learning*. Boston: Harvard Business School Press.

Kim, Linsu, and Richard Nelson. 2000. "Introduction." In *Technology, Learning and Innovation*, edited by Linsu Kim and Richard Nelson, 1–12. Cambridge: Cambridge University Press.

Knight, Chris P. 2011. "Failure to Deploy: Solar Photovoltaic Policy in the United States." In *The State of Innovation: The U.S. Government's Role in Technology Development*, edited by Fred Block and Matthew Keller, 173–95. London: Paradigm Publishers.

Koch, Wendy. 2014. "U.S. Wind Industry Slammed by Tax Uncertainty, Fracking." *USA Today*, April 10.

Kopytoff, Verne. 2014. "Why Foreign Leaders Love Silicon Valley." *Fortune*, February 20.

Kostka, Genia, and William Hobbs. 2012. "Local Energy Efficiency Policy Implementation in China: Bridging the Gap between National Priorities and Local Interests." *The China Quarterly* 211:765–85. doi: doi:10.1017/S0305741012000860.

Kraemer, Kenneth L., Greg Linden, and Jason Dedrick. 2011. "Capturing Value in Global Networks: Apple's iPad and iPhone." Irvine, CA: Personal Computing Industry Center, UC Irvine.

Kreditanstalt für Wiederaufbau. 2006. "Sonderband Innovationen im Mittelstand." *Mittelstands- und Strukturpolitik* 37 (July).

Kremzner, Mark T. 1998. "Managing Urban Land in China: The Emerging Legal Framework and Its Role in Development." *Pacific Rim Law and Policy Journal* 7 (3):611–55.

Kroll, Henning, Marcus Conlé, and Marcus Schüller. 2008. *New Challenges for Germany in the Innovation Competition*. Fraunhofer Institute for Systems and Innovation Research Karlsruhe.

Krugman, Paul. 1979. "A Model of Innovation, Technology Transfer, and the World Distribution of Income." *Journal of Political Economy* 87(2) (April):253–66.

Krugman, Paul R. 1994. "The Myth of Asia's Miracle." *Foreign Affairs* 73 (6):62–78.

Kuntze, Jan-Christoph, and Tom Moerenhout. 2013. *Local Content Requirements and the Renewable Energy Industry: A Good Match?* Geneva: International Centre for Trade and Sustainable Development.

Laird, Frank, and Christoph Stefes. 2009. "The Diverging Paths of German and United States Policies for Renewable Energy: Sources of Difference." *Energy Policy* 37: 2619–29.

Lake, David A. 2009. "Open Economy Politics: A Critical Review." *Review of International Organizations* 4 (3):219–44.

Landrum, Nancy E., and David M. Boje. 2002. "Kairos: Strategies Just in Time in the Asian Athletic Footwear Industry." In *Asian Post-Crisis Management: Corporate and*

Governmental Strategies for Sustainable Competitive Advantage, edited by Usha Haley and Frank-Jürgen Richter, 81–101. London: Palgrave.

Landry, Pierre F. 2008. *Decentralized Authoritarianism in China: The Communist Party's Control of Local Elites in the Post-Mao Era.* Cambridge: Cambridge University Press.

Lang, Johannes. 2003. "Performance Von Photovoltaik Anlagen." *BINE Projektinfo 03/03.* Eggenstein-Leopoldshafen: Fachinformationszentrum Karlsruhe, Gesellschaft für wissenschaftlich-technische Information mbH.

Langlois, Richard. 2002. "Modularity in Technology and Organization." *Journal of Economic Behavior and Organization* 49 (2002):19–37.

Lardy, Nicholas R. 2002. *Integrating China into the Global Economy.* Washington, DC: Brookings Institution Press.

Lauber, Volkmar, and Lutz Mez. 2004. "Three Decades of Renewable Electricity Policies in Germany." *Energy and Environment* 15 (4):599–623. doi: 10.1260/0958305042259792.

Lazard. 2018. "Lazard's Levelized Cost of Energy Analysis." Lazard. https://www.lazard.com/media/450784/lazards-levelized-cost-of-energy-version-120-vfinal.pdf.

Lécuyer, Christophe. 2007. *Making Silicon Valley: Innovation and the Growth of High Tech, 1930–1970.* Cambridge, MA: MIT Press.

Lemoine, Françoise, and Deniz Ünal-Kesenci. 2004. "Assembly Trade and Technology Transfer: The Case of China." *World Development* 32 (5):829–50. doi: http://dx.doi.org/10.1016/j.worlddev.2004.01.001.

Leone, Steve. 2012. "Major Closures for Firstsolar, Sunpower." http://www.renewableenergyworld.com/articles/2012/04/first-solar-closing-plant-30-percent-of-workforce-cut.html.

Levinson, Marc. 2014. *U.S. Manufacturing in International Perspective.* Washington, DC: Congressional Research Service.

Levinson, Marc. 2017. U.S. Manufacturing in International Perspective. Washington, DC: Congressional Research Service.

Lewis, Joanna I. 2014. "The Rise of Renewable Energy Protectionism: Emerging Trade Conflicts and Implications for Low Carbon Development." *Global Environmental Politics* 14 (4):10–35.

Lewis, Johanna I. 2007. "Technology Acquisition and Innovation in the Developing World: Wind Turbine Development in China and India." *Studies in Comparative International Development* 42 (3–4):208–32.

Lewis, Johanna I. 2012. *Green Innovation in China: China's Wind Power Industry and the Global Transition to a Low Carbon Economy.* New York, NY: Columbia University Press.

Lewis, Johanna I. 2013. *Green Innovation in China: China's Wind Power Industry and the Global Transition to a Low Carbon Economy.* New York, NY: Columbia University Press.

Lewis, Johanna I. 2015. *A Better Approach to Intellectual Property? Lessons from the US-China Clean Energy Research Center.* Chicago, IL: Paulson Institute.

Leyden, Dennis Patrick, and Matthias Menter. 2018. "The Legacy and Promise of Vannevar Bush: Rethinking the Model of Innovation and the Role of Public Policy." *Economics of Innovation and New Technology* 27 (3):225–42. doi: 10.1080/10438599.2017.1329189.

Li, Hongbin, Lei Li, Binzhen Wu, and Yanyan Xiong. 2012. "The End of Cheap Chinese Labor." *The Journal of Economic Perspectives* 26 (4):57–74. doi: 10.1257/jep.26.4.57.

Li, Junfeng. 2011a. *China Wind Power Outlook [*中国风电发展报告]. Beijing: China Environmental Science Press [中国环境科学出版社].

Li, Junfeng. 2011b. *Zhongguo Fengdian Fazhan Baogao [China Wind Power Outlook].* Beijing: Zhongguo huanjing kexue chubanshe.

Lin, George C. S., and Fangxin Yi. 2011. "Urbanization of Capital or Capitalization on Urban Land? Land Development and Local Public Finance in Urbanizing China." *Urban Geography* 32 (1):50–79. doi: 10.2747/0272–3638.32.1.50.

Lipp, Judith. 2007. "Lessons for Effective Renewable Electricity Policy from Denmark, Germany and the United Kingdom." *Energy Policy* 35 (11):5481–95.

Liu, Xiaohui, and Trevor Buck. 2007. "Innovation Performance and Channels for International Technology Spillovers: Evidence from Chinese High-Tech Industries." *Research Policy* 36 (3):355–66. doi: http://dx.doi.org/10.1016/j.respol.2006.12.003.

Liu, Xielin, and Peng Cheng. 2011. Is China's Indigenous Innovation Strategy Compatible with Globalization? *Policy Studies*. Honululu: East-West Center.

Liu, Yongzheng, and Jorge Martinez-Vazquez. 2013. "Interjurisidictional Tax Competition in China." *Journal of Regional Science* 54 (4):606–28. doi: 10.1111/jors.12097.

Locke, Richard M. 2013. *The Promise and Limits of Private Power: Promoting Labor Standards in a Global Economy*. Cambridge: Cambridge University Press.

Locke, Richard M., and Rachel L. Wellhausen. 2014. *Production in the Innovation Economy*. Cambridge, MA: MIT Press.

Loferski, Joseph J. 1993. "The First Forty Years: A Brief History of the Modern Photovoltaic Age." *Progress in Photovoltaics: Research and Applications* 1 (1):67–78. doi: 10.1002/pip.4670–10109.

Lubinski, Christina. 2011. "Path Dependency and Governance in German Family Firms." *Business History Review* 85 (4):699–724. doi: doi:10.1017/S0007680511001164.

Lüthje, Boy. 2002. "Electronics Contract Manufacturing: Global Production and the International Division of Labor in the Age of the Internet." *Industry and Innovation* 9 (3):227–47. doi: 10.1080/1366271022000034471.

Mack, Joel H., Natasha Gianvecchio, Marc T. Campopiano, and Suzanne M. Logan. 2011. "All Recs Are Local: How in-State Generation Requirements Adversely Affect Development of a Robust Rec Market." *The Electricity Journal* 24 (4):8–25. doi: https://doi.org/10.1016/j.tej.2011.04.007.

Mai, Trieu, Wesley Cole, Eric Lantz, Cara Marcy, and Benjamin Sigrin. 2016. *Impacts of Federal Tax Credit Extensions on Renewable Deployment and Power Sector Emissions*. Golden, CA: National Renewable Energy Laboratory.

Mair, Peter. 2001. "The Green Challenge and Political Competition: How Typical Is the German Experience?" *German Politics* 10 (2):99–116. doi: 10.1080/772713265.

Mankiw, N. Gregory, and Phillip Swagel. 2006. "The Politics and Economics of Offshore Outsourcing." National Bureau of Economic Research Working Paper No. 12398.

Marigo, Nicoletta. 2007. "The Chinese Silicon Photovoltaic Industry and Market: A Critical Review of Trends and Outlook." *Progress in Photovoltaics: Research and Applications* 15 (2):143–62. doi: 10.1002/pip.716.

Markard, Jochen, and Bernhard Truffer. 2008. "Technological Innovation Systems and the Multi-Level Perspective: Towards an Integrated Framework." *Research Policy* 37 (4):596–615.

Marsh, Peter. 2011. "China Noses Ahead as Top Goods Producer." *Financial Times*, March 13.

Martinot, Eric, Ryan Wiser, and Jan Hamrin. 2005. *Renewable Energy Markets and Policies in the United States*. San Francisco: Center for Resource Solutions.

Matthew L. Wald, 2011. "Energy Firms Aided by U.S. Find Backers." *New York Times*, February 2.

Mayer, Colin, Koen Schoors, and Yishay Yafeh. 2005. "Sources of Funds and Investment Activities of Venture Capital Funds: Evidence from Germany, Israel, Japan and the United Kingdom." *Journal of Corporate Finance* 11 (3):586–608. doi: http://dx.doi.org/10.1016/j.jcorpfin.2004.02.003.

Mazzucato, Mariana. 2013. *The Entrepreneurial State—Debunking Public vs. Private Sector Myths*. London: Anthem Press.

Mazzucato, Mariana. 2016. "From Market Fixing to Market-Creating: A New Framework for Innovation Policy." *Industry and Innovation* 23 (2):140–56. doi: 10.1080/13662716.2016.1146124.

McKenna, Phil. 2015. "Bladeless Wind Turbines May Offer More Form Than Function." *Technology Review*, May 27.

Meckling, Jonas, and Bentley B. Allan. 2020. "The Evolution of Ideas in Global Climate Policy." *Nature Climate Change* 10 (5):434–38.

Meckling, Jonas, and Llewelyn Hughes. 2017. "Globalizing Solar: Global Supply Chains and Trade Preferences." *International Studies Quarterly* 61 (2):225–35.

Meckling, Jonas, Nina Kelsey, Eric Biber, and John Zysman. 2015. "Winning Coalitions for Climate Policy." *Science* 349 (6253):1170–71. doi: 10.1126/science.aab1336.

Menz, Fredric C. 2005. "Green Electricity Policies in the United States: Case Study." *Energy Policy* 33 (18):2398–410. doi: http://dx.doi.org/10.1016/j.enpol.2004.05.011.

Meri, Thomas. 2009. "China Passes the EU in High-Tech Exports." *Statistics in Focus*. Brussels: Eurostat.

Meyer, Timothy. 2015. "How Local Discrimination Can Promote Global Public Goods." *Boston University Law Review* 95 (6):1937–2025.

Minagawa, Tetsuya, Paul Trott, and Andreas Hoecht. 2007. "Counterfeit, Imitation, Reverse Engineering and Learning: Reflections from Chinese Manufacturing Firms." *R&D Management* 37 (5):455–67. doi: 10.1111/j.1467-9310.2007.00488.x.

Ministry of Industry and Information Technology. 2012. "Second Five Year Plan for Solar PV Industry Issued [太阳能光伏产业"十二五"发展规划印发]." http://www.gov.cn/gzdt/2012-02/24/content_2075802.htm.

Ministry of Science and Technology. 2007a. *China Science and Technology Statistics Data Book [中国科技统计数据]*. Beijing: Department of Development Planning, Ministry of Science and Technology.

Ministry of Science and Technology. 2007b. "Industry Establish National Key Labs." *China Science and Technology Newsletter* 481.

Ministry of Science and Technology. 2012. "12th Special Five Year Plan for Wind Power Technology Development." Ministry of Science and Technology: Beijing.

Minks, Karl-Heinz, Nicolai Netz, and Daniel Völk. 2011. *Berufsbegleitende Und Duale Studienangebote in Deutschland: Status Quo Und Perspektiven*. Hannover: Hochschul-Informations-System (HIS), Bundesinstitut für Berufsbildung.

Mitchell, C., D. Bauknecht, and P. M. Connor. 2006. "Effectiveness through Risk Reduction: A Comparison of the Renewable Obligation in England and Wales and the Feed-in System in Germany." *Energy Policy* 34 (3):297–305.

Moore, Bill, and Rolf Wüstenhagen. 2004. "Innovative and Sustainable Energy Technologies: The Role of Venture Capital." *Business Strategy and the Environment* 13 (4):235–45. doi: 10.1002/bse.413.

Moretti, Enrico. 2012. *The New Geography of Jobs*. Boston: Houghton Mifflin Harcourt.

Morris, Craig. 2012. A German Solar Bubble? Look Again! In *German Energy Transition*. https://us.boell.org/sites/default/files/downloads/Morris_GermanSolarBubble.pdf.

Morton, Oliver. 2006. "Solar Energy: A New Day Dawning? Silicon Valley Sunrise." *Nature* 443 (7107):19–22.

Mowery, David C., Richard R. Nelson, Bhaven N. Sampat, and Arvids A. Ziedonis. 2001. "The Growth of Patenting and Licensing by U.S. Universities: An Assessment of the Effects of the Bayh–Dole Act of 1980." *Research Policy* 30 (1):99–119. doi: http://dx.doi.org/10.1016/S0048-7333(99)00100-6.

Mowery, David C., Richard R. Nelson, Bhaven N. Sampat, and Arvids A. Ziedonis. 2004. *Ivory Tower and Industrial Innovation: University-Industry Technology Transfer before and after the Bayh-Dole Act*. Stanford, CA: Stanford University Press.

Mundaca, Luis, and Jessika Luth Richter. 2015. "Assessing 'Green Energy Economy' Stimulus Packages: Evidence from the U.S. Programs Targeting Renewable Energy." *Renewable and Sustainable Energy Reviews* 42:1174–86.

Murphree, Michael, and Dan Breznitz. 2020. "Global Supply Chains as Drivers of Innovation in China." In *Oxford Handbook of China Innovation*, edited by Xiaolan Fu, Jin Chen and Bruce McKern. Oxford: Oxford University Press. https://ssrn.com/abstract=3520159 or http://dx.doi.org/10.2139/ssrn.3520159.

Nahm, Jonas. 2017a. "Exploiting the Implementation Gap: Policy Divergence and Industrial Upgrading in China's Wind and Solar Sectors." *The China Quarterly* 231:705–27.

Nahm, Jonas. 2017b. "Renewable Futures and Industrial Legacies: Wind and Solar Sectors in China, Germany, and the United States." *Business and Politics* 19 (1):68–106.

Nahm, Jonas. 2020. "A Green Economic Recovery: Global Trends and Lessons for the United States." *Statement before the House Foreign Affairs Committee Subcommittee on Europe, Eurasia, Energy, and the Environment*.

Nahm, Jonas, and Edward S. Steinfeld. 2014. "Scale-Up Nation: China's Specialization in Innovative Manufacturing." *World Development* 54:288–300. doi: http://dx.doi.org/10.1016/j.worlddev.2013.09.003.

National Energy Administration (NEA). 2011. "12th Five-Year Plan on Solar Power Development [国家能源局文件, 国能新能(2012)194号]."

National Energy Administration (NEA). 2012. "National Energy Administration Notice on the Issuance of 12th Five Year Plan for Solar Energy Development." National Energy Administration: Beijing.

National Science Board. 2018. Science and Engineering Indicators 2018 (Nsb-2018-1). Alexandria, VA: National Science Foundation.

Naughton, Barry. 2007. *The Chinese Economy—Transitions and Growth*. Cambridge, MA: MIT Press.

Nelson, Richard R. 1993. *National Innovation Systems*. Oxford: Oxford University Press.

Nemet, Gregory F. 2009. "Demand-Pull, Technology-Push, and Government-Led Incentives for Non-Incremental Technical Change." *Research Policy* 38 (5):700–709.

Nemet, Gregory F. 2019. *How Solar Energy Became Cheap*. New York, NY: Routledge.

Neuhoff, Karsten. 2012. "The German Solar Industry." In *Meeting Global Challenges: German-U.S. Innovation Policy*, edited by National Research Council, 154–57. Washington, DC: National Academies Press.

Nolan, Peter. 2012. *Is China Buying the World?* Cambridge, UK: Polity Press.

NREL. 2002. National Renewable Energy Laboratory—25 Years of Research Excellence 1977–2002. Golden, CO: National Renewable Energy Laboratory.

NREL. 2012. "DOE Funds Advanced Magnet Lab and NREL to Develop Next-Generation Drivetrains." http://apps1.eere.energy.gov/wind/newsletter.detail.cfm/articleId=105.

Nussbaumer, Hartmut, Daniel Biro, Helge Haverkamp, and Karsten Bothe. 2007. "Forschung für Neue Technologien und ihre Wechselwirkung mit der Industrie—Vom Mittelständler zum Global Player." Produktionstechnologien für die Solarenergie—Jahrestagung des ForschungsVerbunds Sonnenenergie in Kooperation mit dem Bundesverband Solarwirtschaft, Hannover, September 26–27.

O'Connor, Alan, Ross J. Loomis, and Fern M. Braun. 2010. *Retrospective Benefit-Cost Evaluation of DOE Investment in Photovoltaic Energy Systems.* Washington, DC: U.S. Department of Energy.

O'Sullivan, Marlene, Ulrike Lehr, and Dietmar Edler. 2015. *BruttobeschäFtigung Durch Erneuerbare Energien in Deutschland und Verringerte Fossile Brennstoffimporte Durch Erneuerbare Energien und Energieeffizienz.* Berlin: Bundesministeriums für Wirtschaft und Energie.

OECD. 2005. *The Measurement of Scientific and Technological Activities: Guidelines for Collecting and Interpreting Innovation Data: Oslo Manual, Third Edition.* Paris: OECD, Working Party of National Experts on Scientific and Technology Indicators.

OECD. 2008. *OECD Reviews of Innovation Policy: China.* Paris: OECD Publishing.

OECD. 2012. *Economic Surveys: Germany 2012.* Paris: OECD Publishing.

Ohlhorst, Dörte. 2009. *Windenergie in Deutschland: Konstellationen, Dynamiken, Und Regulierungspotenziale Im Innovationsprozess.* Wiesbaden: VS Research.

Oi, Jean C. 1995. "The Role of the Local State in China's Transitional Economy." *China Quarterly* 144 Special Issue: China's Transitional Economy:1132–49.

Ornston, Darius. 2013. "Creative Corporatism: The Politics of High-Technology Competition in Nordic Europe." *Comparative Political Studies* 46 (6):702–29.

Osnos, Evan. 2009. "Green Giant." *New Yorker*, December 21.

Osterman, Paul, and Andrew Weaver. 2013. "Skills and Skill Gaps in Manufacturing." In *Production in the Innovation Economy*, edited by Rachel L. Wellhausen and Richard M. Locke, 17–50. Cambridge, MA: MIT Press.

Palz, Wolfgang. 2011. "The Rising Sun in a Developing World." In *Power for the World: The Emergence of Electricity from the Sun*, edited by Wolfgang Palz, 1–58. Singapore: Pan Stanford Publishing.

"Peng Fang: Executive Profile." 2014. *Bloomberg Businessweek*, http://investing. businessweek.com/research/stocks/people/person.asp?personId=27714739&ticker=J ASO.

Perlin, John. 1999. *From Space to Earth: The Story of Solar Electricity.* Ann Arbor, MI: Aatec Publications.

Peters, Theodor. 2009. "Das Vensys Konzept." *Wind Kraft Journal* 6:18–22.

Petersen, Bent, and Lawrence S. Welch. 2002. "Foreign Operation Mode Combinations and Internationalization." *Journal of Business Research* 55 (2):157–62. doi: https://doi. org/10.1016/S0148–2963(00)00151-X.

Pierce, Justin R., and Peter K. Schott. 2014. *The Surprisingly Swift Decline of U.S. Manufacturing Employment.* Washington, DC: Federal Reserve Board.

Pierson, Paul. 1994. *Dismantling the Welfare State?* Cambridge: Cambridge University Press.

Pierson, Paul. 2000. "Increasing Returns, Path Dependence, and the Study of Politics." *American Political Science Review* 94 (2):251–67.

Pisano, Gary P., and Willy C. Shih. 2009. "Restoring American Competitiveness." *Harvard Business Review*, July.

Pisano, Gary P., and Willy C. Shih. 2012. *Producing Prosperity: Why America Needs a Manufacturing Renaissance*. Boston, MA: Harvard Business Review Press.

Platzer, Michaela D. 2012a. *U.S. Solar Photovoltaic Manufacturing: Industry Trends, Global Competition, Federal Support*. Washington, DC: Congressional Research Service.

Platzer, Michaela D. 2012b. *U.S. Wind Turbine Manufacturing: Federal Support for an Emerging Industry*. Washington, DC: Congressional Research Service.

Plumer, Brad. 2013. "China May Soon Stop Flooding the World with Cheap Solar Panels." *Washington Post*, March 23.

Porter, Michael E. 1986. *Competition in Global Industries*. Boston: Harvard Business School Press.

Porter, Michael E. 1990. *The Competitive Advantage of Nations*. New York, NY: Free Press.

President's Council of Advisors on Science and Technology. 2012. *Report to the President on Capturing Domestic Competitive Advantage in Advanced Manufacturing*. Edited by Executive Office of the President. Washington, DC.

Publicover, Brian. 2016. "Yingli Agrees to $7.5m Settlement with Solyndra." *Recharge*, September 28, 2016. http://www.rechargenews.com/solar/867428/yingli-agrees-to-usd-75m-settlement-with-solyndra.

QCells. 2005. "Rec Is New Strategic Partner in Everq." http://www.pvqse.de/uploads/media/pm_rec_everq_english_28_11.pdf

Qin, Haiyan. 2013. "Wind Power in China: Chasing a Dream That Creates Value." In *The Rise of Modern Wind Energy: Wind Power for the World*, edited by Preben Maegaard, Anna Krenz and Wolfgang Palz, 589–610. Boca Raton, FL: Pan Stanford Publishing.

Ramaswarmy, Sree, James Manyika, Gary Pinkus, Katy George, Jonathan Law, Tony Gambell, and Andrea Serafino. 2018. *Making It in America: Revitalizing U.S. Manufacturing*. McKinsey Global Institute. https://www.mckinsey.com/featured-insights/americas/making-it-in-america-revitalizing-us-manufacturing.

Raymond, Nate. 2018. *China's Sinovel Convicted in U.S. of Trade-Secret Theft*. Reuters, January 24. https://www.reuters.com/article/us-sinovel-wind-gro-usa-court/chinas-sinovel-convicted-in-u-s-of-trade-secret-theft-idUSKBN1FD2XL.

Redlinger, Robert Y., Per Dannemand Anderson, and Poul Erik Morthorst. 1988. *Wind Energy in the 21st Century: Economics, Policy, Technology, and the Changing Electricity Industry*. Edited by United Nations Environment Programme. New York, NY: Palgrave.

REN21. 2010. *Renewables 2010 Global Status Report*. Paris: REN21 Secretariat.

REN21. 2015. *Renewables 2015 Global Status Report*. Paris: REN21 Secretariat.

REN21. 2020. *Renewables 2015 Global Status Report*. Paris: REN21 Secretariat.

Renewable Energy World. 2000. "Evergreen Solar Has Successful IPO." https://www.renewableenergyworld.com/articles/2000/11/evergreen-solar-has-successful-ipo-4573.html.

Rheinisch-Westfälisches Institut für Wirtschaftsforschung, and WSF Wirtschafts- und Sozialforschung Kerpen. 2010. *Erweiterte Erfolgskontrolle Beim Programm zur Förderung der IGF im Zeitraum 2005–2009*. Essen: Rheinisch-Westfälisches Institut für Wirtschaftsforschung.

Righter, Robert W. 1996. *Wind Energy in America: A History*. Norman, OK: University of Oklahoma Press.

Rithmire, Meg. 2013. "Land Politics and Local State Capacities: The Political Economy of Urban Change in China." *The China Quarterly* 216:872–95.

Rodrik, Dani. 1998. "Has Globalization Gone Too Far?" *Challenge* 41 (2):81–94.

Rogowsky, Robert A., and Karen Laney-Cummings. 2009. *Wind Turbines: Industry and Trade Summary*. Washington, DC: United States International Trade Commission.

Röhl, Klaus-Heiner. 2010. *Der Deutsche Wagniskapitalmarkt—Ansätze zur Finanzierung von Gründern und Mittelstand. IW-Positionen/* Institut der deutschen Wirtschaft: Cologne.

Romer, Paul M. 1994. "The Origins of Endogenous Growth." *Journal of Economic Perspectives* 8 (1):3–22.

Roth & Rau. 2010. "Roth & Rau Ag Schließt Joint Venture Vertrag Mit Chinesischem Unternehmen." http://www.roth-rau.de/fileadmin/user_upload/shared/rr-website/Download/News/03-02-2010_ad-hoc.pdf.

Rothgang, Michael, Matthias Peistrup, and Bernhard Lageman. 2011. "Industrial Collective Research Networks in Germany: Structure, Firm Involvement and Use of Results." *Industry and Innovation* 18 (4):393–414. doi: 10.1080/13662716.2011.573957.

Ru, Peng, Qiang Zhi, Fang Zhang, Xiaotian Zhong, Jianqiang Li, and Jun Su. 2012. "Behind the Development of Technology: The Transition of Innovation Modes in China's Wind Turbine Manufacturing Industry." *Energy Policy* 43:58–69. doi: http://dx.doi.org/10.1016/j.enpol.2011.12.025.

Sabel, Charles, and Gary Herrigel. 2018. "Collaborative Innovation in the Norwegian Oil and Gas Industry." In *Petroleum Industry Transformations: Lessons from Norway and Beyond*, edited by Taran Thune, Ole Andreas Engen, and Olav Wicken, 231–48. London: Taylor and Francis.

Samel, Hiram. 2013. "Essays on Volatility and the Division of Innovative Labor." Ph.D., Sloan School of Management, Massachusetts Institute of Technology.

Samuels, Richard J. 1987. *The Business of the Japanese State: Energy Markets in Comparative and Historical Perspective*. Ithaca, NY: Cornell University Press.

Samuelson, Paul A. 1938. "Welfare Economics and International Trade." *American Economic Review* 28 (2):261–66.

Sandtner, Walter, Helmut Geipel, and Helmut Lawitzka. 1997. "Forschungsschwerpunkte der Bundesregierung in den Bereichen Erneuerbarer Energien und Rationeller Energienutzung." In *Energiepolitik—Technische Entwicklung, Politische Strategien, Handlungskonzepte zu Erneuerbaren Energien und zur Rationellen Energienutzung*, edited by Hans Günter Brauch, 255–72. Berlin: Springer.

Schlegel, Stephanie. 2005. "Innovationsbiographie Windenergie." Diplom, Institut für Landschaftsarchitektur und Umweltplanung, TU Berlin.

Schmid Group. 2013. "Company History." http://www.schmid-group.com/en/company/history.html.

Schneider, Ben Ross. 2015. *Designing Industrial Policy in Latin America: Business-State Relations and the New Developmentalism*. New York, NY: Palgrave Macmillan.

Schultz, Stefan. 2012. "Bankruptcies Have German Solar on the Ropes." *Der Spiegel*, April 3. http://www.spiegel.de/international/business/q-cells-bankruptcy-heralds-end-of-german-solar-cell-industry-a-825490.html.

Schumpeter, Joseph A. 1934. *A Theory of Economic Development*. Cambridge, MA: Harvard University Press.

Schwabe, Paul, Karlynn Cory, and James Newcomb. 2009. *Renewable Energy Project Financing: Impacts of the Financial Crisis and Federal Legislation*. Golden, CO: National Renewable Energy Laboratory.

Schwag Serger, Sylvia, and Magnus Breidne. 2007. "China's Fifteen-Year Plan for Science and Technology: An Assessment." *Asia Policy* 4:135–64.

Schwenn, Kerstin, Henrike Rossbach, and Thiemo Heeg. 2012. "Die Solarförderung Wird Deutlich Gekürzt." *Frankfurter Allgemeine Zeitung*, Feburary 22.

Seemann, Mareike. 2012. *Innovationsnetzwerke in Jungen Branchen—Formation, Morphologie und Unternehmenstrategische Implikationen am Beispiel der Deutschen Photovoltaikbranche.* Marburg: Metropolis-Verlag.

Segal, Adam. 2003. *Digital Dragon: High-Technology Enterprises in China.* Ithaca, NY: Cornell University Press.

Segal, Adam. 2010. *Advantage: How American Innovation Can Overcome the Asian Challenge.* New York, NY: Norton & Company.

Seliger, Bernhard. 2000. "The German Manufacturing Industry Faces Globalization: Old Achievements, New Challenges." *Global Economic Review* 29 (2):48–64. doi: 10.1080/12265080008449787.

SGL. 2013. "Company History." http://www.sgl-rotec.com/cms/international/company/history/index.html?__locale=en.

Shah, Vishal, and Jake Greenblatt. 2010. *Solar Energy Handbook.* New York, NY: Barclays Capital.

Shrimali, Gireesh, Steffen Jenner, Felix Groba, Gabriel Chan, and Joe Indvik. 2012. *Have State Renewable Portfolio Standards Really Worked?* Berlin: German Institute for Economic Research.

Siegfriedsen, Sönke. 2008. *25 Jahre Aerodyn—Den Wind der Welt Einfangen.* Rendsburg: Aerodyn.

Simon, Denis Fred, and Cong Cao. 2009. *China's Emerging Technological Edge: Assessing the Role of High-End Talent.* Cambridge: Cambridge University Press.

Sivaram, Varun, Colin Cunliff, David Hart, Julio Friedman, and David Sandalow. 2020. *Energizing America: A Roadmap to Launch a National Energy Innovation Mission.* New York, NY: Columbia University SIPA Center on Global Energy Polic.

Solar Energy Industries Association. 2014. The Case for the Solar Investment Tax Credit. Washington, DC: SEIA.

Solar Energy Industries Association. 2017. "Solar Industry Expects Loss of 88,000 Jobs in U.S. Next Year if Government Rules in Company's Favor in Trade Case." http://www.seia.org/news/solar-industry-expects-loss-88000-jobs-us-next-year-if-government-rules-company-s-favor-trade.

Solow, Robert M. 1956. "A Contribution to the Theory of Economic Growth." *Quarterly Journal of Economics* 70 (1):65–94. doi: 10.2307/1884513.

Sozialdemokratische Partei Deutschlands, and Bündnis 90/Die Grünen. 1998. *Aubruch Und Erneuerung—Deutschlands Weg Ins 21. Jahrhundert. Koalitionsvereinbarung Zwischen Der Sozialdemokratischen Partei Deutschlands Und Bündnis 90/Die Grünen.* SPD: Bonn.

Spada, Alfred. 2010. "U.S. Metalcasting for Wind Energy." Wind Power Manufacturing & Supply Chain Summit, Chicago, IL.

Stafford, Ned. 2010. "Solar Storms." *Chemistry World*, June, 54–57.

State Council. 2006. "Medium- and Long-Term Strategic Plan for the Development of Science and Technology [国家中长期科学和技术发展规划纲要]."

State Council. 2010. "Decision of the State Council on Accelerating the Fostering and Development of Strategic Emerging Industries [国务院关于加快培育和发展战略性新兴产业的决定]." State Council Document 2010/32.

Steinfeld, Edward S. 2004. "China's Shallow Integration: Networked Production and the New Challenges for Late Industrialization." *World Development* 32 (11):1971–87.

Steinfeld, Edward S. 2010. *Playing Our Game: Why China's Rise Doesn't Threaten the West*. New York, NY: Oxford University Press.

Stokes, Donald E. 1997. *Pasteur's Quadrant: Basic Science and Technological Innovation*. Washington, DC: Brookings Institution Press.

Stokes, Leah C. 2020. *Short Circuiting Policy: Interest Groups and the Battle over Clean Energy and Climate Policy in the American States*. Oxford: Oxford University Press.

Stokes, Leah C., and Christopher Warshaw. 2017. "Renewable Energy Policy Design and Framing Influence Public Support in the United States." *Nature Energy* 2:17107. doi: 10.1038/nenergy.2017.107 https://www.nature.com/articles/nenergy2017107#supplementary-information.

Streeck, Wolfgang. 1989. "On the Institutional Conditions of Diversified Quality Production." In *Beyond Keynesianism: The Socio-Economics of Production and Full Employment*, edited by Egon Matzner and Wolfgang Streeck, 21–61. Hants: Edward Elgar.

Streeck, Wolfgang. 2009. *Re-Forming Capitalism: Institutional Change in the German Political Economy*. Oxford: Oxford University Press.

Streeck, Wolfgang, and Daniel Mertens. 2010. "Politik im Defizit: Austerität als fiskalpolitisches Regime." MPIfG Discussion Paper 10/5, Cologne.

Streeck, Wolfgang, and Kathleen Ann Thelen. 2005. *Beyond Continuity: Institutional Change in Advanced Political Economies*. Oxford: Oxford University Press.

Stromag. 2016. "Company History." http://www.stromag.com/unternehmen/historie.html.

Strum, Harvey, and Fred Strum. 1983. "Solar Energy Policy, 1952–1982." *Environmental Review: ER* 7 (2):135–54.

Stuart, Becky. 2012. "Dupont and Yingli Sign $100 Million PV Materials Agreement." *PV Magazine*, February 14.

Sturgeon, Timothy J. 2002. "Modular Production Networks: A New American Model of Industrial Organization." *Industrial and Corporate Change* 11 (3):451–96.

Sustainable Business News. 2012. "Jinkosolar Gets $1 Billion Infusion from Chinese Development Bank." *SustainableBusiness.Com*, February 12.

Sutherland, Dylan. 2005. "China's Science Parks: Production Bases or a Tool for Institutional Reform?" *Asia Pacific Business Review* 11 (1):83–104. doi: 10.1080/1360238052000298399.

Swank, Duane. 2002. *Global Capital, Political Institutions, and Policy Change in Developed Welfare States*. Cambridge: Cambridge University Press.

Swanson, Richard M. 2011. "The Story of Sun Power." In *Power for the World: The Emergence of Electricity from the Sun*, edited by Wolfgang Palz, 531–54. Singapore: Pan Stanford Publishing.

Tacke, Franz. 2003. *Windenergie—Die Herausforderung*. Frankfurt: VDMA Verlag.

Tan, Xiaomei, and Zhao Gang. 2009. *An Emerging Revolution: Clean Technology Research, Development and Innovation in China*. Washington, DC: World Resources Institute.

Tang, Ziyi. 2020. "China's Next Five-Year Plan Downplays Rapid GDP Growth, Emphasizes Tech Independence." *Caixin*. https://www.caixinglobal.com/2020-10-30/chinas-next-five-year-plan-downplays-rapid-gdp-growth-emphasizes-tech-independence-101620854.html.

Tassey, Gregory. 2010. "Rationales and Mechanisms for Revitalizing U.S. Manufacturing R&D Strategies." *Journal of Technology Transfer* 35 (3):283–333.

Taylor, Zachary M. 2004. "Empirical Evidence against Varieties of Capitalism's Theory of Technological Innovation." *International Organization* 58 (3):601–31.

Theile, Charlotte. 2012. "Ärger Unter der Sonne." *Süddeutsche Zeitung*, March 5.

Thelen, Kathleen. 2014. *Varieties of Liberalization and the New Politics of Social Solidarity*. Cambridge: Cambridge University Press.

Thun, Eric. 2006. *Changing Lanes in China: Foreign Direct Investment, Local Governments, and Auto Sector Development*. Cambridge: Cambridge University Press.

Thüringer Allgemeine. 2012. "Ostbeauftragter Lobt Arbeit Von Solarvalley." July 12. http://www.thueringer-allgemeine.de/web/zgt/wirtschaft/detail/-/specific/Ostbeauftragter-lobt-Arbeit-von-Solarvalley-881367561.

Tianjin Yearbook [天津年鉴]. 2010. Tianjin: Tianjin Yearbook Publishing [天津年鉴社编辑出版发行].

Tibken, Shara. 2012. "Applied Materials Trims Solar Business." *Wall Street Journal*, May 10.

Traufetter, Gerald. 2013. "Wirtschaftsminister Rösler im Silicon Valley: Philipp Was Here." *Spiegel*, May 22.

Trina Solar. 2008. "Annual Report 2008—Form 20-F."

Trina Solar. 2010. "Annual Report 2009—Form 20-F."

Trina Solar. 2012. "Annual Report 2011—Form 20-F."

Trina Solar. 2013. "Annual Report 2012—Form 20-F."

Trina Solar. 2016. "Annual Report 2015—Form 20-F."

Trumbull, Gunnar. 2004. *Silicon and the State: French Innovation Policy in the Internet Age*. Washington, DC: Brookings Institution Press.

Turner, Greg. 2011. "Evergreen Solar Files for Bankruptcy, Plans Asset Sale." *Boston Herald*, August 15.

Tushman, Michael L., and Philip Anderson. 1986. "Technological Discontinuities and Organizational Environments." *Administrative Science Quarterly* 31 (3):439–65. doi: 10.2307/2392832.

Ulrich, Katrin. 2017. "German Exports Are Dominated by Automobiles." *Economics in Brief*, KfW Research. Frankfurt: KfW.

UNIDO. 2020. *World Manufacturing Production: Statistics for Quarter I*. Vienna: UNIDO.

Uriu, Robert M. 1996. *Troubled Industries: Confronting Economic Change in Japan*. Ithaca, NY: Cornell University Press.

Urumqi Year Book [乌鲁木齐年检]. 2000. Urumqi: Xinjiang People's Press [新疆人民出版社].

Urumqi Year Book [乌鲁木齐年检]. 2007. Urumqi: Xinjiang People's Press [新疆人民出版社].

US Department of Energy, 2006. "Wind Energy Program Portfolio." http://nrel.gov/docs/fy06osti/37937.pdf.

US International Trade Commission. 2011. "China: Effects of Intellectual Property Infringement and Indigenous Innovation Policies on the U.S. Economy." Investigation No. 332–519, USITC Publication 4226.

US International Trade Commission. 2012. *Crystalline Silicon Photovoltaic Cells and Modules from China*. Washington, DC: USITC.

US-China Energy Cooperation Program. 2014. "Ogin Wind Turbine." http://www.uschinaecp.org/en/Members/FloDesign.aspx.

US-China Business Council. 2013. *China's Strategic Emerging Industries: Policy, Implementation, Challenges, and Recommendations*. Washington, DC: USCBC.

Vasseur, Véronique, and René Kemp. 2011. "The Role of Policy in the Evolution of Technological Innovation Systems for Photovoltaic Power in Germany and the Netherlands." *International Journal of Technology, Policy, and Management* 11 (3/4):307–27.

VDA. 2019. "Facts and Figures." https://www.vda.de/en/services/facts-and-figures/facts-and-figures-overview.html.

Vensys. 2012. "Geschichte und Gegenwart." http://www.vensys.de/energy/unternehmen/historie.php.

Vensys. 2017. "About Us." http://www.vensys.de/energy-en/unternehmen/unternehmen.php.

Vernon, Raymond. 1966. "International Investment and International Trade in the Product Cycle." *Quarterly Journal of Economics* 80 (2):190–207.

Vernon, Raymond. 1979. "The Product Cycle Hypothesis in a New International Environment." *Oxford Bulletin of Economics and Statistics* 41 (4):255–67.

Vogel, David. 1995. *Trading Up: Consumer and Environmental Regulation in a Global Economy*. Cambridge, MA: Harvard University Press.

Wade, Robert. 1990. *Governing the Market: Economic Theory and the Role of Government in East Asian Industrialization*. Princeton, NJ: Princeton University Press.

Wade, Robert. 1996. "Globalization and Its Limits: Reports of the Death of the National Economy Are Greatly Exaggerated." In *National Diversity and Global Capitalism*, edited by Suzanne Berger and Ronald Dore, 60–88. Ithaca, NY: Cornell University Press.

Wallace, R. L., J. I. Hanoka, A. Rohatgi, and G. Crotty. 1997. "Thin Silicon String Ribbon." *Solar Energy Materials and Solar Cells* 48 (1–4):179–86. doi: http://dx.doi.org/10.1016/S0927-0248(97)00101-3.

Wang, Qiang. 2010. "Effective Policies for Renewable Energy—The Example of China's Wind Power—Lessons for China's Photovoltaic Power." *Renewable and Sustainable Energy Reviews* 14 (2):702–12. doi: http://dx.doi.org/10.1016/j.rser.2009.08.013.

Wang, Ucilia. 2011. "Dupont Buys Solar Ink Maker Innovalight." *Reuters*, July 25. http://www.reuters.com/article/2011/07/25/idUS165538390720110725.

Wang, Zhengming. 2010. *The Evolution and Development of China's Wind Power Industry [中国风电产业的演化与发展]*. Zhenjiang: Jiangsu University Press.

Wenzelmann, Felix, Gudrun Schönfeld, and Regina Dionisius. 2009. "Betriebliche Berufsausbildung: Eine Lohnende Investition für die Betriebe." *BiBB Report*. Bonn: Bundesinstitut für Berufsbildung.

Wesoff, Eric. 2013. "Rest in Peace: The List of Deceased Solar Companies." *Greentech Media*, April 6. https://www.greentechmedia.com/articles/read/Rest-in-Peace-The-List-of-Deceased-Solar-Companies.

Wessendorf, Florian. 2013. "VDMA Photovoltaik Produktionsmittel: VDMA Begrüßt Einigung im Solarhandelsstreit." http://www.vdma.org/article/-/articleview/1989046.

West, Joel. 2014. "Too Little, Too Early: California's Transient Advantage in the Photovoltaic Solar Industry." *Journal of Technology Transfer* 39:1–15, 487–501. doi: 10.1007/s10961-012-9291-6.

The White House. 2009. "Remarks by the President Challenging Americans to Lead the Global Economy in Clean Energy." Edited by Office of the Press Secretary. Washington, DC.

Whitford, Josh. 2005. *The New Old Economy: Networks, Institutions, and the Organizational Transformation of American Manufacturing*. Oxford: Oxford University Press.

Whitford, Josh. 2012. "Waltzing, Relational Work, and the Construction (or Not) of Collaboration in Manufacturing Industries." *Politics and Society* 40 (2):249–72. doi: 10.1177/0032329212441600.

Whiting, Susan H. 2004. "The Cadre Evaluation System at the Grass Roots: The Paradox of Party Rule." In *Holding China Together: Diversity and National Integration in the Post-Deng Era*, edited by Barry Naughton and Dali L. Yang, 101–19. Cambridge: Cambridge University Press.

Whiting, Susan. 2011. "Values in Land: Fiscal Pressures, Land Disputes and Justice Claims in Rural and Peri-Urban China." *Urban Studies* 48 (3):569–87. doi: 10.1177/0042098010390242.

Whittaker, D. Hugh, Timothy Sturgeon, Toshie Okita, and Tianbiao Zhu. 2020. *Compressed Development: Time and Timing in Economic and Social Development.* Oxford: Oxford University Press.

Wieczorek, Anna J., Rob Raven, and Frans Berkhout. 2015. "Transnational Linkages in Sustainability Experiments: A Typology and the Case of Solar Photovoltaic Energy in India." *Environmental Innovation and Societal Transitions* 17:149–65.

Windolph, Melanie. 2010. Innovationskooperationen 2010—Mit Kooperativen Projekten Ideen Erfolgreich Umsetzen. *Schriftenreihe der Professur für Unternehmensrechnung und Controlling*, edited by Klaus Möller. Göttingen: Universität Göttingen.

WindGuard. 2007. "Evaluierung Des 4. Energieforschungsprogramms Erneuerbare Energien." Berlin: Progos AG.

Windpower Monthly. 1997. "American Giant Moves into European Market." November.

Windpower Monthly. 2005a. "A More Conservative Approach." November.

Windpower Monthly. 2005b. "Who Supplies to Whom—Wind Industry Gearboxes and Bearings." November.

Windpower Monthly. 2006. "Gearbox Supply in Asia and Europe Expands—Wind Power Now an Industry Worth Making Investments For." October.

Windpower Monthly. 2008. "China Gearbox Factory Orders 5000 High Capacity Bearings." September.

Winston & Strawn LLP. 2012. "Complaint for Violations of §§ 1&2 of the Sherman Antitrust Act, the California Unfair Practices Act, the Cartwright Act, and for Tortious Interference." Oakland, CA: United States District Court Northern District of California.

Wiser, Ryan. 2017. *2017 Wind Technologies Market Report.* Washington, DC: U.S. Department of Energy.

Wiser, Ryan, and Mark Bolinger. 2008. *Annual Report on U.S. Wind Power Installation, Cost, and Performance Trends: 2007.* Washington, DC: Department of Energy.

Wiser, Ryan, Mark Bolinger, and Galen Barbose. 2007. "Using the Federal Production Tax Credit to Build a Durable Market for Wind Power in the United States." *The Electricity Journal* 20 (9):77–88. doi: http://dx.doi.org/10.1016/j.tej.2007.10.002.

Wiser, Ryan, Mark Bollinger, Galen Barbose, Kathy Belyeu, Maureen Hand, Donna Heimiller, Debra Lew, Michael Milligan, Andrew Mills, Alejandro Moreno, Walt Musial, Ric O'Connell, Kevin Porter, and Zack Subin. 2008. *Annual Report on U.S. Wind Power Installation, Cost, and Performance Trends: 2006.* Washington, DC: Department of Energy.

Wittenberg, Jason. 2015. "Conceptualizing Historical Legacies." *East European Politics and Societies* 29 (2):366–78. doi: 10.1177/0888325415577864.

Wolman, Paul. 2007. "The New Deal for Electricity in the United States, 1930–1950." In *The Challenge of Rural Electrification: Strategies for Developing Countries*, edited by Douglas F. Barnes, 259–92. Washington, DC: RFF Press.

Wong, Edward. 2015. "China Blocks Web Access to 'Under the Dome' Documentary on Pollution." *New York Times*, March 7, Section A, Page 6.

World Bank. 1993. *The East Asian Miracle: Economic Growth and Public Policy*. Washington, DC: World Bank.

Wübbeke, Jost, Mirjam Meissner, Max J. Zenglein, Jacqueline Ives, and Björn Conrad. 2016. *Made in China 2025: The Making of a High-Tech Superpower and Consequences for Industrial Countries*. Berlin: Merics.

Wuxi Yearbook [无锡年检]. 2003. Shanghai: Pudong Electronic Press [浦东电子出版社].

Wuxi Yearbook [无锡年检]. 2006. Beijing: Gazetteer Press [方志出版社].

Wuxi Yearbook [无锡年检]. 2008. Beijing: Gazetteer Press [方志出版社].

Yang, Yungkai. 2006. *The Taiwanese Notebook Computer Production Network in China: Implication for Upgrading of the Chinese Electronics Industry*. Personal Computing Industry Center, University of California, Irvine.

Yeh, Emily T., and Johanna I. Lewis. 2004. "State Power and the Logic of Reform in China's Electricity Sector." *Pacific Affairs* 77 (3):437–65.

Yingli Green Energy Holding Company Limited. 2008. "Annual Report for Fiscal Year Ending 12/31/2007—Form 20-F."

Yudken, Joel S. 2010. *Manufacturing Insecurity: America's Manufacturing Crisis and the Erosion of the U.S. Defense Industrial Base*. Washington, DC: Industrial Union Council, AFL-CIO.

Zademach, Hans-Martin, and Christian Baumeister. 2013. "Wagniskapital Und Entrepreneurship: Grundlagen, Empirische Befunde, Entwicklungstrends." In *Wertschöpfungskompetenz Und Unternehmertum. Rahmenbedingungen für Entrepreneurship und Innovation in Regionen*, edited by H. Pecklaner, B.C. Doepfer, and S. Märk, 122–42. Berlin: Gabler.

Zaleski, Andrew. 2019. "Battery Start-Ups Are Raising Millions in the Battle to Crush Tesla." *CNBC*, March 17. https://www.cnbc.com/2019/03/15/battery-start-ups-are-raising-millions-in-the-battle-to-crush-tesla.html.

Zhang, Kevin. 2006. *China as a World Factory*. New York: Routledge.

Zhang, Sufang, Philip Andrews-Speed, and Meiyun Ji. 2014. "The Erratic Path of the Low-Carbon Transition in China: Evolution of Solar PV Policy." *Energy Policy* 67:903–12. doi: http://dx.doi.org/10.1016/j.enpol.2013.12.063.

Zhang, Xiliang, Shiyan Chang, Molin Huo, and Ruoshui Wang. 2009. "China's Wind Industry: Policy Lessons for Domestic Government Interventions and International Support." *Climate Policy* 9 (5):553–64. doi: 10.3763/cpol.2009.0641.

Zhao, Pengjun. 2011. "Managing Urban Growth in a Transforming China: Evidence from Beijing." *Land Use Policy* 28 (1):96–109. doi: http://dx.doi.org/10.1016/j.landusepol.2010.05.004.

Zhao, Xin-gang, Guan Wan, and Yahui Yang. 2015. "The Turning Point of Solar Photovoltaic Industry in China: Will It Come?" *Renewable and Sustainable Energy Reviews* 41:178–88. doi: http://dx.doi.org/10.1016/j.rser.2014.08.045.

Zhao, Zhen Yu, Jian Zuo, Tian Tian Feng, and George Zillante. 2011. "International Cooperation on Renewable Energy Development in China: A Critical Analysis." *Renewable Energy* 36 (3):1105–10.

Zhi, Qiang, and Margaret M. Pearson. 2017. "China's Hybrid Adaptive Bureaucracy: The Case of the 863 Program for Science and Technology." *Governance* 30 (3):407–24.

Zimmermann, Volker, and Christoph Hofmann. 2007. "Schaffen Innovative Gründungen Mehr Arbeitsplätze?" *Zeitschrift für KMU und Entrepreneurship* 55 (1):48–70.

Zysman, John, and Mark Huberty. 2013. *Can Green Sustain Growth?* Stanford, CA: Stanford University Press, xi–58.

Zysman, John, and Abraham Newman. 2006. "Frameworks for Understanding the Political Economy of the Digital Era." In *How Revolutionary Was the Digital Revolution? National Responses, Market Transitions, and Global Technology*, edited by John Zysman and Abraham Newman, 3–22. Stanford: Stanford University Press.

Index

For the benefit of digital users, indexed terms that span two pages (e.g., 52–53) may, on occasion, appear on only one of those pages.

Tables and figures are indicated by *t* and *f* following the page number